Christina Baldwin "First read this book carefully, perhaps aloud to a friend. Then dance with it. Then draw in it. Then bundle it in a leather pouch and take it someplace sacred—like under a large tree, alongside clear water, into the temple of a coffee shop, into a circle of women. Then read this book again. There is wisdom here that women and companioning men need in order to make the world anew. Bravo to Kris Steinnes for holding the vision, calling the gatherings, and harvesting these voices and images." (Author of *Life's Companion, Calling the Circle, The Seven Whispers*, and *Storycatcher*).

Joan Borysenko, Ph.D. "This anthology of wisdom from some of the greatest women thinkers and writers of our time is a rare treasure. It inspires, informs, and gives us hope for the future in which the best potential of all people, and of our precious Earth, can be realized." (Author of *Inner Peace for Busy Women* and *A Woman's Book of Life)*.

Angeles Arrien "*Women of Wisdom* offers a wide range of possibilities, images, and visions for galvanizing a better world for future generations. This compilation is a timely and invaluable resource for all ages, cultures, and disciplines." (Author of *The Four-Fold Way* and *The Second Half of Life*).

Jean Shinoda Bolen, M.D. "*Women of Wisdom* (the book) is a distillate of the spirit from *Women of Wisdom* (the conferences that go back to 1993), both inspired by Kris Steinnes, a woman of wisdom. This anthology is an expression of the sacred feminine as voiced through individual women who have keynoted the conferences. It is a rich and inspiring women's spirituality anthology. Women who have felt a deep yearning for the return of the divine feminine, or had a significant dream of a numinous woman or goddess, or value the feminine principle will find insights and encouragement to bring what they know into the world." (Author of *Goddesses in Everywoman and Urgent Message From Mother*).

Dr. Pat Baccili "I should have known that what we were going to get some of the most significant conversations we've had with women on the leading edge on this planet. What I didn't expect that we would get is this beautiful book that is so filled with pictures and poetry. For me, all books should be done like this. But mostly what I love about this is how you share the personal stories of the people and also how you integrate their message." (The Dr. Pat Show*)*.

Testimonials from Amazon.com

Dr. Judith Orloff "*Women of Wisdom* is a beautiful book that reveals the stories of a cross section of women and the wisdom they have to share. Kris Steinnes has lovingly compiled these stories with fascinating details. I recommend this book to anyone looking for inspiration, insight, and courage. Kris also is the tireless founder of the powerful *Women of Wisdom* organization in Seattle that is dedicated to empowering women and providing conferences to support feminine power in the deepest sense. (Author of *Emotional Freedom*).

Christine Agro "WOW! The *Women of Wisdom* book is beautiful, empowering and inspiring. Reading through it my own knowingness was affirmed. I felt both encouraged to continue my work and embraced for the work I do in supporting women through all stages and phases of Womanhood. It is a book that I have and will recommend to those I work with to help them claim their own voice and their true place in this world. The book is so beautiful both visually and through the written words that it sings. Women of Wisdom is truly like having your own personal Women of Wisdom conference. I highly recommend this book. (*The Conscious Mom's Guide*).

Pamela D. Blair "I love *Women of Wisdom* and Kris Steinnes' writing is excellent! This book includes almost every woman who has ever inspired me, including Rianne Eisler and Angeles Arrien. I'm thinking about starting a women's book discussion group and this book is at the top of my list. If nothing else, I'm highly recommending it to my women friends and clients who are looking for inspiration for their own spiritual journey. (Author of *The Next Fifty Years: A Guide for Women at Midlife and Beyond*).

Cari LaGrange Murphy "This brilliant and inspiring compilation of female voices offering their personal tales of empowerment, glory, and illumination is a true gift for the feminine spirit. The celebration of these remarkable women of wisdom will serve to open the door of your heart and allow the dreams of your soul to awaken and request expression. This unique collection of work from highly respected women of power and accomplishment will inspire you to explore your deepest passions and tap into the limitless, divine spark of consciousness that resides within you. I highly recommend it." (Author of *Create Change Now: Reflections for Personal Transformation*).

Women of Wisdom

empowering the
dreams. AND
spirit
of women

Published by
Wise Woman Publishing
PO Box 30924
Seattle, WA 98113

Wise Woman Publishing is dedicated to promoting women's empowerment, the Divine Feminine and artistic expression.

Printed in the USA

First Edition May 2008

Library of Congress Control Number: 2007943896

ISBN 978-0-9800622-0-5

Cover and interior design by Drai Bearwomyn McKi
Front cover art by Deborah Koff-Chapin
Back cover art by Diana Denslow
Edited by Kris Steinnes, Hilary Hart and Annalisa Steinnes
Index by Christine Frank

This book is dedicated to the memory of my mother, Jeanette Hesby Steinnes, who lived to be 91, and my Aunt Verna Hesby White, for their love and for modeling professional women leadership which was uncommon in their time.

Jeanette Hesby Steinnes

Verna Hesby White

Kris Steinnes

Author, Editor, Collaborator.
Founder of the Women of Wisdom Foundation.

Hilary Hart

Editor. Author and teacher about feminine
aspects of mystical consciousness.

Annalisa Steinnes

Transcriber, Editor, Proofreader, Researcher.
Creative Writing and Geography
Cum Laude, University of Washington.

Deborah Koff-Chapin

Cover Illustrator.
Interpretive Touch Drawing Artist.

Drai Bearwomyn McKi

Graphic Designer of Cover and Content.
Founder of Wild Redhead Design. Mother.
Ceremonialist and Keeper of the Song.

Women of Wisdom

empowering the dreams and spirit of women

Kris Steinnes

A percentage of the profits from the sale of this book benefits
Women of Wisdom Foundation, a not-for-profit organization.

Wise Woman Publishing™
Seattle, Washington

Acknowledgments

There are so many people who have contributed to Women of Wisdom. I am forever grateful to all the women who have served in all the diverse ways the past sixteen years: conference committee members, board and now council members, presenters, volunteers, artists, healers and vendors. A list of committee members, board/council members, presenters and supporters from all the years are listed in the Contributor Resource Chapter. As you can see it has taken many hands to create this event. I apologize if I have missed anyone, I searched for as many old lists as possible.

I particularly want to thank the current WOW Council members who have supported me emotionally and spiritually through this process this year: Roberta Sherwood, Bergith Kayyali, Julie Charette Nunn, Karen Fletcher, Jennifer Lund, and Janeal Stevens.

A heartfelt thank you to everyone who donated their contributions to this book—the keynote presenters, participants, artists, songwriters and key WOW personnel. The names are listed in the table of contents and the contributor pages. Thank you so much for making this book possible.

Beyond the community of Women of Wisdom, I want to thank the people who have supported or contributed to my journey: Danaan Parry and Victoria Castle for their inspiring workshops that changed my life, Rev. Steve Towles, Rev. Karen Lindvig and Seattle Unity Church for their support from the very beginning to sponsor this conference and to allow us to become our own organization, Faye Fitzgerald, Training in Power, healing partners: Georganne Oldham, Ginette Bedsaul, Juli Butler among many others, friends and family, and my husband, Chris Prall, who not only is a key volunteer with his technical computer expertise, he is one of our steadfast supporters of this work we do.

Thank you to the assistance of these people to make this book a reality: Christina Baldwin, for a fabulous writer's retreat where sacred space allowed words to flow for the first chapter, Sally Vaillette & Chiara for a lovely retreat in Sicily where I started writing, Annalisa Steinnes, for her wise assistance in the English language, Drai Bearwomyn McKi, for her fabulously talented graphic skills, editor Hilary Hart for her assistance in word crafting. Thank you to the organization Ladies Who Launch, and Melody Biringer for their support to launch new enterprises. I want to thank ewomenpublishingnetwork.com's Jan King and Gail Richards of authorsmart.com for the expert training in developing, writing and publishing that led me through this process.

There are several organizations I would like to thank who have been connected to Women of Wisdom's community for several years: Pacific Women's Circle Association, (pwcacamp.org), creates a 5 day women's camp retreat in British Columbia, Women's Summer Solstice, (www.womenssolstice.com), takes place every June in Cle Elum WA, Sacred Fire Choir, (sacredfirechoir.org), provides wonderful sacred music and performances at WOW, Gaia's Temple, (gaiastemple.org), where many of our members attend the Goddess worship services, and a professional network organization, (eWomennetwork.com) which I attend monthly.

Thank you to those who supported me through reading the book and giving their feedback: Suzanna McCarthy, Patty Zeitlin, Rev. Judith Laxer, Joan Borysenko, Jan King and Christina Baldwin. Thank you to Jean Houston for her reflections on *Women of Wisdom* in the foreword.

Finally, thank you to Sherry Anderson and Patricia Hopkins for writing the book, *The Feminine Face of God*, which sparked the inspiration of Women of Wisdom in 1992! And a big thank you to Sophia, the Goddess of Wisdom, for guiding me through this process, as I felt her presence with me daily.

–Kris Steinnes
Founder, Women of Wisdom Foundation

Table of Contents

Foreword

thoughts from Jean Houston

> The world within becomes as important as the world outside.
>
> —Jean

Women of Wisdom is in the forefront of the biggest change in human history—the only change that will assure our continuity as a species. Those who organize and participate in the Women of Wisdom experience know that for a new world to be born we have to bring a new mind to bear. Critical to this is the rich mind style of women that has been gestating in the womb of preparatory time, lo, these many millennia. In their ebullient and evocative conferences WOW demonstrates a tremendous change in who we are and how we do things.

Playing their part to usher in feminine mind, WOW emphasizes process rather than just product, and making things cohere, relate, and grow. Cultures in which the feminine archetype is powerful are almost always non-heroic; they tend to make things work together, each piece has its part to play. The feminine principle expresses itself as an unfolding of levels of existence, not as conquest of facts. The relationships between people and things become more important than final outcome. The world within becomes as important as the world outside.

Let us not forget that women hold the Mother-Mind—a mind that is not primarily linear, sequential, and objective, but is rather circular, empathic, and narrative.

If, for a hundred thousand years or so, you've been stirring the soup with one hand and holding the baby with the other, kicking off the wooly mastodon with one foot and rocking a cradle with the other, watching out for the return of the hunters with one eye and determining with the other on which cave wall you will paint a magical bison, then you are going to develop a very complex consciousness.

In each and every WOW conference women discover ways to manifest this consciousness, embrace their power, challenge the way things are done, and build a new social order. They learn how women are more geared to team building and leading enterprises through natural growth stages.

The conferences demonstrate that governance, games, education, work, health–society itself–can be held to a new standard, one that promotes and honors the fullness of who and what we can be rather than just collective rights and liberties. They empower women to challenge the most sexist institutions from the medical establishments to business institutions, and at long last, allow their full creativity to be set free.

The women's movement as a whole, and events such as the Women of Wisdom Conference in particular, may be the outward manifestation of what is happening on depth levels in essential, mythic, and archetypal space-time. Whether the women's movement has evolved because the crisis of the eternal world is calling for the rise of the Goddess to restore the balance of nature, or because the release of women into full partnership demands a similar release of its archetypal principle, or even because, in the cosmic cycle of things, the time of the Goddess has come around, we cannot say. But all the evidence indicates that the feminine archetype is returning.

This is perhaps the most important event of the last five thousand years, and its consequences may well have an immense, unimaginable effect on cultural and ecological evolution.

artwork
Snake
Sue Coccia
©2001

Men and women will be released from the old polarities of gender that force them into limited and limiting roles, and qualities of intelligence will be added to the human mind-pool that will render most previous problem solving obsolete. Linear, sequential solutions will yield to the knowing that comes from seeing things in whole gestalts, in constellations, rather than in discrete fact. In fact, the emphasis will probably be more on affirming things that are true but not accurate, rather than that of being accurate but not true! The appreciation of process will be celebrated along with the seeking of end goals.

And it will bring an ecological ethic, along with a new partnership between men and women, in which the human acts in concert and in partnership with Nature to bring about more symbiotic ecological relationships.

The Earth is a living organism and its nervous system is nearly in place with the spread of the human "neurons." Women's role's must necessarily be expanded in all fields of endeavor as they were in the old partnership societies, both to allay population growth and to make women available for the complex requirements of the emerging planetary culture.

Because its approach is systemic rather than systematic, because it sees things in constellations rather than as discreet and disconnected facts, the feminine mind view is supremely concerned with the networking of the individual with the larger social organism. This is most important as we try and create a planetary society with deepening of individual cultures.

As I have had the opportunity to talk with many of the participants at these conferences I am moved to celebration and gratitude for what these remarkable women have done and how they have served in the creation of this new society.

–Jean Houston, Ph.D.

> All the evidence indicates that
> the feminine archetype is returning.

—Jean

artwork

Nut and Isis

Robin
Maynard-
Dobbs
©1994

Preface

the vision by Kris Steinnes

> " I hope this book sparks a new way of thinking and empowers you to embrace your calling.
>
> —Kris

I was called to create this book just as I was called to found the Women of Wisdom Conference. Three years ago I was leading a short workshop on the principles of leadership, which I've written about in this book, and a man from Toronto was ecstatic–here was a new paradigm model of leadership. He said, "You need to copyright this, write a book, and I see you on Oprah!"

In that moment I had a glimpse of my future—not unlike when I had a vision of bringing women spiritual authors to Seattle, which began my Women of Wisdom journey in 1993. I saw how I was going to be an instrument to bring feminine consciousness forward in our society, beyond the women's movement, even into mainstream business.

I'm not the only person doing this, there are many and that's what's so great about this era—the collective consciousness of women is on the march—for change. Change in how we are doing things, so we will live and act from a fundamentally different place than what we've experienced in our lifetime.

So it's a calling for me, and you'll read in the book from women leaders about the importance of finding and following your calling. I heard the voice of this book in 1999, knowing we had a wellspring of knowledge from this feminine viewpoint in all the tapes of our keynote talks from the Women of Wisdom Conferences and I wanted to share them with others.

During the process of listening to the tapes, transcribing these talks, reading and editing this material and designing this book, memories of these important transformative talks exploded in me through tears of joy and amazement. Words from these powerful women are as relevant today as they were when they were spoken–anywhere from 1993 to 2006.

As I read and listened, I was struck how political these talks are. WOW already had a strong overall foundation in women's spirituality, and in the early 2000's there was a call to bring women social activists to the conference. But going back to some of these talks I could see there always was an element of activism—always a call for change. Regardless of their specific topic or viewpoint, each of these authors bring an important message to us—a message of change.

It's time for women to unite, stand up and speak for what they believe in. It's time for women to be leaders, and it's time for women's values to be honored.

What are these values? What is this wisdom? You will discover them in these pages. But you know them already, for they are everywhere, and have been throughout time. In the Bible She is, Sophia, She is called Shekhinah in the Talmud, Shakti (and so many other names!) in Hinduism, She is Prajnaparamita in the Buddhist scriptures, and in Sufism every heart is Her—receptive and full of longing for Her Beloved.

artwork
White Tara
Robin
Maynard-
Dobbs
©1995

Always She is found deep within. Within ourselves, within our hearts, within the Earth, and within life itself. She is with us, regardless of our conditioning or our beliefs, and She guides us. She is intuition, She is receptivity, She is that divine spark in our hearts, She is soft, loving, caring, and knows that we must take care of everyone, children, women, and men. With Her guidance She can lead us through these times of turmoil if we only listen. She calls to us to find Her.

When we awaken in Her wisdom and power, we can live in balance with the masculine energies that have ruled for so long. We all have this responsibility—"to know the masculine and cleave to the feminine," as stated in verse 28 of the Tao Te Ching. It is up to all of us to become balanced and help create a balanced world. So this book is written for men as well, to see that there are other ways of being; that they've nothing to loose and everything to gain by embracing the feminine knowledge and even into the political and economic systems. It's time for a change, don't you agree?

My wish is that this book helps you to wake up to Her gifts, and claim a life in balance. I hope it sparks a new way of thinking and empowers you to embrace your calling, find the support you need to manifest your dreams, and fulfill your purpose—just as these women in this book have found and followed their own paths. For it is only from this place of balance that we can live our destiny and play our part in the whole.

These women have contributed to this book as an offering to you and to the feminine consciousness within us all. It's time for the feminine to come forward and lead us into the next stage of evolution. This book reflects the feminine and all Her voices— expansive, intuitive, loving, inclusive, nourishing, wrathful and perhaps most of all, present. She is not concerned with power over another, or how you can get ahead of everyone else. She will bring everyone along with you so we can all succeed together.

If we let Her.

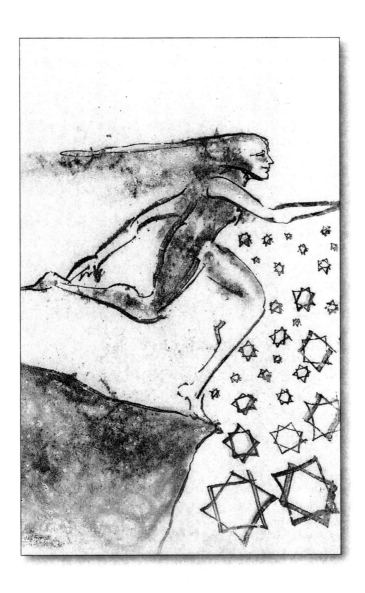

artwork

Women of Wisdom Art Series

Deborah Koff-Chapin
©2004

"Women of Wisdom is for any woman
who desires to connect with other women
& be inspired by the spirit that links us.

We join hands in a circle, we sing,
we dance and we lift our arms
to embrace everyone in our community.

Our sisters, our daughters, our mothers,
our grandmothers and our ancestors before us.

We express the Divine Feminine,
which is the spirit of women within all of us.
We explore her wisdom & her many diverse expressions.

We welcome all of you into our circle of Women of Wisdom!

Spirit of Woman Poem, Kris Steinnes ©1998. *Mandala: WOW Logo*, April Cody ©1996
Background Art: *The Cosmic Dreamer*, Montserrat ©1997

CHAPTER 1

What is Women of Wisdom?

Women of Wisdom

a sharing by Kris Steinnes

> Foremost for us has been creating a safe environment for women to speak.
>
> —Kris

Women of Wisdom began in 1993 as a conference in Women's Spirituality, sponsored by Seattle Unity Church, and grew to be one of the largest women's spirituality conferences in the country. That first year included twenty-four events over a period of seven days, and by 1998 this had grown to over ninety events in eight full days and nine nights! In 1998 we became our own not-for-profit organization, Women of Wisdom Foundation

Every year a circle of women craft and create the conference considering the needs of the women who will attend. From the very first year, as a guiding principle, we developed the idea of a sacred vessel designed to contain very specific elements that we felt were essential and they continue to this day. Foremost for us has been creating a safe environment for women to speak, allowing for the important element of sharing our stories, which contribute to empowering women to seek their dreams. Several of these stories from participants are shared in this book.

We also made sure to include elements that created a transformative experience for people. We didn't want to hold a traditional conference, where participants sit with five hundred plus people for one and half hours, listening to one person talk. Instead, we made sure experiential workshops formed eighty to ninety percent of the conference presentations. These three to six hour workshops take place in an intimate setting allowing women to share their feelings, move in their bodies, create through artistic expression, and have a transformative experience. Our conference evenings, which are attended by men and women, include music, concerts, performances, and inspiring lectures from our featured presenters, some of which you will get to read in this book.

One wise woman, Flor Fernandez, a presenter who's been with us since the first year, advised us not to bring only famous, well-known speakers to the conference. She suggested that we utilize the gifts of local women as well—so seventy-five percent of our presenters are women from our local community with diverse backgrounds. We place a call for new presenters every year, and are blessed with an abundance of wonderful women who share their gifts and wisdom.

We also gave careful attention to the issue of affordability. We wanted everyone to have the opportunity to attend. Therefore we created a price structure where people could pay for events separately. We realized that if we had had one price for the week, we would maybe have two hundred attendees. Offering separate prices would allow more women to share this unique experience. If someone could only afford to go to one lecture, that's what they could do; or they could create their own conference, choosing to go to one or twenty events during the week. You could arrive mid-week and still feel part of the community. You didn't have to be there on the first day to feel connected to the spirit and essence of the conference. And the flow of energy from women coming and going was a wonderful and unexpected result of this policy.

So that was our first year–defining our purpose and creating the conference structure. Each following year we determine what will improve the program. We begin our planning in the spring, choosing a theme for the next year that will inspire women and speak to that which is calling us to discover even more about ourselves. Researching and selecting our keynote presenters formed an important part of my job.

Much of the time spent preparing for the conference is just hard work: finalizing the presenters and programs, creating brochures, marketing, dealing with obstacles and meeting with the steering committee. These sixteen years have involved managing a lot of details and held many lessons for me to learn about collaboration and team dynamics, in addition to forming a business. Who in their sane mind would dream of holding a conference that lasts eight days! I wouldn't advise it, but I also don't regret it.

As we near our February conference date, we get excited to host our presenter potluck, which gathers together the committee, staff, key people and local presenters. This is when the energy really starts to build, as we visualize the larger community—

> We sense
> the unique
> essence of
> everyone
> involved.
>
> —Kris

beyond the core contributors—joining us as a part of Women of Wisdom. We sense the unique essence of everyone involved, and in our ceremonial circle we visualize the participants who will be arriving in a month. We also call to others who are seeking their spirit and a connection with other women—to help them find us.

Aside from sharing food and conversation with each other, the potluck is also an important time to circle and share our gifts that we are bringing to the conference. The diversity of these women and their sharing is magnificent; we all look forward to attending each other's workshops. During the potluck I lead a meditation from which everyone creates a blessing reflecting on the theme of that year. Later, one of our faithful volunteers creates a scroll with these blessings and ties them with a ribbon, as a gift to each attendee.

Gifts come in many forms through this experience, and we are blessed to have the opportunity of a personal experience with the presenters who mentor us. Many people have expressed that they don't feel a separation between the speakers and the attendees; perhaps because we are all so present and generously giving of ourselves to each other. Everyone understands the value of women coming together in such a sacred atmosphere, and how important it is to empower each other to step into our power and manifest our dreams. As Jean Houston said in 2001,

"There is nothing like this in the world!"

> WOW is not an ordinary event but a path of experiences linked together through the commonality of women and spirit on a journey seeking the Divine.
>
> —Kris

WOW is not an ordinary event. It is not just a workshop, a lecture, or a concert, but a path of experiences linked together through the commonality of women and spirit on a journey seeking the Divine, seeking purpose in life, seeking our dreams. It is this linkage that makes it non-ordinary. It is the bonds formed between the women, during and between events, as they connect with other women who seek similar and diverse resolutions to the transitions they face in their lives.

WOW is a story that unfolds creatively in our midst, a story with a life and a voice. It is as though WOW connects to the Divine Feminine Herself, who speaks to us with a resonance we can all hear and feel. She expresses Herself through the diversity of individual voices, through the moving songs, and all the tones and colors of the fabric that make Her presence known. We hear an ancient wisdom that exists beyond time, beyond our known history. She is calling us to gather once again. This book is a channel to bring Her voice to others, to anyone who is longing for Her in their heart, who doesn't have access to a circle in their community and desires to create one.

Women of Wisdom is a journey, and this book is designed to be a journey as well, helping you to discover your path. Throughout the book you will find extracts from the inspiring talks our presenters have given over the years. These different speakers were chosen to represent the variety of women's voices who are leading us today such as: novelist Isabel Allende who shares personal life stories; activist Frances Moore Lappé inspiring us toward change; Riane Eisler, illuminating the history of patriarchy and how we can shift to a partnership model; the feminist voice of Jean Shinoda Bolen, calling us to build women's circles to change the world; and Marion Woodman, who leads us through a meditation and inspires us to embrace Sophia and the Divine Feminine.

artwork
Bag Lady
© Denise
Kester

"May this book call you to your circle, to your ancient wisdom, to the Divine Feminine within.

—Kris

Additionally, different women from our Women of Wisdom Community have written their stories for this book, sharing how they were empowered through their experience at WOW. Another chapter allows women who have led certain aspects of the conference to share their experiences of interpretive conference art, musical directing, ceremonial directing, and Ritual Theater. One chapter explores the importance of circles and circle leadership, and outlines the role that it plays as WOW grows its organization and creates the conference.

Art, music and poetry created by our talented WOW community is woven throughout the book, bringing a full expression of the Divine Feminine that I hope will bless and inspire you. At the end of each chapter exercises guide you for your very own WOW experience.

So this book is created to mirror our experiences at Women of Wisdom: not just wise words from our featured presenters, but also personal expressions that reflect women's experiences during the week. Memories of personal connections, revelations, and friendships formed are all key ingredients.

Lastly, I felt it necessary to share with you the contributor's information, so you can go to their websites, connect with their work, and their organizations, and discover the treasures that are out there for women—it's a large, loosely interwoven community. Think of the power we would have if we joined forces!

You are entering a journey—a journey that begins as we take you through an experience of the opening circle, so you can feel for yourself what it was like to enter Women of Wisdom.

May this book call you to your circle, to your ancient wisdom, to the Divine Feminine within. Many blessings on your journey as you discover your passions and your dreams for the beautiful self within you.

Veronica Appolonia ©2005
Art: *Crone May,* Joanna Powell Colbert ©1993

Call to Circle

Listen to the Lady call
It's time to begin.
Listen to the Lady call
It's time to circle in.

Join hands, sisters all,
Listen to the Lady call.
Join hands, sisters all.
Listen to the Lady call.

Lorraine Bayes ©2002
Art: *Cosmic Dreamer*, Montserrat ©1997

Women of Wisdom

Women of Wisdom, Women of Wisdom (1993–1994)
Women of Wisdom
Rise and Shine Sisterkind
Spirit of Woman Rise and Shine

Women Remembering Who We Are (1995)
Following the Moon and the Stars
Honoring Our Wholeness Body and Soul (1996)
Mother We Are Healing
Weaving Our Tapestry
Sharing Our Stories (1997)

Ancient Fires in the Belly of the Earth
Hearts and Hands Gather Round
Sacred Circles of Life, Death, Rebirth (1998)
Mother We Are Healing
Dancing Our Passion Strong and Wild
Birthing Our Power to Bless Every Child (1999)

Choosing Our Future in the Beauty of the Day
Grounding Our Love in Gratitude
Changing Our World in a Wise Woman Way (2000)
Mother We Are Healing
Holy Life in Reflection
Deepening Our Connections (2001)

To fire, water, Earth and air
Witnessing the Sacred everywhere
Transforming our World in the presence of love (2003)
Calling to Community
Tides of hope reach every shore
We Are the Ones We've Been Waiting For. (2004)

Living Boldly! With Heart! Intention and Commitment (2005)
Return to the Well (2006)
Return to the Well

Women of Wisdom, Women of Wisdom
Celebrating the Circle of All Life
Living Our Dreams in Spirit Divine, (2002)
Spirit Divine, Spirit Divine
Wings of Wisdom Taking Flight
Spirit of Our Love Shining Bright

Women of Wisdom, Women of Wisdom
Women of Wisdom
Rise and Shine Sisterkind
Spirit of Woman Rise and Shine

*Lorraine Bayes, music director for Women of Wisdom,
wrote this lovely song, incorporating the themes of the Women of
Wisdom Conference. These are highlighted in the words above, with
the year of the theme in parenthesis at the end of the phrases. This
song really speaks about the work women have done during these ten
years of gatherings; remembering, honoring, weaving, sharing,
healing, creating, dancing, changing and celebrating.*

"The circle is timeless.

I will wait as long as it takes for you to discover me.

I am all of you.

I have been with you in every circle that has met
around the ancient fires and candles of today.

I am at the center of the divine spark of feminine energy.

Now with a sense of urgency I call you to the circle,
to anchor it here on this Earth plane.

Anadolu Twinns, Lydia Ruyle ©1995. The Circle Poem, Kris Steinnes ©2006

CHAPTER 2

Enter into Women of Wisdom

Enter Into Women of Wisdom

a sharing by Kris Steinnes

I am WOW: the Weaver of Webs
I spin my web in a circle that contains everything:
The silvery gossamer threads that light our path,
The spaces between the threads that
open us to our infinite possibilities,
The threads that bond and strengthen
our connections to each other.
I hold together the concentric circles,
Surrounding the center where the circle is cast.
We are all in this circle; we are all part of this web.

–Kris Steinnes Poem ©2006

> " There is a stirring in my DNA that remembers I have been here before.
>
> —Participant

Women of Wisdom was created for women to gather with each other, to become a rich tapestry of spirit and community exploring the Divine Feminine through our creativity and our connections to one another. This is the story of WOW, and I invite you to enter into the circle we cast. The story will unfold as in a spiral, starting from the center, and curving its way around, not knowing what will come with each new turn. Enjoy the journey!

Having traveled from far and near, women walk towards Seattle Unity Church, where for many years Women of Wisdom has gathered. They wait in the sanctuary in eagerness for the opening ceremonies, until at last they are invited to step through the door that will lead them down the staircase. If they listen carefully they can hear the heart beat of the drums and the chant by Shawna Carol calling them in *"Carried by the Love of My Sisters, I am Carried by the Love of My Sisters."*

As if spiraling down through time, women return to this ancient sacred circle, entering into the darkened ceremonial room through a channel of women holding candles, dressed in flowing goddess gowns. As torchbearers, responsible for creating this gathering for the past year, we are holding the energy for these women to enter this circle.

As we hold our candles to light the way for these arriving women, we feel the familiarity of this ritual. We have waited a long time for the gathering of women to return. We prepare ourselves to enter this channel that leads us to the sacred womb. The birthing process into the Divine Feminine has begun.

Women continue to file into the room and join hands, creating a large circle. They stand silently until the last woman comes through the door. They gaze into the center where an altar stands, a round low table, adorned with decorations expressing the theme of the conference, candles and elements representing the directions: air, fire, water, Earth. The women look across the center altar into faces reflecting the excitement they are also feeling. The ceremony begins as the last women join their hands to complete the circle.

Many women have expressed how important this ritual is for them. Every year we dress in colorful, long, flowing goddess raiment, adorned with our special jewelry and scarves. Draped fabric in orange, fuchsia and purple streams from the ceiling and strings of lights surround the room, creating the sacred space for women to enter into. Expressions of the feminine are everywhere, including the scarves, art, and altars around the building; we know we are in sacred feminine space.

One participant shares her experience with these words: *"To transcend time and enter into the womb of the ancient circles, where stories were shared, rituals performed and healings transacted, is to recognize and feel that I am a part of this sacred vessel. There is a stirring in my DNA that remembers I have been here before."*

Another woman expresses her entry into Women of Wisdom: *"As I entered through the door into the circle, a deep unexpected longing for the sacred feminine stirred within me. I had picked up a WOW brochure and found something that spoke to my heart, but I could not identify what it was that called me, or why I responded in the way I did. When I arrived, I looked around the circle of women, breathed it in, and said, yes. I am here. I have found my tribe."*

artwork
Spider
Sue Coccia
©2003

"

Music
expresses
the heartbeat
of who
we are.

—Kris

We sing, dance and drum together, to call forth the energy, to create the ambiance and purpose of this week. The ceremony calls us together and includes ritual components designed each year to bring meaning to the theme and our week together.

At the close of the opening ceremonies, everyone is led in a spiral dance, and as they are about to exit the room, committee members line up on each side of the door and hand each person a scroll with the blessings created at our potluck meal one month before. Earlier in the ceremony I share how each scroll has a message especially written with love for each woman. It will speak to what they need to be receptive to, or what will assist them in their experience at WOW during the week.

Blessing scroll in hand, the women head back upstairs to anticipate the opening keynote presenter. There's always a buzz of activity, a hum of excited voices, as old friends greet each other and new people, while gazing at the art in the church sanctuary. At last, someone stands before them and the audience is welcomed as we sing beautiful chants led by our talented musical director.

There are many fond memories of feeling the excitement in the sanctuary, sitting in the ready room with the speakers, and then leading the presenter out to sit in the audience to experience the music along with everyone else. Music has been instrumental in bringing us together and expressing the Divine Feminine. It expresses the heartbeat of who we are and is a foundation for the tapestry we are weaving. To walk onto the stage with an audience already joined together by song and a sense of community is a gift for our presenters that I have felt as well.

I remember one evening in particular. Marion Woodman was the featured presenter, and when she arrived she asked for a piece of apple pie, needing a little energy boost. As she ate it in the ready room, I could feel the electric excitement of the audience. We had over 700 people eagerly waiting to hear Marion speak. This was in 1995, her first speaking engagement since having recovered from cancer. She said she felt more energy now, (of course she was speaking of the pie), but I knew it was also the energy of the audience. They were on the edge of their seats waiting to hear her. I heard people say it didn't matter what she said; they just wanted to be there. Marion is a petite woman, but speaks with a powerful voice for the feminine. She shared with us a collective dream of a chocolate colored goddess coming on a tidal wave. That was an amazing statement that has remained with me all these years, one that profoundly affected more than one person that night.

Many other speakers have inspired the same excitement among the audience: Isabel Allende, speaking with her lovely accent, told her vivid personal life story; and Iyanla Vanzant, with grace and humor, inspired the audience with ways to turn your life around from the worst circumstances to a life that will serve others. When a presenter captivates an audience, keeps them excited and in awe, magic happens that allows for a personal experience, which transcends the everyday ho hum of life. These gifted authors have changed lives through their books, and in person they come to inspire us in a deeper way, touching the lives of many, empowering all of us to claim our own stories, to claim our gifts and our place in the world.

We welcome you as part of this circle; you have entered into Women of Wisdom through reading this opening experience. Drink deeply as you read the words, and experience the different elements of women experiencing the Divine Feminine. Embrace your mind, body and spirit and allow yourself to be taken back to your roots, and into your future to discover the purpose of why you are here.

" We welcome you as part of this circle.

—Kris

artwork

Women of Wisdom Art Series

Deborah Koff-Chapin
©2004

Our call in the 21st century is to bring meaning, magic and enchantment back into the world.

meaning, magic and enchantment

meaning, magic and enchantment

The Star, Joanna Powell Colbert ©2002

meaning, magic and enchantment

magic and enchantment

Photo, Marianne Gontarz York

CHAPTER 3

Angeles Arrien

Biography

Angeles Arrien is a cultural anthropologist, award-winning author, educator, and consultant to many organizations and businesses. She lectures and conducts workshops worldwide, bridging cultural anthropology, psychology, and comparative religions. Her work is currently used in medical, academic, and corporate environments. Angeles is the President of the Foundation for Cross-Cultural Education and Research. Her books, including *The Four-Fold Way*, *The Signs of Life*, and *The Second Half of Life*, have been translated into nine languages, and she has received three honorary doctorate degrees in recognition of her work.

Reflections Today

Two primal energies coexist inside the human spirit. Whether we reside in a male or female body, these dynamic and magnetic energies seek equal development and expression for full individuation. Many cultures have described these two energies as yin-yang; sun/moon; animus/anima; and left brain/right brain. For purposes of this book, I would like to explore what constitutes the healthy feminine energy that resides within each human being, (as does the healthy masculine).

In the following address, I have used selected stories, questions, and historical examples to illustrate some of the positive functions of the healthy feminine, such as: befriending the feminine in others by committing to the spirit of collaboration and cooperation (*The Miracle Bridge Story*); to reclaim the true self and no longer abandon oneself (*Florence Chadwick Story* and *Old European Story* of self-abandonment); to have a strong sense of personal choice and effectiveness (the *Toll Booth Story*); to sustain a profound respect for human life by maintaining rituals, ceremonies, and traditions; and to awaken the world by modeling ways we can increase strength, compassion, wisdom, and self-responsibility. The healthy feminine within the human spirit has released patterns of denial and indulgence; control and appeasement tendencies, and seduction and special attention needs. Women of wisdom have a profound respect for nature and human life. Theirs is always a commitment to meaningful action, fostering community, and making a contribution, whether it is measured by public or non-public impact.

Psychologist Carl Jung reminds us that the feminine principle reclaimed within every man and woman will create the intermediary bridge needed to reconcile the existing human needs and collective learnings surrounding the unsolved conflicts, dualities, polarities and oppositions present within the human psyche. It is this wisdom energy that will ignite the soul's fire and restore meaning, magic and majesty back into the world. Will we seize the opportunity? Women and men of wisdom will and must!

–Angeles Arrien

artwork

Women of Wisdom Art Series

Deborah Koff-Chapin ©2003

The Soul's Fire:
Bring Meaning, Magic and
Majesty into the World

a talk with Angeles Arrien

I'd like to begin with a story written by Dr. Charles Garfield*, found in the *Chicken Soup for the Soul* series:

I've been through every one of the seventeen tollbooths on the Oakland-San Francisco Bridge on thousands of occasions, and never had an exchange worth remembering. But late one morning in 1984, I drove through one of the booths, and I heard loud music. It sounded like a party or a Michael Jackson concert. I looked around and finally looked inside the tollbooth where a man was dancing. I said, "What are you doing?" And he said, "I'm having a party!"

I looked in all the other booths lined up and nothing was happening in there, and I said, "Well, what about the rest of these people?" He said, "They're not invited."

I made a note to myself to find this guy again. There was something in his eyes that said there was magic in his tollbooth.

Months later, I found him again. Still with the loud music, still having a party. Again I asked, "What are you doing?" And he said, "Oh, I remember you from the last time. I'm still dancing; I'm still having the same party." And I said, "Well, what about the rest of your colleagues in the other booths?"

"Stop," he said to me, pointing down the row of tollbooths. "What do those look like to you?" I answered, "Well, they look like tollbooths." He said, "No imagination! No imagination!"

*Used with permission by Dr. Charles Garfield.

And I said, "Okay, well I give up. What do they look like to you?" And he said, "Vertical coffins. I can prove it. Every morning, live people get in and then they die for eight hours. At 4:30 like Lazarus from the dead they reemerge and then they go home. For eight hours their brains are on hold, dead on the job, going through the motions."

I was amazed. This guy had developed a mythology and philosophy about his job. I could not help asking the next question: "But why is it different for you? You're having a great time!" He looked at me and he said, "I knew you were going to ask me that question. You see, I'm going to be a dancer some day." And he pointed to the administration building and he said, "My bosses are in there, and they're paying for my training!"

Sixteen people dead on the job, and the seventeenth in precisely the same situation figures out a way to live. That man was having a party where you and I would probably not last three days. Imagine the boredom! He and I did have lunch later and he said, "I don't understand why anyone would think my job is boring. I mean, I have a corner office, glass on all sides; I can see the Golden Gate, San Francisco, the Berkeley hills; half of the western world vacations here, and I get to stroll in every day and do what I absolutely love—dance, dance, dance."

This is a powerful story about not letting anything get in the way of our fire, the visionary fire, the heart fire, the creative fire and the soul's fire.

Our call in the 21st century is to bring meaning, magic and enchantment back into the world, and we can only do that by coming forward with our gifts and our talents. This century is really a call to courage and character; a deep, deep remembering of why we're here, our life dreams and our life calling. It takes a lot of courage to walk that road of authenticity in order to stand behind our dreams, to stand up in that tollbooth and dance. It takes a lot of courage to stay in our integrity, honesty and truth-telling instead of giving ourselves over to our need to look good, or to appear other than who we are. It takes a lot of courage to love, and to express what's in our hearts. But that's what we're being called to do in this 21st century—to walk the road of authenticity.

Life-affirming actions are so needed at this time, especially as we're beginning to move out of the archetype of the journey of the hero and the heroine. We're beginning to move into another archetype, the journey of partnership, which is collaboration. The spirit of cooperation opens the vast door to the journey of the tribe, to community and to teamwork. There is a lot that I can do by myself, and there's a lot that I can do with a partner, but there's a thousand and one things that I can do in a community, team, or collective.

In our circles of affection and truth, and in our councils of wisdom, we can begin to bring spirit into action, bring spirit to the sweet face of Mother Nature. It's a calling to bring the Blessing Way back into our family lives, our organizational lives, and our deep interior lives—to bring our great dreams, and stop colluding to that first lie that we don't make a difference. If we truly believe that we don't make a difference I'd like for each of us to think about one stalled car in eight o'clock traffic. That one stalled car has a huge impact!

A very favorite source of inspiration for me is that petite woman who with great grace and no malice put her purse on her lap and she chose not to move. She believed she had every right to sit there. And Rosa Parks changed the South.

Each one of us has a great dream and a great calling. Many of us have put our dreams on the back burner. We say, "Someday when I have enough time, when I have enough money; then I'll do what I really want to do, what has fire for me." At this time there is such a wonderful opening in history, in evolution, if we will just come and take our place.

What I've found among many of the indigenous peoples of the world is that they know how important it is to bring our medicine and our dreams to this world. If we want the Earth to get better we need to show up and take our place, not with our shrouds of insufficiency, but with our long tall bodies and our deep, deep roots. The warrior's way or the leader's way is to show up. And then I can pay attention to what has heart and meaning, which is the healer's way. I can't know what has heart or meaning until I choose to show up, until I choose to be present.

I think it is absolutely essential that each one of us is able to answer yes to one important question. I think it's an act of irresponsibility if we cannot answer yes to this question every day.

CD: *Ignite*, Pamela Gerke ©1996
Edited for poetry

Doin' What You Do

Doin' what you do,
Doin' what you can,
Doin' for the Spirit
in all women and men!
Making people happy,
Making people smile,
Makes the Spirit sing,
even if only for awhile.
If music be your business,
then music be so fine.
Music is the glory of the Spirit,
Spirit divine!

St. Francis of Assisi taught
that everything sings.
Do you love singing?
Is a smile your style?
Then smiling can bring
All the glory of the Spirit, (Glory!)
Everywhere you go,
in everything you do, (Glory!)
in every time and place (Glory!)
in every person, every little thing!
(Glory!)

Doin' what you do,
Doin' what you can,
Doin' for the Spirit
in all women and men!
Making people happy,
Making people smile,
Makes the Spirit sing,
even if only for awhile.
If singing be your business,
then singing be so fine.
Singing is the glory
of the Spirit, Spirit divine!

What do you do?
Do you dance, child?
Then dancing can sing.
Do you love dancing?
When the beat is sweet,
Then dancing can bring
All the glory of the Spirit, (Glory!)
Everywhere you go,
in everything you do, (Glory!)
in every time and place (Glory!)
in every person, every little thing!
(Glory!)

Doin' what you do,
Doin' what you can,
Doin' for the Spirit
in all women and men!
Making people happy,
Making people smile,
Makes the spirit sing
even if only for awhile.
If dancing be your business,
then dancing be so fine.
Dancing is the glory
of the spirit, Spirit divine!

" I know I'm on fire when I've connected to something numinous and extraordinarily beautiful.

—Angeles

I'm going to ask the question in a contemporary form first, and then I'm going to say it as many traditional people may say it: *Is my self-worth as strong as my self-critic?*

This is how it's said in other old traditions: *Is the good, true, and beautiful in my nature as strong as the whispers of the demons and the monsters?*

I have a responsibility to my soul's fire and my character to say yes to that question every day, so I can be a healing catalyst in my life and also to be a change agent.

Among the shamanic traditions of the world, if you go to a shaman or a medicine person, and you are dispirited, disheartened, or depressed, many of them will ask you one of four questions: "When in your life did you stop singing? When in your life did you stop dancing? When in your life did you stop being enchanted by stories, and particularly your own life story? And when in your life did you stop being comforted by the sweet territory of silence?"

Wherever we stop singing, dancing, being enchanted by stories or deeply comforted by silence, we begin to experience soul loss. There's not a culture in the world that does not have song, or dance, or story, or doesn't recognize that in the sweet territory of silence we connect to the mystery in our contemplative and reflective practices.

I know I'm not at home when I'm in appeasement, weak-heartedness, seduction, drama or exaggeration. I know I'm not at home when I am playing the martyr or the victim and wanting someone else to be responsible for my life and therefore guilt induce others. I'm not at home when I'm controlling, because the opposite of control is trust.

I am at home when I have fire; when I am deeply connected to what has heart and meaning, the heart's fire; when I'm seized by a vision that I want to manifest and bring to the sweet face of Mother Earth. I know I'm on fire when I've lost time through some creativity, and when I've experienced a moment of tender sweetness and intimacy in a relationship that has substance and depth. I know I'm on fire when I've connected to something numinous and extraordinarily beautiful that can only be found when trusting in an unshakable part of myself, in a sacred refuge that I can find in my deep interior.

We get smarter and we get wiser about claiming and living our gifts, and moving away from our tendency to abandon ourselves. We know we're in a different place in our journey when we no longer flirt with self-abandonment. I want to tell you just a very old European short story about self-abandonment. We always come back wiser from a detour, to the point that we'll stop self-abandonment.

This is a story that didn't happen a long time ago; that happened in ordinary time, where a woman just couldn't believe the last two months of her life. Everything was working like clockwork, all of her appointments were on time, her bills were all paid. She was in such a state of grace that she just couldn't believe it. So she decided that two weeks from Saturday night, she'd have a party and invite all her friends to celebrate this state of grace. Her life seemed like it was all coming together, that it was all ease and effortless effort. And sure enough, two weeks from Saturday night all her friends were available—that was just how her life had been working. So she decided to call her favorite caterer who was usually booked a year and a half in advance and somebody had just happened to cancel that weekend, and so also with her favorite dance band. All her friends could come, her dance band could come, and her caterer could come.

Two weeks from Saturday they were all there having a wonderful time, when there was a knock at the door. And she wondered, "My, I wonder who that could be. Everybody who's supposed to be here is here." She went to the door and this man said, "Hello, I'm a stranger in the town." All her friends whispered, "He's a stranger in the town. He's a stranger in the town." And he said, "I just heard so much joy and laughter coming from this place that I wondered if I could be so presumptuous as to invite myself in."

Now she thought, "Well, he is very dashing. I mean, really dashing. I mean, the hunk variety." So, she said, "Oh sure, why don't you come on in?"

She introduced him to all her friends, and then she went to the hors d'oeuvres table and would kind of sneak these peeks at him from across the room. And then their eyes locked and she gasped, "He caught me looking at him!" She turned around to the hors d'oeuvres table and said, "Be still my beating heart," because she was flushed purple. She began to fill her plate, and she turned around and it was him. He said, "Would you care to dance?"

" The world is hungry for a healthy feminine.

—Angeles

And so she calmed herself down and very coolly said, "I'd love to dance." And they danced, and they danced, and they danced. Pretty soon, he said just what she thought he might say: "Let's go to my place." She looked around and all her friends were having a wonderful time—no one would notice. And so they went out the back door and he put her in the car. And he had a very nice car! They zoomed off and roared up in front of his house. She looked at this house, and she looked at him, and she thought, "Very interesting man that would live in a house like this. I mean, how many men do you know in ordinary time who live in a tower?"

He helped her out of the car and took her to the front door, and the door was beautifully carved mahogany. There was this white marble spiral staircase that was just gleaming and he said, "Please go on up." And she went up, up, up and came out in this fantastic room with wood parquet floors, and an oriental rug that looked like a magic carpet that could go out the windows, that were arched, overlooking the bay.

He said, "Would you care to dance?" And she said, "Oh, I'd love to dance." He went over to his very fabulous stereo equipment, and he put on slow dance music. And they danced, and they danced, and they danced. And they'd been dancing about an hour when she just decided, "Oh, I've just been so gone here, I haven't even been listening to what we've been dancing to."

So she decided to listen, and she thought, "This is very unusual music." Because what they were dancing to, gliding around the room and slow dancing to, was like a high pitched "ooooo" sound, like wolves howling. That was the music that they'd been dancing to.

She decided to look around the room. And she looked around the room, and don't get me wrong, it was a very attractive room, but extraordinary would be a bit of an exaggeration. And she decided to look at him. Don't get me wrong—he was very attractive, but dashing and of the hunk variety would be an exaggeration. And before she knew it, she found herself dancing with a skeleton, and in that very ordinary time, not so long ago, last week some time.

They say that they lived well, and they died well. And it is said

that an old famous saying comes from that town: "Remember,
the journey first, and relationships will fall into place.
Remember, the journey first, and relationships will fall into
place. Remember, the journey first, and relationships will
fall into place."

I want to quickly peel that back, because when we begin to come
home to who we really are, when we really trust our hearts, and
follow what really has heart meaning, our life can work like
clockwork, with effortless effort, and we experience a state of
grace and fluidity. And when we're at home with who we are,
many parts of ourselves want to come home. And when a lot of
our parts of ourselves are at home, and we're having a wonderful
time at the bedrock of who we are, there's always a knock at the
door. Because any disowned part of our nature, any part of
ourselves that we have kept away, comes knocking: "Hello, I'm
a stranger in this town and I heard so much joy and laughter
coming from this place that I hope it won't be too presumptuous
that I invite myself in." So any disowned part wants to be
included, and we are always enchanted, fascinated, and seduced
by the unfamiliar. And the moment of choice always comes up
whether we're going to stay at home with ourselves or not. She
read his lips, and he said, "Let's go to my place."

At that moment of choice we often think that we only have three
options: "yes," "no," or "I don't know." But the truth is that we
have multiple options. She could say, "Oh, what a great idea! A
progressive party—we'll just take the whole party to your
house." Or: "You know, I really don't trust myself because I
have an enormous crush on you. In fact, I'm so attracted to you
that I'm reduced to a fourteen year old in droolsville, and I'd
like to take it a little slow." Or: "Sure I'd love to come to your
place right now, but I'm not going to until I get to know you
better." The truth is always an option, always an option. Or: "We
don't have to go to your place or my place—we could go to a
creative third place, a neutral place." There are all kinds of
options and one option is always the truth.

The world is hungry for the healthy feminine, and the healthy
feminine is the feminine that does not move to the extremity.
The healthy feminine is one that doesn't test love, or manipulate
for love, attention, acceptance or approval. The healthy feminine
doesn't go into drama or victimization. The healthy feminine
does not go into appeasement patterns, or collapse, or control, or

seduction. Those are all behaviors of the covert feminine that lives in every man and woman. It's amazing what the covert feminine will do to get attention. It's not a pretty sight.

We need to wean ourselves away from the underlying belief that "I can't have what I want unless I employ these behaviors." That's the collective lie that women collude to. It's the ultimate self-abandonment, and keeps us out of our emotional integrity— saying what's so when it's so, saying what I mean, and doing what I say. Whenever we abandon ourselves we always go out the back door. And then we begin to fall out of the fascination, the seduction and the enchantment. There's often a haunting that starts taking place. We begin to feel empty and kind of sick. This kind of sickening feeling comes over us—it's called the hounds of heaven that say, "Don't you think you've been away from home long enough?" I love the saying from Montana, Idaho and Wyoming that when you turn over on the pillow the next morning, you would almost chew through your own arm to get out of there, which is called "Coyote Ugly."

When we look at things as they are, we begin to wake up to what's really there rather than what we want to be there. And when we begin to wake up out of the illusion—and I love the word collusion because it means "co-illusion"—we are always left dancing with the bones of the illusion, dancing with the skeleton of the illusions, because we never saw it as it really was in the first place.

We must trust the old saying, "Remember, the journey first, and relationships will fall into place. Remember, the journey first, and relationships will fall into place." Because when we abandon ourselves, our hearts, and our emotional integrity, we step out of the river of love.

The river of love is about learning about love and expressing love, staying in our emotional integrity, saying what's so when it's so, and saying what I mean, and doing what I say. Telling the truth without blame or judgment. The river of love is the place where we can access the healthy feminine, and be totally connected to the sacred mystery. On the river of love there comes a place at the last doorway, which is our death, where we see that it has always been about love. It's never about achievement or our success in life; it's all about love. And we defy medical records at the last doorway, because we want those who we are leaving behind to know how much they were valued and cherished, and also that we were valued and cherished.

We all need to grow into a place that honors our gifts and our character more than the shroud of insufficiency. We know we're starting to move more toward the healthy feminine when we stop carrying our wounds in front of us as if they are us. We know that we are on the river of love when we take responsibility for really showing up with who we really are in this moment

There's nothing more powerful than the healthy feminine, and a group of women and children saying, "No, this has to stop. This has to stop." Women will not be taken seriously until they come back home to the deep power that they hold. As women move forward with that power and peace, and begin to really model that for other women, we will gain a critical mass. This will be extraordinary.

Florence Chadwick knew her dream when she was five years old. She insisted that her family flank her whole bedroom with fish and aquariums, because she was fascinated with how they would swim through water. She would watch their every move, and then she would go into the bathtub and practice moving like that in water. This is a story about where she put her dream down and picked it up again. She knew all her life that this was what she wanted to do—it seized her. It's a wonderful true story, again from the Chicken Soup for the Soul series, that I think can inspire all of us who have put our dreams down.

The river of love is the place where we can access the healthy feminine, and be totally connected to the sacred mystery.

—Angeles

artwork

Women of Wisdom Art Series

Deborah Koff-Chapin ©2006

When she looked ahead, Florence Chadwick saw nothing but a solid wall of fog. Her body was numb. She had been swimming for sixteen hours. Already, she was the first woman to swim the English Channel in both directions. Now, at age thirty-four, her goal was to be the first woman to swim from Catalina Island to the California coast. On that Fourth of July morning in 1952 the sea was like an ice bath, and the fog was so dense she could hardly see the support ropes. Sharks cruised through the water toward her lone figure, only to be frightened away by rifle shots. Against the frigid grip of the sea she struggled hour after hour after hour, while millions watched on national TV. Alongside her in one of the boats, her mother and her trainer offered encouragement. Her mother told Florence it wasn't much further. But all she could see was fog. They urged her not to quit. She had never quit, until then.

With only a half mile to go she asked to be pulled out. Still thawing her chilled body several hours later, she told a reporter, "Look, I'm not excusing myself. But if I could have only seen land, I might have made it." It was not fatigue, or even the cold water that defeated her. It was the fog. She was unable to see her goal and she stopped swimming.

Two months later, she tried again. This time, despite the same dense fog, she swam with her faith intact, and her goal clearly pictured in her mind. She knew that somewhere behind that fog was land and this time she made it. Florence Chadwick became the first woman to swim the Catalina Channel, eclipsing the men's record by two hours.

And that's a healing story.

The last topic that I want us to end on is commitment. We have to have a commitment to our dream; that we won't stop no matter what. We won't stop. This is really fighting the good fight for our dreams.

Here is a really amazing story about commitment. Five years ago I was asked to do some consulting work outside of New York, and they said, "We'll meet you outside down by the Miracle Bridge." I said, "The Miracle Bridge? What bridge is that?" And they said, "Oh, it's the Brooklyn Bridge."

I said, "Well, why do you call it the Miracle Bridge?" And they said, "Oh, we don't know—us natives, we've always called it that since the late 1800's." I thought, "Oh, there's a story." It took me 18 months but I finally found the story, again in the Chicken Soup for the Soul series*, about commitment to a dream, and not letting anything get in the way—fog, negative voices, anything.

The Brooklyn Bridge that spans the river between Manhattan and Brooklyn is simply an engineering miracle. In 1883 a creative engineer named John Roebling was inspired by an idea for this spectacular bridge project. However, bridge building experts told him to forget it; it just wasn't possible. Roebling was not convinced that it couldn't be done, and he immediately began pressuring his son Washington, an up-and-coming engineer, that the bridge could be built.

Washington, after his father had showed him all the plans, knew that it could be built too. So the two of them conceived the concept of how it could be accomplished and how they could overcome the obstacles. Somehow they even convinced the bankers in New York to finance the project. There was unharnessed excitement and energy; they hired their crew and began to build their dream bridge.

The project was only underway a few months before a tragic on-site accident killed John Roebling and injured his son Washington. Washington was severely brain damaged, and everyone thought the project would have to be scrapped, since the Roeblings were the only ones who knew how the bridge could be built. Washington Roebling was unable to move or talk, but his mind was as sharp as ever. One day as he lay in his hospital bed, an idea flashed through his mind about how to develop a communication code. The only part of his entire body that he could move was one finger. So he touched the arm of his wife Mary with that finger, and he tapped out in code to communicate to her what she was to tell the engineers who continued building the bridge.

* Adapted from "The Miracle Bridge" in *Fresh Packet of Sower's Seeds* by Brian Cavanaugh, TOR. Copyright ©1994 by Brian Cavanaugh, TOR. Paulist Press, Inc., New York/Mahwah, NJ. Used with permission of Paulist Press, Inc. www.paulistpress.com

For thirteen years Washington tapped out his instructions on Mary's arm with one finger, and she delivered the message to the engineers until the Brooklyn Bridge was completed.

That's commitment! And that's the commitment that the healthy feminine has to her children. That's the commitment that the healthy feminine has to her husband. That's the commitment that the healthy feminine has to her community. That's the commitment that the healthy feminine has to her own dreams, her own emotional integrity, and her own creativity.

We must ask for what we truly want, and be open to outcome, not attached to outcome. To know that we've planned well, we've prepared well, we've done everything we possibly can, but if the doors shut, then the spirit world is saying maybe it's not the right time, or it's not the right place, or that we need to be open to other options. And it's about carrying both the "what I want" and, "I'm open to other options."

The mystery cannot be answered by repeating the question. Nor can it be bought by going to amazing places. It means continuing to ask the question, and knowing it might not make a difference. I can keep going to other cultures or countries and feeling that maybe it's there, but I cannot be attached to finding it. Not until the eyes and desires have been stilled for many years. Not until then will I cross over from confusion. Not until the eyes and desires have been stilled, not until the eyes have turned inward, and not until I stop grasping for my desires will I meet the call of the 21st century and come home to the inherent wisdom within my nature.

artwork

Women of Wisdom Art Series

Deborah Koff-Chapin ©2002

...come home to the inherent wisdom...

Excerpt from Coming Home,
Robin Maynard-Dobbs ©1999

Coming Home

Sisters,
Answers will not be found
in glossy pictures of hard bellies
that have no room to breathe.
Our bellies will never
be flat enough.
We will waste our lives,
forever waiting for someone else
to say we're o.k.
Come home.

Be still long enough to hear
where the only real answers
can be found here in the dark.
This sacred dark place
inside our own bellies
will always speak the truth
a singular, inconvenient truth
that may upset the status quo.

Dare we listen, dare we begin
to feed our own hungers
with the only nourishment
that will ever sustain us…
self love
self trust
self honoring.

Unless we care for ourselves
starting right here with
our own bodies,
we cannot begin
to care for anyone else.
Let us start now to do the most
important work we will ever do.
Next time you feel hunger,
listen to your belly, let it speak.

If the voice is too soft to hear,
then act on what you think
it might be saying.
You and your belly need practice
in trusting one another.

The more you listen,
the clearer its messages
will become.
This body you inhabit
is a living miracle…
treat it with reverence
by honoring its wisdom.

As women, we were given
the power to create life
inside of our bodies.
As humans, we were given
the power of choice.

Will you choose to
keep searching endlessly
for answers outside yourself?
Or will you begin to trust
the truth that can only
be found within?

Let us be as fierce on
our own behalf.
Let not anyone take away
the most precious part of us,
our center point, our own truth.

Only when we find our
authentic voices
and live from there
will we satisfy our restless hunger.
Only then will we come home.

Empower Your Self

explore your dreams and spirit...

1   What are your gifts?

2   What gets in the way of your fire?

3   When do you feel most at home with yourself?

4   What illusions do you dance with?

5   What is your commitment to your dream?

_____

_____

_____

_____

_____

_____

_____

_____

_____

_____

_____

_____

"Part of the healing is healing ourselves, that's true;
that's a life long endeavor.

a life long endeavor
a life long endeavor
a life long endeavor
a life long endeavor
a life long endeavor

She is the Source, Montserrat ©1999

a life long endeavor
a life long endeavor

CHAPTER 4

Judith Orloff

Biography

Judith Orloff, M.D. is a psychiatrist, intuitive, and author of the bestseller *Positive Energy: Ten Extraordinary Prescriptions For Transforming Fatigue, Stress, and Fear Into Vibrance, Strength, and Love.* She is an Assistant Professor of Psychiatry at UCLA with a private practice in Los Angeles. Her other books are *Second Sight, Guide to Intuitive Healing: Five Steps to Physical, Emotional, and Sexual Wellness.* Her upcoming book, *Emotional Freedom*, will be released in September, 2008. She leads workshops on the interrelationship of intuition, energy, emotions and medicine. For more information visit www.drjudithorloff.com.

Reflections Today

I feel more strongly than ever that feminine consciousness is the force that will save the Earth and restore inner peacefulness. To me, the feminine is the deep, flowing, receptive part of each of us, in women and men, that is constantly processing intuition. I feel this force moving within me every day, growing more and more, trusting the truths that come from it. Developing the feminine is a treasured part of my ongoing spiritual growth, my connector to spirit and the Earth. Over the years, I feel proud to say I've grown more confident in my own feminine side. Since I first spoke at the Women of Wisdom conferences, I am blessed to feel increasingly more connected with feminine energy, and feel honored to be able to continue to transmit this to my patients and workshop participants. The Goddess Quan Yin, the protector of women and Goddess of compassion, is a presence I turn to and draw strength from. She is on my altar, next to my candles and incense. She is in my office. Many of my patients have found connecting with this yin energy through her very meaningful. I believe the more we connect with the feminine, and balance it with the yang (the more aggressive, efforting masculine forces), the richer and more powerful our lives can be.

–Judith Orloff, M.D.

artwork

*Sea
Priestess*

Diana
Denslow
©2001

Second Sight

a talk with Judith Orloff

> Finding my voice and coming out in the world with it was healing for me.
>
> —Judith

Intuition is a still small voice inside that tells us the truth about things; the essence of our power. It's been called Second Sight. Intuition flows like water; it amplifies like water. Two-thirds of the body is water, so we resonate with the fluidity of life through our intuition—the moon, the tides, all the natural elements. Intuition is not just about information; it is where the answer is. It's a spiritual awareness of the higher Self. Nothing is divorced from that knowing inside. When you go inside you find the whole universe and you discover how it connects to the divine.

I'm a psychiatrist and I also work as an intuitive. Patients come to me and they tell me why they're coming, and at the same time I tune into any images, impressions, sights, smells, poems, sounds, knowings, songs, energy body sensations that I have as I'm listening. I love listening this way. It's a beautiful thing to be able to listen to someone one hundred percent and to focus on them and not think of anything else except the moment. This is how I listen. I live and breathe it. I walk it. It's the way I live my life. It's my passion.

Intuition is not elusive; it's very concrete. It is that still small voice inside that we must access to learn the absolute truth about things, without any kind of questions, ambivalence, or uncertainty. This is the voice that has been with you through the centuries, through the lifetimes, through everything you've ever experienced before. With intuition you're tuning in to the timelessness of your spirit, for the knowledge you've accumulated over all of this experience is in you.

We're born into this human life without a memory of who we were. Part of the spiritual path is reclaiming that memory, and reclaiming who we are in a deeper sense as it connects to something greater. And that something greater begins in here, inside ourselves.

All you have to do is want it. If you really want it, it will be there for you. It is your Self. It doesn't matter how old you are. You can be one year old, you can be a fetus, or 110 years old—that higher Self is there. If you want to get in touch with this you must go inside and learn how to be quiet. If the mind is active all the time, and you can't experience that inner stillness, you're never going to find it.

I've gone through years of medical training and so I have a very highly developed analytic mind; I love to analyze things. Yet I profoundly realize how limited the mind is in terms of understanding things like love, death or intuition. I like to balance many sides of myself—the analytical mind with the flowing, intuitive side.

The intuitive realm doesn't obey the same laws as the physical universe. It isn't sequential—it's non-time, non-space. In the silent space there is no past, present or future. Sometimes this disorients people. Mystics have described this as oneness, and when you begin to feel this oneness—this flow that's between everybody, every living thing, and every nonliving thing—there's a relationship going on. You can feel it as a pulse and it's very real. You can have many levels of awareness at once.

Freedom is the great gift that can come from speaking your voice. For me, speaking out has been a healing path. As a child I had many premonitions and my parents didn't encourage me to develop my intuition at all. When I was eleven, they told me to never mention them again in our home. So part of my early process was suppressing my gift, being shamed into thinking there was something wrong with me. It does tremendous violence to children if their voices and creativity are stifled, if their parents don't see who they are and don't honor their intuitions.

Finding my voice and coming out in the world with it was healing for me. I had so many questions: Why use it? How do I use it? Is it something I should use with patients? When is it appropriate? Can I trust it? We all have these questions; we all face a collective kind of angst when it comes to embracing our visionary side, because it has been so divorced from who we are.

My intention is to help make intuition a conscious spiritual practice available in every second of your being here. Tune into this conscious connection by communing with the inner voice, listening to dreams, listening to the body, sensing energies—all ways to interrelate with the world.

I know a lot of people dream. They remember something and they have a longing. There's something that calls out in one's sleep and in one's spirit that brings one towards the water flow. I really encourage you to move towards that flow, because if you fight it, it creates problems. It can cause depression, anxiety, or physical illness. If you've had intuitive gifts since you were young and you squash them, it can cause so many difficulties. It's a big power surge that comes through you, so it's not a good thing if you try to hold it down. So bring it up, gently.

Beliefs are essential to intuitive healing, and you must be clear on this. Having the correct beliefs is the first step to developing your intuition. And one of the most important beliefs is that love is the most powerful healing force in the universe. There's nothing that doesn't come from love. Every cancer cure, every depression lifting: it all ultimately comes from love. Love is the healing force.

You must know this in every bit of your being, because you will be tested. If you believe in the tenets of love, you must apply them. Everything must be looked at as a call to love. What happens if you get cancer? How are you going to apply that love to yourself and your body? Illness can be a fierce teacher and a very powerful path. You'll be put into situations and you have to ask yourself: Is this call to love in such dire circumstances more significant than any one event or loss in life, no matter how painful?

> One of the most important beliefs is that love is the most powerful healing force in the universe.

—Judith

Body is the Temple words and music by
Libby Roderick. CD: *If You See a Dream*.
© Libby Roderick Music, 1984.
Art: *Butterfly*, Sue Coccia ©1997

Body is the Temple

The body is the temple of the spirit
The body is the window to the soul
If you listen lowly you will hear Her
Whispering the truths that must be told.

Lava flow, raging river, windblown trees, moonlit nights,
Ocean tides, desert canyons, mountain lakes, arctic lights

The body passes life on to the young ones
The body is the cradle of desire,
The Goddess sends Her breath across the embers
Kindling the sparks into a fire.

Lava flow, raging river, windblown trees, moonlit nights,
Ocean tides, desert canyons, mountain lakes, arctic lights

Come down and hear Her, Time will abide
Come down and touch Her, Time will abate
Time will have to wait.

For the body is the temple of the spirit
The body is the window to the soul
If you listen lowly you will hear Her
Whispering the truths that must be told
Whispering the truths that make you whole
The body is the temple of the soul.

Living an intuitive life means having your arms open and diving in. It doesn't mean guarding yourself; it means trusting what life gives you and going in and trying your best. Apply everything you know about love in every situation you are put in. Sometimes you fall short and sometimes you can't do it. Sometimes when I'm gripped with fear and I can't contact that love in myself, I pray for the fear to be lifted. I pray to find the love in my heart when I can't get there on my own. You must remember to make these requests.

So love as the healing source is the first belief in developing intuitive healing. The second belief that is absolutely crucial is a commitment to make fear release its grip in your life. It must be absolute. Otherwise your fears can sneak in there and take you away from your intuition in any given moment. Fear is the antithesis of intuition. Intuition is pure truth; fear is not. You have to consciously make the shift to go into the intuition whenever the fears come up.

The third tenet of intuitive healing is that healing has a very wide definition. It can mean vibrant health and wellness, and it can also mean illness. Sometimes you get an illness and that is the healing. There is something about the experience that brings healing. I've seen this with many people who get ill. They come into their heart, and grow more spiritually through an illness than when they were not ill. For some reason, this is the catalyst. So if you bring this attitude of love, compassion and intuition, you can help people through whatever it is they're going through.

Healing can come from illness, and in some instances death. Dying at the moment when it is time to go is the proper healing. Let the dying go, help them over with love and ease; don't try to pull them back. It's not your job to revive life when it's time to go. You might not understand why a thirty-year-old mother has to go, but you help her over and that can be the healing.

I feel very strongly that we need to learn about death. The western mind is very death phobic, and sees death as taking you away from your body into some black hole. I have written quite a bit about death, and worked with many terminally ill people, and I think that working with the dying and contemplating death are amazing ways to open up your spirituality and intuition.

I've had a fascination with watching the spirit as it leaves the body, as I wanted to see with my eyes what goes on in this process. I wanted to sense, I wanted to know. What I've seen is that death is an energy that comes in when you're born and it stays with you. It's a creative, affirmative, positive force. It's so creative. In fact, it helps with the dissolution of your body, it helps you out; but this is not its only function.

Knowing about death is an intuitive knowing and experience, not an intellectual understanding. You need to feel it in order to know it. It's an experience in your body that is unforgettable. It's like going home. It is life, it is love, and it is a distillation of all goodness you've ever found. It's the most positive energy; it is like everything that you need not be afraid of.

You can invite death in and trust your intuition and your experience around death. You can do this in meditation or however you feel like doing it. Trust your inner guidance and your intuition, and trust your experience of energy. Trust the dreams that might come. Then, you can have a positive experience of what death is, and this can lift fear like nothing I've ever seen.

Intuition can show you that you are much more after this life; your spirit is huge and it will go beyond this body. You can discover that it is so luminous, so bright and so resilient, that you need not be afraid of losing yourself through death. When you leave here, you take yourself with you. You take your spirit, your inner Self, and your intuition. This is the most valuable thing in the world. You can't take your money, you can't take your friends, you can only take your Self. So we're here on Earth cultivating ourselves. This is a valuable thing.

You must learn about death; it's part of basic human training. If you go through life unsure about this, in some way it can cause a lot of confusion.

My father was going through a very serious illness during a time that I was writing my book *Second Sight*. I was there with a yellow pad at his deathbed, writing down the details because I didn't want to miss out on anything. I wanted to get down all the intuitions I had around my father's death. I wrote quite a bit about death, and emotions and relationships. And it was interesting that my father died right before I began a chapter on sex.

> Intuition demands that you stay awake and aware in every moment.
>
> —Judith

I asked myself—how am I going to get from the death chapter to sexuality? But during the time of my father's death, I experienced an awakening of my sensual self. A certain womanliness was coming into me as a result of helping him pass on. So it felt very natural to write a chapter about my feather's death and then move on to sexuality. You see, you can uncover so many unexpected things when you look at death, and when you use intuition to look deep into your experiences.

While my father was going through this illness and death I saw an incredible white light around him, and the white light said to me, "All is well."

I felt this so deeply. And this is a paradox: somebody goes through a supposedly irredeemable experience, and yet there is white light present with a sense of wellbeing. Intuition helps resolve the paradox. On the surface it looked like one kind of terrible situation, but my intuition revealed something much deeper.

Intuition can allow you to penetrate surfaces, and go beyond accepted responses to situations. Intuition helps you see the mystery within the paradoxes. The mystery is not straightforward; it's always surprising. It's always deep and it's very rarely what you expect. Intuition demands that you stay awake and aware in every moment, whether you're going through the death of a parent, or suffering from an illness or depression, or you want to awaken sexually and you feel things blocking you.

There are also beliefs that get in the way of healing—for example, the belief that we create our own reality. I've seen people come into my office and say, "I meditate, I'm a good person, I do everything right." And they feel they've done something wrong because they've got cancer. They ask, "How did I create this cancer in my body?" If you get cancer, do you want somebody saying that to you, that you created your cancer?

So beliefs are very important and they are the first step to developing intuition. The second step is that you must have a total commitment to be in your body. Being in your body means listening to the signals your body sends. Most people live from the neck up. When you start your day, notice *how* you are in your body and *where* you are in your body. Notice if your attention starts to go to your mind, and you're thinking and worrying about your list of things to do, and suddenly you don't have feet, knees, stomach, breasts, or genitals anymore. People go unconscious; people don't notice they lose their body when they are in their mind.

If you want to be an intuitive person all the time, you can't leave the body. I floated above my body for many years because I never really liked being in a body. I always fantasized when I was little that a space ship would come and take me to some place where I belonged. We're all huge spirits that get born into these bodies and we need some education about how to be in our bodies, but very little is ever said about it. So at a certain point I made a commitment to be in my body. I realized I was

artwork

Women of Wisdom Art Series

Deborah Koff-Chapin
©2006

> " You must
> listen to
> your body
> as a form
> of intuition.
>
> —Judith

missing a lot of intuitions and wholesome life experiences by floating outside.

Many psychic children have suffered traumas in their life or they've suffered abuse, so they've learned to dissociate from their bodies and have out-of-body experiences at a very young age. If you want to be intuitive, part of the healing is coming back again to your body and dealing with the trauma.

Everybody has traumas, and the healing is going through the traumas and coming back in the body and teaching about it. Dealing with the traumas is one thing, but I encourage you to go out and teach. The healers and the teachers that I trust the most are the ones who have gone through the ups and downs of life, have kept their eyes open and have healed themselves in some way. Part of the healing is healing ourselves, that's true; that's a lifelong endeavor. But then getting out and circulating what you know with others is very important.

Being in the body helps you know so much. If you ask your body, "How do I like this person?" and your stomach goes into a knot or the shoulders get tense—that's a good answer! If your heart opens and you feel relaxed and comfortable, that's another answer.

You have to ask: How does my body feel about this situation? Your mind might say, "This is a good job, I'm getting paid lots of money for it," but if your body is feeling sick, it is giving you a different message. Most people take the job and they live with it, and then they have real problems. Don't take the job! Something better will come along—something your body likes. You have to have faith in that. Taking a path that your body is uncomfortable with will create a problem.

I had a patient who had a dream of being a real estate broker; she wanted to sell houses by the ocean and have time for herself. She was a school administrator for a long time even though her body felt awful as an administrator. But for practical reasons she decided to stay in the administrative job, and a couple of years later she developed a malignant tumor in her breast. While she was getting chemotherapy, she said to me, "I'm going to go be a real estate broker. Life is too short."

It took an illness for her to make the decision to follow her dream, and now she's been in remission for many years and her body feels good. I'm not saying that if you don't listen to your body that you're going to get cancer, but you will be drained in some way. So you must listen to your body as a form of intuition.

A great way of listening to your body is to learn its anatomy. You have these precious vehicles for a certain time, and you have no idea of what's inside. If you want to send energy to your body you have to know how you're made. I suggest you find *Gray's Anatomy Coloring Book*. Color in your organs. Learn where your organs are and what they do. This way, if you need healing, you know where to send the energy and you'll know how to visualize it. Otherwise it's a big blur in there. So visualize where your organs are and begin to know there's an intuitive intelligence in your organs that is very powerful.

Each organ speaks an intuitive language and you can speak to it. I don't mean a metaphoric language or visualization, I mean your organs actually speak; your organs encode information. This is the concept of cellular memory. Claire Sylvia wrote this wonderful book called *A Change of Heart*, where she talks about her heart transplant. After the transplant, she suddenly experienced new tastes in food, new desires for things to do, and new thoughts, and she didn't know where it was coming from.

She got psychic impressions that it was from her donor, and through her intuition she tracked down the donor's parents and found out these were his tastes, his likes and dislikes. So the heart itself actually carried the memories of its owner at the time. Our organs hold who we are and we can speak to these organs and get information. We always have the opportunity to commune with our bodies, but we must know about our bodies in order to do this.

The next step in developing intuition is sensing subtle energies—our energy bodies. We're made of light, and this light extends many feet beyond our physical bodies. We can sense it and feel it. And we must, because it can tell us about people and it can indicate subtle energetic changes in ourselves.

One way to understand subtle energy is through the concept of energy vampires. These are people who suck you dry. You're around them and suddenly you have no more energy. So you can sense energy by being around people who drain you. They can look good, but if you're standing there and you're feeling nauseous or you have a headache, know that this is a real subtle energetic phenomenon. Don't question yourself; just accept it. If you're not sure, back off about 15 to 20 feet from the person and see if you feel better. Take care of yourself—don't choose to be with people who drain your energy. Don't marry them or choose them as business partners.

You may have friends who are energy vampires—you love them, but they keep you on the phone for three hours talking about breaking up with their boyfriend for the third time. You're just listening, but you feel drained afterwards. What you need to do with people like this is not listen. Don't do it anymore; it's not good for you. What you need to say to them is, "I'll listen for ten minutes but then I have to go, because I feel drained when you go around and around." Don't say it angrily, don't punish them, just say it. Say, "I love you; you're my friend, but I can only listen for ten minutes. Then I have to go. If you want to get into this illusion, I'll talk to you about that, but until then it's just ten minutes." It'll do wonders for you in terms of protecting your energy. It can take years off your life listening like that.

If you feel you drain other people, then you need to courageously take a look at why. Often, early life traumas cause this kind of energy drain. The trauma causes something like a leak in your energy field, and you are constantly reaching out to another to get it filled, but you can't contain it. The secret is to heal that trauma and patch it up so you can learn to contain who you are. Learn to feel the inner self and root it. This rooting phenomenon happens in meditation. Let your meditation help you feel grounded, feel strong inside. Let it help you go deep into the Earth until the holes get plugged up. It is not good to go on in life with this issue because people won't respond to you well. They'll feel it. They might not know what they're feeling, but they won't want to be with you.

The alternative of this, energetically, is when you meet somebody who comes from their heart. They exude this tremendous sense of heart, and you love to be around them. These are the people to choose as friends or mates.

The next step in developing intuition is to ask for inner guidance—to go inside and ask over and over again. Have a constant ongoing inner dialogue with what's inside. Let's say you have a question: How can I heal myself? My body isn't feeling well. You go in and you wait. The whole posture of intuition is asking, and then waiting. It's not getting nervous if nothing comes. it's not trying to force it if nothing comes. It's simply waiting.

This is the essence of intuition: ask, and then wait. We're not taught this in Western culture. It's hard to wait; it's hard to be patient and just sit there. Some people go into a panic because they're so afraid that nothing will come and that will mean they don't have an inner self.

If nothing comes to me, I go on with my life; I go about my business, and then I ask again. I go back and I ask again, and if it still doesn't come I go about my business. There are some circumstances where you do ask and ask and you get nothing, and in those cases just stop asking. Maybe you're not meant to know at that moment.

Most of the time you really get a very informed response to your inquiry. But don't get too fixated if you ask in meditation and the answer doesn't come then. It might come in a dream, or you ask in a dream and then you're walking down the street and you overhear a conversation and that's your answer.

Intuition is very fluid—it's not linear or predictable—it's flow, it's surprises. If it's not here, it's there. Keep looking; keep your eyes open; keep your antennae active. That's intuition. It's about being alive. You have to trust it. You ask, you wait, practice non-action, be the mountain, and let it come to you. Trust that something will come to you. Be open and receptive.

" Intuition is very fluid—it's not linear or predictable —it's flow, it's surprises.

—Judith

Intuition is very feminine. The feminine in both men and women is extremely receptive like this. It doesn't go out and do big conquering things.

If you ever want to know what feminine energy is, I strongly suggest renting a video called *The Miracle of Life*. It's a close up of the egg and the sperm meeting and it shows the incredible energy when a man ejaculates into a woman—this flow of sperm going into the vagina. You can see millions of sperm, really active, conquering, going directly to the egg. It's important for you to see the sperm move; it epitomizes male energy.

The woman's environment is acidic and it tries to kill the sperm because it sees it as alien. Isn't that interesting? If you want to know about male and female dynamics go into biology: you'll see everything. Most of the sperm drop out, but a few get up there, and then they reach this luminescent egg. The egg is a huge, beautiful, white, radiant orb and it's flowing. The little tiny sperm goes up to the edge of the egg and it needs the egg to reach out and pull it into the egg. Then you see the sperm dissolving in this feminine egg. If anyone wonders what motivates this fear of commitment with men, look at the biology of the egg and the sperm—you can learn so much from our bodies!

So this egg is the feminine. Have a vision of this egg just waiting, undulating, huge and beautiful—this is who you are when you're waiting intuitively. You are like this egg: feminine spirit waiting for the intuition. Man or woman, it doesn't matter. Just feel receptive, waiting, flowing and being like water. That's all you do—you wait and then something comes. And when something comes it is so beautiful! It can be a very light kind of pressure that comes over you—you get an impression, you get a dream, or maybe you get a memory from the past.

The impressions will come like flashes; you'll get an image quickly or a transmission will come. You don't have to think, you just get it; it's a knowing. That's how intuitions come in, and it doesn't require that linear process. It's very dynamic. You might get a body sensation; you might feel that your stomach doesn't feel good right now; you might feel an opening of energy like a great sun in your heart; or you could get a voice. I've had a voice that has come to me over the years. It is a genderless voice that tells me things, very straightforward things, like:

CD: *ReUnion*, Susan Osborn ©1987

She Speaks

She speaks in the rushing of a river
She speaks in the crying of a child
She speaks in the glances of lovers
She speaks in the footsteps of the wild

She speaks in the quiet of the morning
She speaks in the ringing of the bell
She speaks in the colors of the dawning
She speaks in the heart of this prisoner's cell

And when she speaks
I can hear if I listen
There's music everywhere
And in that moment
Past and future forgiven
That moment is here

I call to the night wind through pine boughs
I call to my heart's own stillness
I call to the pounding of sea waves
I call to the calm beyond the storm

Written after moving to Orcas Island as a celebration of the
power and beauty of nature. She speaks so clearly here.

You're going to go get an MD in order to have the credentials to help legitimize intuition in medicine. You might get some directions, so remember to ask, remember to listen, and remember to act.

Ask, listen and act.

Don't forget the third part—you must come to trust all this.

The last thing I want to talk about is asking for dreams. If you want to learn about intuition I really encourage you to navigate the dream world. Every night when you go to sleep travel to many places, go to different realms. You don't have to worry about gravity. You can fly; you can get imagery, impressions, knowings, and you don't have to speak. It's totally telepathic in dreams; you just know. This is our natural way of being.

You can ask dreams for guidance about anything. You can have ongoing dialogues with your dreams. When I have a question I'll ask a dream what I should do, and sometimes I'll get the most ingenious solutions. Get used to asking, to listening, and to remembering. Keep a dream journal with the pen by the bed. The key to remembering dreams is not to talk to anyone the first five minutes when you wake up. The minute you start talking, you've gone to linear mode and you lose the dreams.

These are the steps I hope you will try and enjoy if you want to develop intuition. They are: to have productive beliefs, and let go of the unproductive beliefs; to commit to being in your body; to learn to sense subtle energies; to ask for intuitive guidance; to listen; to act; and to work with your dreams. These are all ways to help you go deep into your power, your essence. This is the person you were meant to be.

artwork

*Wolf
Maiden*

Diana
Denslow
©1993

Empower Your Self

explore your dreams and spirit...

1   What is your memory of having intuitive gifts as a child?

2   How do you know you are in the grip of fear and what causes your fear?

3   What messages do you receive from your dreams?

4   On what occassions do you find yourself leaving your body?

5   What messages does your body send you?

6   When have you experienced energy vampires around you?

7   What would you like guidance on that you can go inside and ask?

_____

_____

_____

_____

_____

_____

_____

_____

_____

The most precious gifts women can
give to each other are their personal stories.

precious gifts
precious gifts

precious gifts
precious gifts

Photo, Lori Barra ©2007

CHAPTER 5

Isabel Allende

Biography

Isabel Allende sprang from the obscurity of political exile to world-wide popularity in just a few years. One of Latin America's most celebrated writers, her numerous international best sellers include *The House of the Spirits, Of Love and Shadows, Eva Luna, The Infinite Plane, Paula* and her latest book, *Inés of My Soul.* Considered the finest female practitioner of magical realism, Allende has a rare ability to blend fantasy and legend with political fact. In 2004 she was inducted into the American Academy of Arts and Letters.

Reflections Today

I have come to the conclusion that the most precious gifts women can give to each other are their personal stories. By sharing our experiences, our pains and joys, our fears, hopes and desires, we create a sacred space where we can find new strength. Allow me to tell you about the only subject that I know really well: my own life. In doing so, I hope to encourage you to do the same and share your stories.

I tried to look as honestly as possible inside myself, to go deeply into my memory and my heart, to search in the dark place where all the fears come from and in the luminous place where the creative force is generated, looking for the motivations that have driven me forward and the uncertainties that have pulled me back. What are the fundamental issues that define my personality and determine my life? Two themes come to my mind: love and losses.

–Isabel Allende

artwork

Women of
Wisdom
Art Series

Deborah
Koff-Chapin
©1998

Love and Losses

a talk with Isabel Allende

I should start with the most solid love in my life, who was my mother. She says that when she was expecting me she had a dream in which I appeared as a beautiful, smart and charming girl. Obviously, she was very disappointed when I was born! But she quickly got over it, and she surrendered to the biological calling of most mothers, which was to love me. I suppose the reproductive instinct is to blame for such an unreasonable behavior. Actually, the more I live, the more I marvel at this thing that females have—this capacity to love another being more than they love themselves.

My melodramatic mother took upon herself the task of loving me more than she ever loved anybody—more than any man in her life or any other of her own children. Why? Nobody knows; I was just the lucky chosen one. Her love for me is like having permanent central heating; the world is never too cold with such a stove.

A few other people have loved me too along the way: my grandfather, who wanted me to be a boy and never got over the shock when two small plums appeared on my chest at puberty, but loved me all the same; half a dozen men who did not complain about the plums on my chest, especially when they got bigger; my children Paula and Nicholas, who really didn't have much of a choice; some loyal old friends; my three grandchildren, who think that I am cool; and of course Willie, my second—and I hope my last—husband, who doesn't seem to notice that the plums have turned to prunes.

I have been lucky in matters of the heart. I have not been abused or abandoned. Due to the abundant love I received, it was easy for me to give some love back. But it was not until I turned fifty and a tragedy hit my family that I learned the most important lesson about love.

On December 6th, 1991, my only daughter Paula fell very sick in Madrid, where she lived with her husband Ernesto. She had a rare condition called porphyry, that should not be fatal; but a series of misfortunes and neglect in the hospital caused Paula to fall into a deep coma. The specialist assured us that she would come out of the coma and that she would recover completely. But time passed: weeks, months, and Paula did not wake up. Finally, almost six months later, the doctor told us what he probably had known for a very long time: Paula had severe brain damage and she would never recover.

We realized that we could not keep Paula connected to a machine; she would never have chosen that kind of life for herself. At that point Ernesto told me that a few months before, during their honeymoon in Scotland, Paula had had a nightmare. He said that she woke up very upset and wrote a letter, put it in an envelope and sealed it with wax from a candle. *She wrote on the envelope: To be opened when I die.*

After much agonizing, we decided to disconnect Paula from life support. When we did, she started breathing, very faintly at the beginning, but enough to keep her alive. I spent that year—which happened to be the year I turned fifty, an important threshold in any woman's life—sitting at my daughter's bedside, holding her, desperately trying to save her, to bring her back to life with the force of my will; praying for a miracle that would trade my life for hers, that I would die instead of her. During that awful year I gave my daughter all the love I had, and I suppose she received it, but I am not sure, because she could not make any sign; she could not even smile or blink or give me a glance of recognition. During those twelve months I slowly lost her.

The day came when we also had to let go of her body. I remember exactly when it happened. Ernesto and I went to Paula's room and proceeded to improvise a brief ritual of parting. We told Paula how much we loved her; we reviewed the wonderful years we had lived together in this world, and assured her we would find her again in another place, because in fact we would not be separated.

Shortly after I decided to finally open my daughter's letter, I asked myself why a young, healthy, deeply in love woman on her honeymoon would write a letter to be opened after her death. What did she see in her nightmares? What mystery lied hidden in my daughter's life? Shakily I broke the wax seal, opened the envelope, took out two pages written in Paula's precise hand, and read it aloud. Her clear words came to me from another time:

I do not want to remain trapped in my body. Freed from it, I will be closer to those I love, no matter if they are at the four corners of the planet. It is difficult to express the love I leave behind, the depths of the feelings that join me to Ernesto, to my parents, to my brother, to my grandparents. I know you will remember me, and as long as you do, I will be with you. I want to be cremated and have my ashes scattered outdoors. I do not want a tombstone with my name anywhere. I prefer to live in the hearts of those I love, and to return to the Earth. I have a savings account—use it to help children who need to go to school or eat. Divide my things among any who want a keepsake—actually, there is very little. Please don't be sad, I am still with you, except I am closer than I was before. In another time, we will be reunited in spirit, but for now we will be together as long as you remember me. Ernesto... I have loved you deeply and still do; you are an extraordinary man and I don't doubt that you can be happy after I am gone. Mama, Papa, Nico, grandmother, Tío Ramón; you are the best family I could ever have had. Don't forget me, and... let's see a smile on those faces! Remember that we spirits can best help, accompany, and protect, those who are happy. I love you dearly. Paula.

After reading this letter I felt, for the first time during that year of agony, a certain peace, and I could accept Paula's unavoidable death. In that letter, written a year and nine months before, she already spoke of herself as a spirit: *we, the spirits*, she wrote. A week later, on December 6th, 1992, exactly a year after she fell into a coma, my daughter died softly in my arms.

After Paula's death I felt as if I had fallen into a sort of emptiness, a void. I felt that I had lost everything, even the good memories, because I could only remember her suffering. I could not remember her healthy or happy, as a child, a teenager or a bride. I would close my eyes and see her only in the coma or dead. It seemed I had finally lost everything. Only some ashes in a tiny box remained of my daughter.

CD: *Toward Home*, Rhiannon and
Betsy Rose ©1990

Say a Prayer

Dawn is breaking slowly
From a night of fear
The light comes so soft, it's holy
Burns away my tears
Rise up precious one
Greet the morning sun
Lift up your head
Are you ready, to take the next step into the light
It's gonna be all right, all right if you will
Say a prayer
While you're just standing there
No one is ever gonna tear your dreams in two
If you will say, say a prayer for you
Oh, say a prayer
One step is gonna take you there
One note's gonna fill the air
But you gotta let it come through
You gotta say a prayer just for you.

Some have called you crazy, I know they have
Some have hurt your pride
Right now, right now, there's not even one voice that is embracing
The song you just keep hearing inside
Well, you gotta sing out in the dark
Reach out for a spark that's getting ready in flame
Make your claim to the morning
The hush of early dawn is waiting right here, right here for your song
Say a prayer
Out in the open air
That's when that old despair steps in your view
Never mind, just go on and say a prayer for you
Oh, say a prayer
Nothing is too much to bear
The more you dare, the more you can do
If you will say a prayer just for you

No, no, don't ever worry
Just say what you know, just say what you feel
Say a prayer
No one says it quite like you
So say a prayer just for you.

But then, slowly, I came to understand that I had not lost everything—by no means! I had something extraordinary with me: the love I had given Paula and the love that I would always have for her. So that was Paula's gift to me, the most important lesson about love: the love you give is more significant than the love you receive. And the only thing you have is what you give. In other words, it is by spending oneself that one becomes rich.

This brings us to the other issue that I wanted to talk about today: losses. From the very beginning there have been great losses in my life. The first one was probably my father, who one day went to buy cigarettes and never returned. He left the family when I was around three years old and we never saw him again.

We went to live in the large house of my grandparents, but after a short while my grandmother died suddenly. That was an even a greater loss than my father, because she was a fantastic character. She spent her days experimenting with paranormal phenomena, like telepathy—moving objects without touching them, and conversing with the souls of the dead. This wonderful woman was raising me to become an Illuminata; teaching me Esperanto, the universal language of the future; and training me for her séances. But she died without any warning. This happened almost fifty years ago, and to this day I can't quite get over it.

The house became a sad place without my extravagant grandmother. My grandfather dressed in black from head to toe; music, deserts and flowers were banned, and the household entered into a mourning mood that would last several years.

When I was around ten, my mother married a diplomat and we started traveling. We never spent more than a couple of years in a country. The rest of my childhood was about saying good-bye to places, to people—even to languages. I was always moving, losing friends, trying to adapt, only to be uprooted again. Finally we ended up back in Chile. By then I was fifteen and I had decided that I would never move again; I would stay in Chile, plant my roots there and someday be buried in my own garden.

I worked as a journalist, married, had two kids and for a while everything seemed fine. Then in 1973 there was a brutal military coup. At the time, Chile was the longest and most solid

artwork
Women of Wisdom Art Series

Deborah Koff-Chapin
©2006

democracy in the whole of Latin America; we had no idea what a dictatorship was, and therefore didn't know what to expect or how to act.

President Salvador Allende died in the presidential palace the first day of the coup. I was the only member of the Allende family that remained in Chile. Those who did not die or were in prison went into exile immediately. Like most people, I didn't expect the dictatorship to last. I was convinced that in a few weeks, maybe months, the soldiers would go back to their barracks and we would have elections again. Little did we suspect that the military regime would last seventeen years! In the meantime I got in trouble by helping people find asylum or smuggling information out of the country. Slowly, the circle of repression closed around me. It is not easy to live in fear. Eventually my husband, my children and I escaped to Venezuela. Needless to say, exile is not an easy experience. We lost our extended family, our jobs, our house, our country and our friends. For a while we didn't even have a proper visa or a permit to work.

However, out of that experience came my writing. In Venezuela I could not find a job as a journalist and had to make a living with all kinds of odd jobs, most of them rather unpleasant. For years I felt that my life was meaningless; that I was a failure. Only my children and the fact that I had to support and take care of them kept me going.

But then something happened that would change everything for me: on January 8th, 1981, we received a phone call from Chile that my beloved grandfather was dying. I started a letter for him; a sort of spiritual letter that probably he would never read. He died and I continued to write every night in the kitchen of our apartment in Caracas. By the end of the year I had five hundred pages and it didn't look like a letter anymore. I had written my first novel: *The House of the Spirits*. Losses triggered that book. Through writing I had recovered the world I had lost—my family, my memories.

We all go through losses of one kind or another, and my life has been like a roller coaster—ups and downs, great success and great losses. The pattern is so clear that I am always expecting a dramatic shift. When I am up, I enjoy it while it lasts, knowing that the house of cards will collapse any minute. When I am

We're the Ones Who Can't Outrun the Lion

I.
This is one strange-looking army!
Gray-haired and dyed,
fat-waisted,
flat-footed, slow-moving wrinkled
soldiers with sagging tits.

II.
Pretend the enemy is a Lion.
Pretend it's a Lion who waits
patiently in the dark doorways,
licking its chops
While we scurry by,
trying to look invisible.
Pretend the Lion leaps out,
claws extended, fangs bared,
and begins to chase us,
its shadow covering the sky.
Pretend we try to run, but our
bones creak, and our breath is
labored, and the Earth beneath our
feet holds us to her with jealous
desire.

III.
We're the ones who can't
outrun the Lion.
So what do we do as we
feel it bearing down?
Fall into a pile, weeping?
Start pleading for our lives?
What do we do when we feel its
hot breath on our necks?
Pull our collars up higher?
Huddle together, or split up
and take our chances
alone in our rooms at night?
Put more locks on the door

or put on camouflage–
lipstick and rouge…
try to blend in with the scenery?

IV.
But the Lion can smell
who we are,
even through all that
cheap perfume.

V.
How about a little bribery?
Go to church, say a prayer,
make a donation.
Say "God" or "Spirit" often
in tones that make it appear
we know what we're talking about.
Act humble but look proud.
(Or is it the other way around?)

VI.
The Lion doesn't care.

VII.
In the end, all battles are lost.
Maybe that's the wisdom that
eludes us.
It's not about winning,
it's not about losing.
It's about being Lion food,
as tasty and juicy as we can be.

> Security does not come from outside myself; it comes from within.
>
> —Isabel

down I know that it will not last forever; I keep on walking blindly and stubbornly, trusting the life force and my own capacity for survival.

Everything passes. And you know what? For me everything passes in about two years. Two years seems to be a magic time for me. I have learned not to fear the ups and downs because I always have in the back of my mind that magic number: two years. My karma has been to lose what I most cherish and gain what I never aimed for. It's like a joke!

When I was very young I thought that the journey would be like going up a gentle hill. In my childhood I had experienced insecurity; therefore as soon as I had some independence I looked for safety. I believed that if I followed the rules and had good intentions, nothing could go wrong. Where did I get that silly idea? In my eagerness to do the right thing, I overworked myself like a slave, caring for and protecting everybody around me. I was so hyperactive—I had to be in order to cope with all my self-imposed tasks—that being in the same room with me was like getting an electric shock.

From the outside, people might have thought that I was a loving and concerned person, always ready to help and give; but really my motivations were not selfless at all. I wanted desperately to be loved, and I was in fear. I was afraid of separations, failures, pain, humiliations, you name it!

When my kids were born, that fear became a monster watching over my shoulder permanently. What if they got sick, or were kidnapped, or the roof fell on their heads during an Earthquake? What if I was not raising them properly and they would become fundamentalist pricks? What if I couldn't make enough money to support them? Money was such an important issue then! Not that I ever had illusions of grandeur; I just wanted to give my kids the best education and opportunities, and I thought that only money could buy those. Little did I know that the really essential gifts of life can't be bought, and that the only inheritance I can leave for my children is the good memories of the time we spend together.

There's a saying: God respects us when we work, but loves us when we sing. Sing? I never had much time for that. My plans of being good and making everything right for everybody worked for a while; but then the roller-coaster started again and life took over, as it always does, no matter how much we protect ourselves.

Five years and two books have passed since my daughter died. The pain washed me clean inside, but I am back in my body, back in this world. In my journey to the underworld I learned much and I changed. I lost the fear of death, and once it's gone, there are very few fears left. I feel much stronger than ever before. I don't take life for granted. Every morning when I wake up and every evening before I go to sleep, I rejoice. I am grateful for whatever comes to me.

Losses, separations and failures represent the dark side of my life, and love is the light, the redeeming force that always saves me at the end. Don't get me wrong, I am not complaining about the darkness. On the contrary, I welcome it. I am not a masochist, but I am as grateful for the pain as I am for the joy and the love, because it is through struggle and suffering that I have grown and learned the most important lessons.

I have also become more detached. So many things have happened to me, good and bad, that I simply gave up trying to keep track of everything, let alone trying to be in total control of my life. Now I am more relaxed and open.

Most of the time happiness depends on our disposition, not our circumstances. Now I know that I don't control anything. I could not protect my daughter from death; how could I protect my son, or my grandchildren, from life? This doesn't mean that I love them less; only that I love them in a more optimistic way. I believe that they will be all right with or without me. Before I thought that if I didn't have three jobs my family would starve to death. The first few years when we went to Venezuela we were poor, but nobody in my family starved; in fact we gained weight. I learned that poverty is not desirable, but it is not the end of the world either.

It took me several decades to understand that security does not come from outside myself; it comes from within. Strength had always been there; I just had not trained the muscles properly. Now I trust that I will always be able to feed my family, unless there is a nuclear cataclysm; then of all us will perish, and who wants to be alive and alone in a radioactive dump of a planet?

I used to think that if something bad happened to my kids I would certainly die. It took the terrible experience of my daughter's death to teach me that no matter how great the pain, the human capacity for endurance is even greater. Everything dies, even the stars. It is the cycle of the physical world—birth, growth, deterioration, death—all parts of the same journey. We are fragile creatures. Death is another stage of life, and we will all go through it. What will last forever is love.

" *Our souls are drops of one infinite ocean of spirituality and consciousness.*

—*Isabel*

Where is my daughter Paula now? I believe that our souls are drops of one infinite ocean of spirituality and consciousness; they are all particles of the same eternal substance. These particles of the one and only Spirit are incarnated for a while on this planet; they take the forms of people, animals, vegetables or minerals, or they incarnate in any of the innumerable galaxies of the universe and take forms that we can't even imagine. Maybe a particular physical form allows the soul to experience something that could not be experienced otherwise. In the case of human beings, maybe it is through the senses, through intuition and imagination, through love and other fundamental emotions that the soul gathers experience or knowledge.

Why? What for? I don't know. Will I see Paula on the other side when I die? Will she be waiting for me at the end of a tunnel of light, as some gurus say? I don't think so. I think that we will be just water of the same ocean: identical and impossible to separate.

I was raised a Catholic, but walked away from that church at age fifteen. After trying a couple of other traditional religions, I ended up making up my own private church—so private, in fact, that it has only one member. What bothers me in most traditional religions is that they are run by males. They make the rules to their advantage. How can the divinity be male? If God has gender, it probably has a digestive system too. The whole concept is preposterous! But I need a spiritual practice; therefore, I have to invent my own ways of connecting with the divine, as I am sure most of you have. Saint Catherine of Seina wrote: *Make two homes for thyself, my daughter: one actual home and another spiritual home, which thou art to carry with thee always.*

This idea of the common spirit is very useful to me. It allows me to identify with everyone and everything that exists, including the skunks that often spray my basement, or the majestic trees in the woods where we scattered Paula's ashes. If all people are made from the same spiritual matter, we are all potentially capable of the greatest deeds as well as the worst evil. I can be a saint or a sinner; I can be Mother Theresa or a serial killer. It is only my good luck that I am none of the above. I admire Mother Theresa, but I like fancy clothes and I look terrible with no makeup.

Since Paula died I have come to terms with the fact that life is painful. But life is not only painful. It is also full of pleasure, light, joy and laughter—bittersweet, like the best chocolate. The very nature of life is change, transformation, and losses. Life is about cycles, movement, beginnings and endings, birth and death; it is essentially messy and chaotic. If that is the case, then it is useless to worry. Let's be content in eternal insecurity, knowing that whatever comes to us we will find ways of coping; most of the time we will.

Now that I am over fifty, I can tell you that there is nothing more liberating than age. As we get older we can be ourselves, wear sensible shoes and speak our minds; we don't have to please everybody anymore, only those we really care for. At fifty we have more cellulite, but we are also wiser. If we had a choice, maybe most of us would rather have thin thighs than wisdom; but we don't have a choice, so we better make the most of wisdom.

The year 2000 is right here, and we can all feel that the world is changing. In the United States alone, there are at least forty million people that think and feel like you and I do; only we still don't have a name for our emerging movement. Two-thirds of those forty million are women. Some sociologists are calling us the cultural creatives, because we are creating the new culture for the next century. I am no New Age junkie, but I am very optimistic about the future; I feel we are at the threshold of a culture where spirituality, relationships and concern for the planet will be crucial issues. It will also be a time of peace and tolerance. The world where my grandchildren will live is going to be a much better one than the world I knew as a child. We have come a long way, baby!

Are you expecting some advice from me? I don't blame you. When I was younger I thought older people had all the answers.

Now I realize that as I grow older I have less answers and many more questions. But there are a few things that I have learned along the way:

First, I don't care too much about my personal future, because the real troubles are things that are unpredictable and unavoidable.

When listing my priorities, relationships come first. In the long run they are much more rewarding than achievements.

The process is always more important that the goal. In fact, the process often determines the goals. I don't believe that the end justifies the means. If you believe that the end justifies the means, you are ready to justify anything, including the Inquisition.

I am happier when I do something for others. Getting involved with the community is better than therapy—and cheaper. Getting involved in protecting our planet, the victim of such unrelenting desecration, makes a lot of sense, and you meet nice people.

This I can tell you with absolute certainty: look for your own truth; don't accept what the predominant culture tells you is true or is good. Most of the time what they tell you is bullshit.

And I can throw in some practical advice, if you want: wear sunscreen, don't smoke, drink little but expensive; read, sing, cherish your friends, and make love as often as you can, because as you get older the opportunities diminish considerably.

I am looking forward to the future. It will be a great time for the feminine forces to emerge in full blossom. We can work magic; we can change the culture. Women are potential witches. Allow me to finish this evening with an invitation: let's all of us become benevolent and powerful witches and let's start practicing right now. Let's polish our broomsticks and dance in the moonlight with other pagan women, invoking the winds and the forces of water and Earth. Let's learn ancient spells and healers' secrets. Let's start right now, training for wisdom, for generosity and for joy.

" We can work magic;
     we can change the culture.

—Isabel

artwork

*Keeping a
Lid on the
Beast While
Loosening
the Ties
That Bind*

Denise
Kester
©2000

Empower Your Self

explore your dreams and spirit...

1   Who is the solid love in your life?

2   What lessons have you learned through your losses?

3   What gifts have you discovered through
    your experiences?

4   What do you do to be desperately loved?

5   Describe the roller coasters of your life.

6   What strengths do you have within yourself?

"We all have moments in our lives when we find our depth. Reflection on those times helps to create a story that defines how we live our lives. The more deeply we carry the story, the more we can recognize wisdom in our lives and the lives of those around us.

—Christina Baldwin
Quote from
Storycatcher
©2005

Limbs of Reason, Ashley Adams ©2006

CHAPTER 6

The Power of Stories
at Women of Wisdom

The Power of Stories
at Women of Wisdom

introduction by Kris Steinnes

Stories have always been an important part of Women of Wisdom. As I shared in the introduction to the book, Women of Wisdom's birth was inspired from reading a book of stories. We created a format that allows women to tell their stories, and with this sharing, we have found and continue to find healing. It is probably the most transformational element of Women of Wisdom–telling your story. Many women find or enhance their voices through participating in this annual event.

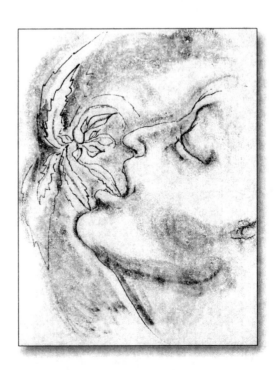

Stories draw us together, and in my experience, truly successful workshops and events always allow women to share their personal stories and experiences. And the stories are not just told during WOW workshops. Throughout the Conference, many informal gatherings take place such as when women sit in the teahouse and chat over a cup of special brew. The teahouse serves as a great opportunity for women to share their conference and life experiences with each other. As we listen to others we allow ourselves to speak as well.

Telling Your Story.

It sounds easy, but for many of us it's not. For a long time, I wouldn't allow myself to think I had an interesting story to share. Inside I knew I did, but when I listened to the exciting and inspiring tales other women told, mine never seemed interesting enough. I doubt I'm unique in that kind of thinking. Many women do not think they live interesting enough lives to tell their story.

I remember being at Women's Camp in British Columbia, and midway through the week they held a story night. They would ask everyone in camp for a story to tell. Each year my mind would go blank. *Surely I must have a story*, I thought. *I've traveled the world; I founded a huge conference.* But for some reason I discounted these experiences. I envied those women whose stories sparked something within me and made me laugh, but as much as I wanted to, I couldn't bring myself to raise my hand. I just felt that my story could not compare with theirs.

I attended women's camp for five years in a row, and at last, during the fifth year, I gathered my courage and shared my story about how Women of Wisdom was birthed, and what my dreams held for the future. I found out it was inspiring for others. Many women came up to me afterwards thanking me. So I learned that it is important to share this story of mine.

I attended camp five years later, and was asked to tell this story again. That time I even sang a song! *"We are going, heaven knows where we are going, we know within"*–by Sol Amarfio. It expressed my journey of not knowing my destination, but knowing I was moving forward, confident that I would get there. It was the lesson of sharing my story–not always knowing what the outcome would be, but trusting and taking one step at a time led to where I am today.

artwork

Women of Wisdom Art Series

Deborah Koff-Chapin ©1995

> Story is the song line of a person's life.
>
> We need to sing it and we need someone to hear the singing.
>
> Story told, story heard, story written, story read create the web of life in words.
>
> —Christina Baldwin from Storycatcher

Why tell our stories?

So many of us doubt the power of our own experiences. When we share stories and see the flash of recognition on someone's face, or see how we move another, we find a validation that cuts through our doubt and isolation. We often find meaning through this process of reflection. And stories help us make life transitions, for we learn to recognize patterns, pitfalls and opportunities in our own lives when witnessing them in others.

So much happens when we share our stories. A sacred honoring and nurturing can occur when we are listened to, and in turn this honoring gives us strength to make tough decisions. And it is a way for our own courage and strength to touch the lives of others in service.

We all seek meaningful experiences; we have a need to sing, to reflect, to share, and to embody what our life is about. We don't want to be talked at, as though we don't exist–we want opportunities to find our existence, our ground, our hearts, and identify what truly matters to us. We each have something to offer; we have gifts to bring to the whole group as well. In the sacred circle of women being together, we learn to give ourselves to the world.

At the Women of Wisdom Conference all the workshops are experiential and from the beginning we intended women to be held in a safe container, where there was a place for sharing our personal stories. This helps women know they are supported in both who they are and also in who they want to become. People leave the conference inspired to make the changes in their lives they've always wanted to–go back to school to study, create a new career, start a business, change their name, leave their partner, or quit their job. This is not just a psychological process, as it comes from a spiritual depth, it's a spiritual transformation that allows the women to make these changes.

Those of us who come year after year witness this mystery. We see women become more powerful, contribute more to their outer lives, and receive more nourishment from their inner lives.

Stories can also heal deep wounds in ourselves and in the collective consciousness of women. When we cry in a group, we come to know that others have felt the same pain, and they

Linda Castine ©2005 written from experiences
at Women of Wisdom
Art: *Fulfilling Promise*, JoAutumn Brock ©2000

An Unknown Future

An unknown future is calling to me
A place I want to applaud and cheer
Held deeply in the grip of life's complexities
Letting go creates an unwelcome fear.

Insecurity is like a sealed envelope
From which I forgot to place a stamp
I wish to retreat from the dry, desert storm
And find a sunny, new spot to camp.

It's like the lights have all gone out
To the path that I long for
I am here today to find the switch
And find my way back to shore.

> Story is
the mother
of us all.

—Christina
Baldwin
from
Storycatcher

can cry as well–both for us and for themselves. In this protected space, we can also cry for the Earth, for the abuse done to Her. It is in these tears that we remember Her divinity.

As women heal ourselves individually, we heal the greater wound to the feminine in our culture and in our world. As we share who we are, we awaken new consciousness in the collective, forging a way for the Divine Feminine to manifest. As we grow, She grows. In this way, sharing our individual stories serves a much greater unfolding.

Deep spirit is expressed at Women of Wisdom; women get in touch with their inner selves, with each other; and with the divinity that runs through all life. We yearn to feel connected to others, for touch, for meaningful exchanges, for heart to heart talks. In our every day lives many of us feel so isolated, we go to work, eat and sleep, and it can feel so mundane. But when we feel the spirit of women empowering us; when we feel the divine expression of the feminine that says, "we are all in this together"; when we feel supported by others, we can expand through creativity and Self-expression.

This chapter is composed of stories from different women who have participated at Women of Wisdom and want to share their unique experiences with you. I believe that if a story touches one person's heart, changes one person's perspective, then it has fulfilled its mission. I hope these stories will open up something in your heart and your life that can lead to positive transformation, allowing you to move into the next stage of your journey. As you read them, know that you join in the sacred circle of sharing, and remember that your story also has the power to bless and enrich other women's lives.

CD: *Shadow of the Moon,* Marita Berg ©1993

Stories

All I have to give is to share my story
All I have to give is to sing my song
Sometimes you'll like it
And sometimes you won't
The lesson for me is to let go and trust that...

All you have to give is to share your story
All you have to give is to sing your song
Sometimes I'll like it
Sometimes I won't
The lesson for me is to let go and trust that...

All the threads of story weave a fabric that's whole
All the songs when sung make a symphony
Sometimes I feel it and sometimes I don't
The lesson for me is to let go and trust...

Descant:

All the stories, all the songs
Time there's plenty of time
Let go, let go, let go and trust
All the threads of story, all the lines of song
Time, there's time to feel
Let go, let go, let go and trust

Bass:

I stand under, understand

The Power of Stories:
A Sacred Document

Photo, Kathy Admire ©2007

Melissa Layer
Writer, WOW participant
From Port Townsend, WA
lissalayer@yahoo.com

a talk with Melissa Layer

> The spiraling
> energy in
> the room
> gathered and
> quickened;
> the stories
> flowed.
>
> —Melissa

When I was ten years old, my fourth grade teacher introduced my class to traditional cursive writing, utilizing pen nibs dipped into bottles of black ink. Kinesthetic in a way I hadn't experienced before–dizzying circles and angular slashes flowing from the wet tip of my pen across the blue lines of the paper–this emerging skill tapped an inner spring. One evening, a story blossomed inside of me and pressed insistently against the tips of my small fingers. I opened a yellow, spiral notebook and wrote *"Once upon a time..."*

Thirty-five years later in February of 2001, at the annual Women of Wisdom conference in Seattle, I sat in a circle of women awaiting the start of a two-day writing workshop with author and healer Deena Metzger. The sterile meeting room at the Holiday Inn, where we had gathered, had been transformed into a sacred space. A colorful altar cloth had been spread in the middle of the circle, anchored with a large vase of early spring flowers, softly flickering candles, and sacred objects.

With the exciting and diverse array of workshops to choose

from, I was not entirely clear why I registered for a class facilitated by a woman I knew very little about. Why was I drawn to this particular workshop suggesting I might "deepen my connection with language?" Since that original story in fourth grade, I had journaled sporadically for years, and occasionally written a short story; but at some unidentified moment I began to print neat letters and abandoned all cursive writing except for my signature.

At the WOW conference, the door to the Holiday Inn conference room opened and Deena entered. I was unprepared for and surprised at my immediate response. A wave of feeling arose and washed over and through me. My eyes filled with tears and my throat felt tight. She stood much smaller than I had imagined, but a crackling energy surrounded her. She walked briskly across the room; her deeply tanned and wrinkled face intent and inscrutable beneath her long white hair. The soft hum of conversation subsided completely. I knew instantly that I sat in the presence of a powerful teacher, a wise and fierce Grandmother. I recognized immediately my previously unidentified longing for such a crone to see and mentor me as I entered midlife.

Over the next two days, Deena wove us together. My pen flew across the pages of my journal, my neat and precise print attempting to capture her words: "We gather here to see what we can recover and what we can bring in. In other cultures people walk in an air that is thick with ancestors and spirits. In exorcism when a spirit is cast out, it needs a place to go. It can find its place in a story. Remember that this work we are doing has consequences in other dimensions."

Deena challenged, encouraged, confronted, and called us forth. The spiraling energy in the room gathered and quickened; the stories flowed. In that space I reflected: once upon a time in a remote forested corner of the Pacific Northwest, I wrote a story about a rogue wolf terrorizing a small pioneer town, and a feisty ten-year-old girl who secretly befriended him.

At the end of the first day, I went home and opened a storage closet. I found the yellow spiral notebook titled *Shilo, Wolfdog* that my ten-year-old hand had transcribed from some ancient voice flowing through me. As I re-read the words, a veil lifted from my eyes: Furtively offering food and water, the pioneer girl met the wolf at the well where her daily chore was to draw water for her family. When her mother discovered the secret, she locked her daughter in her bedroom, but the spirited girl escaped and ran away with the wolf. The bold, symbolic content, written as I teetered on the threshold of pre-pubescence, became piercingly clear to me now as a mature woman in midlife. This was a rite-of-passage journey, an initiation story.

That pioneer child's story ended happily—the townspeople eventually located the determined girl and her wild companion. With grudging respect, they acknowledged the devoted bond between the girl and the dark animal of chilling fairy tales. She and the wolf returned to the village. The wolf bred with a domestic dog and they produced a litter of pups with riveting gold eyes. As for the young author, her story continued far beyond the pages of the yellow spiral notebook, not yet fully understood or embraced until a small, white-haired Grandmother stirred her simmering creativity among a circle of women in Seattle.

"*Go deeply within yourself,*" Deena invited, "*where supplication and prayer come together. May you ask for something so deep that you can meet the Divine.*" I closed my eyes and breathed deeply. My hand began to print neat black letters: "*Courageous ...brave...broken heart...voice...permeable... message ... messenger...boldness...compassion...healing...balance... immediacy...Don't stop, don't stop...these words* (and then, like a wave, the cursive arising and rolling through me) *have meaning! They have waited so long to come forth...go, go—Go! Awaken! No— Reawaken! Time is of the essence. Ears are aching to hear the messages. Say what you know. Give me your hand. Let me feel your heartbeat. Let's breathe together. Let the healing in my life extend out to all Beings. May speaking my truth empower you to speak yours. What does it mean, how does it feel to yield to the words that come?*"

My hand stumbled across the page, finding the flow and rhythm of longhand writing once again: tight, tense, uncertain, but compelled. I felt aware of loss, anger, curiosity, and a growing excitement. Was it possible, that the words I could offer, the stories I could tell, were only birthed and borne in this powerful cursive current?

"*Think about the life that supports the creative. Consider carefully the inner voice and the outer authentic voice. Call forth the Spirit—ask that the greatest good be done. Ask for healing. Words can be description and invocation at the same time.*" Deena's compelling words seemed to come from a great distance, and my hand kept moving.

As women began reading their stories aloud, the depth and diversity of the work was stunning—bringing us to tears, sighs of appreciation, gasps of horror, and laughter. I felt a tension gathering within me. I had brought my yellow notebook with me, and it was *this* story that I longed to share in the circle of women. Would it be all right to invite a ten-year-old girl who ran away with a rogue wolf to share her story? Could she find her place in this circle?

On the final day of the workshop I found myself standing at the front of the room, the tattered yellow notebook pressed against my chest. My voice shook as I explained how the story had bubbled up within me as cursive letters formed, connected, and rolled across the page. When Deena invited me to read from the curling pages my voice steadied and was clear and strong.

artwork

Dancing With Bear

Suzanne Cheryl Gardner
©1997

"Susan had the job of getting the water from the well in the woods. As she went into the woods she saw something black and hairy with yellow eyes and a black nose. She peeked around the well and there lay Shilo, the killer wolf, but he was now a terrible thirsty wolf and a tired one. Susan was afraid and she wanted to run but she didn't like to see the wolf suffer, so she filled the water pail with cold water and set the pail out on a strong stick to the wolf. Shilo stumbled over and drank the water."

> I recognized that this story belonged to all of us.
>
> —Melissa

I closed the notebook and took a deep breath. The room was completely quiet, but I felt something pulsing, pushing just beneath the surface. I looked into the circle of women, my vision sharpening and clear, and saw the faces streaked with tears, saw the box of tissues being passed from one woman to another. Deena stood at the edge, and when I met her eyes, I thought I saw sorrow, tenderness, and joy there. She shook her head incredulously, and after a long moment she said, *"This is a sacred document."*

"Do you know what happened to this ten year old girl when she chose to give a thirsty wolf a long cool drink of water?" I asked the group. "She befriended and bonded with him in secret and chose to run away with him, to the complete horror of her mother and the community in which she lived. And unlike the Susan I had birthed in the story, I began to hide my stories and staunch the cursive flow, returning to tight, isolated, solitary letters. The risk was too great."

Women haltingly began to share their own stories of emergence from childhood to young maidens. Stories of repression, wounding, shame, and withdrawal. Of silence. I recognized that this story belonged to all of us, and I passed it to the woman on my right. I asked that each woman hold the yellow notebook and bless the ten-year-old girl within each of us, allowing her to step forward confidently, speaking her truth, and taking her rightful place in the circle.

"Only the prayers of a broken heart can open the gates to heaven. When you really call out, open your heart, then Spirit enters."

The Power of Stories:
Growing Up Professionally

Coleen Rhalena Renee, CSH
WOW presenter, performer
and past council member
www.coleenrenee.com

a talk with Coleen Renee

I had heard about the Women of Wisdom Conference for several years before I was able to attend. Each year I poured over the brochure, feeling inspired by workshop titles and the idea that powerful women gathered in community for an entire week.

Finally, my schedule allowed me to sign up for the conference. That was seven years ago. Although I had a good job teaching massage at a technical school, my heart wanted to teach my own material in a more natural environment. This unfulfilled dream had created an ever-deepening sense of discontent. But at the time I had no models for how to get started, and felt too unprepared to risk going for it. I hoped that attending the Conference would provide a spark of inspiration.

> She changes everything she touches,
> and everything she touches changes.
>
> —Starhawk

The first conference event I attended was *Temple Dreams*, a ritual theater performance. It was water to my parched spirit. The ritual piece honored the power of dreams, the ability of ancestral knowledge to speak through us, and the beauty of the divine feminine. This was no spark of inspiration—I was on fire!

Throughout the conference, what most impressed me was the beautiful community woven around the workshops and performances. I found a spiritual family, a musical family, and a wealth of professional models. That same year, I birthed my dream to teach healing and empowerment classes in the oral tradition, outside of a formal classroom setting. Though I still felt scared, I knew it was possible, and that I had support when I needed it.

> In serving the organization we ourselves are deeply served.
>
> —Coleen

The success of that first year opened the door to other opportunities: I began performing with the Sacred Fire Choir–a choir that honors Earth and celebrates spirit–at the WOW conferences; acted in and helped write ritual theater pieces; and for several years presented my teachings in workshops. I might even say that I grew up professionally at the WOW conferences.

Each year at the conference I find myself called to a higher level of professionalism. This is due in part to self-expectation, but also due to the community's ability to inspire. The conference has become a time for self-evaluation. It's a professional marker for me. Have I achieved my goals in the last year? What goals do I have for the coming year? What inspiration and support do I need to achieve these new goals?

Last fall, Spirit asked me to move across the country to northwest Ohio. I had just become a WOW Council Member six months earlier. WOW was seeking new ways to serve the community more consistently throughout the year, and serve women who might be isolated by circumstances or distance. Moving across the country would allow me to serve these goals and represent our growing part membership outside of the Northwest.

Through the move I have come to experience and understand a truly magical aspect of Women of Wisdom. WOW grew me professionally, and now I am growing WOW. In serving the organization we ourselves are deeply served. I can now see so many instances where individuals in WOW grew into their own power and used that power to ignite the potential in other women and the organization.

As I now explore ways to teach my work via the Internet, I'm finding there is a growing network of personal and professional connections. As a result of my own experience in Women of Wisdom, I know people in California, New Mexico, Montana, Washington, Wisconsin, Michigan, New York, Massachusetts, Pennsylvania, Texas, Toronto, and England. Whenever I feel alone or uncertain, I reach out to the community and remember the magic I have the privilege and honor of sharing. Women of Wisdom has changed our lives, and in turn, our lives have changed Women of Wisdom.

artwork

Women of Wisdom Art Series

Deborah Koff-Chapin ©2003

The Power of Stories:

Finding My Calling

Photo, Taddeusz Charette Nunn ©2007

*Julie Charette Nunn, Crow's Daughter
Herbalist, Goddess Market Vendor,
WOW presenter, WOW council member
julie@crowsdaughter.com
www.crowsdaughter.com*

a talk with Julie Charette Nunn

I have had many helpers in my life. I feel blessed to live in a community of people that really nourishes my soul. But about fifteen years ago I lived a very different life. I was a schoolteacher—hard working, dedicated and stressed out. I had a longing to find more of myself, and embarked on a quest to bringing spirituality into my life on a daily basis. I had attended a few women's workshops on Earth spirituality and healing, and then discovered Women of Wisdom. I remember one of the first years I attended–I would stop at the conference on my way to work to have a cup of tea. Just being in the space of this the conference nourished me.

It was my husband that encouraged me to attend the Susun Weed evening talk on Menopause at the WOW conference. *I certainly didn't need this*, I thought. *I wasn't anywhere near old enough*! Well, at his urging we both attended.

Susun was incredible. She spoke about women becoming powerful and fully connected *to ourselves and to life*, and related this to food and nourishment. She said, "How can milk and eggs be bad for women? We are milk and eggs!" This simple statement changed my life. I became very interested in Susun Weed's teachings, and I met another woman at the conference named EagleSong, a student of Susun Weed's, who offered Wise Woman teachings at her home and garden.

At the following year's conference I attended a workshop with EagleSong. She entered the teaching space, dressed in black, hobbling in on a long walking stick. She threw french-fries around the room as an offering of the salt of the Earth! She spoke her name and her lineage and I woke up. I began to cry.

We all spoke in turn; in a circle of women, we spoke our names and our lineage. That is all I remember of that workshop. Through this one experience, EagleSong opened the doorway for me into the realm of possibility.

Sixteen years later, I am no longer a schoolteacher. Instead, I am passing on the teachings of those before me, the shamanic herbal tradition of the Wise Woman. I see through the eyes of one who lives her spirituality woven into each moment. Women of Wisdom offered the gift of this opportunity, offered me solace from my stress, offered me teachers who showed me who I really am. I feel blessed to live in a community of people who truly nourish my soul.

Women of Wisdom imparts a subtle gift - a treasure sought and found by women who are searching for themselves.

artwork
Buddha
Montserrat
©2002

The Power of Stories:

Fueling My Creativity

Photo, Frank Coccia ©2006

Sue Coccia
Artist, Goddess Market Vendor,
past WOW council member
www.earthartinternational.com

a talk with Sue Coccia

> *I felt empowered to know I was finally on my way.*
>
> —Sue

Fall 1997 marked the beginning of my journey as an artist. At an evening typing class I met a woman named Gloria Taylor Brown. Her marketing company, Alchemy Arts Inc., was literally the first of many that I used to begin my business. Little did I know at the time that Gloria was involved with Women of Wisdom. Prior to meeting her, I had joined a meditation group in my neighborhood, and as my artwork developed I became very interested in learning more spiritually. No coincidence that I should meet Gloria!

Women of Wisdom was holding a Fall Festival at Seattle Unity Church, and Gloria suggested I display my art at the festival. I had not shown my work to anyone except family and friends, and I was terrified. It felt like jumping off a cliff with my eyes closed. I had no need to be worried though. What a perfectly safe place among women to show my work for the first time! To my honest surprise, my totem style animal work was received very well. My confidence increased, and I felt empowered to know I was finally on my way. Attending the festival also helped me understand my work, and how it was emerging from within.

The friendships and bonds I formed with other artists from this first event are still a vital part of my life. At the February conference we crowded our booths quite close to each other, creating a wonderful and intimate Goddess Market where we could sell our tributes to the divine feminine. This conference gave me the "juice" to carry through the year, as I participated in the workshops and heard wise women speakers from around the country.

And at every conference that followed I could count on learning, laughing, singing, crying and growing with the support of such amazing women! It gave me the spiritual strength to go out into the world and develop my business. After a few years, I began to volunteer for WOW, and to help other women starting out on their journeys, just as I had been helped starting out on mine.

Today, I'm a successful artist. My work is sold through stores, aquariums, zoos, and museums around the world. I've had several one-woman exhibits, and sell my work through art fairs and festivals as well. Traveling with my husband Frank helps keep me inspired to meet local wildlife and Nature, and fuels my creativity. And I remember how it all started—with women just like me, with a longing to know, celebrate and honor the divine power within us all as we gathered together at Women of Wisdom.

Thank you Kris, and Women of Wisdom!

Love, Sue Coccia

artwork
Frog
Sue Coccia
©1998

The Power of Stories:

Rituals of Connections

Photo, John Holzwart ©2007

Linda Conroy
Volunteer, Goddess Market
vendor and WOW presenter
Founder and proprietress of
www.moonwiseberbs.com

a talk with Linda Conroy

> It was the
> informal
> interactions
> with other
> women.
>
> —Linda

I remember clearly the first time I walked into the busy office at Women of Wisdom. It was early in January of 1996, I had just returned from a two-year trip to the Arctic. I was on a journey of self-discovery and was looking for experiences that would expand my horizons.

A mentor/friend who was teaching me about plants and the wise woman tradition suggested I participate in the Women of Wisdom Conference. At the time I was not familiar with the conference, but the idea of women gathering in one place intrigued me. I was curious enough to contact Kris Steinnes and offer to volunteer. At the time I was not aware of the journey that would ensue, a journey of growth, self-discovery and community.

The first day of my scheduled volunteer shift was full of sound and energy. As I entered the cramped office, I could hear phones ringing and see women scurrying to answer them, while at the same time making copies and taking time in between to connect with each other. The conference was a month away and I was quickly initiated into this ritual. This was the first of many Women of Wisdom rituals that I became a part of.

Attending the conference was similar to volunteering. Lots of activity was constantly happening: workshops and performances, which were transformative on many levels. And of course, the ritual that started the day I began volunteering—the time in between when women connected with each other. The aspect that is the most memorable for me are those spontaneous visits in between scheduled activities.

artwork

Women of Wisdom Art Series

Deborah Koff-Chapin ©2006

After the first year, I knew I would be participating in this community for a long time to come. And I did for over a decade. The weeklong conference provided me with a wide spectrum of opportunities to expand my horizons. I had the opportunity to show my beadwork in the art show; I was able to participate on the planning committee; and I presented workshops on herbs, the wise woman tradition and basketry. I offered my handcrafted herbal wares as part of the Goddess Market and I attended a host of workshops with some of the most influential women of our time.

When I reflect on these experiences, it always comes back to that first day volunteering, which set the stage for the most transformational aspect of the Women of Wisdom Conferences. It was the informal interactions with other women, the familiar as well as new faces. It was the phone conversations while registering participants; it was visiting between workshops; it was dancing together during performances; it was conversations in the tea house; it was the shared tears and smiles that have left the biggest impact on me.

It was the ordinary women, or as coined by singer songwriter Celia, "The Everyday Goddesses," that impacted me the most. It was the simple ritual of anticipating the conference and looking forward to spending the week with women that has etched itself in my memory. My heart fills with warmth as I remember the rituals of connection that have left this lasting imprint on my soul.

WOW Big Bear Lake, CA:

www.womenofwisdomca.com

Photo, Kris Steinnes ©2007

Chandra Smith
Psychotherapist, ceremonialist,
Founding committee member
Women of Wisdom CA

a talk with Chandra Smith

In 2000, two young women from Big Bear Lake attended the Governor's conference on "Women in California" and while they thought it was helpful and well organized, they missed the spiritual component. Upon returning to Big Bear they sought me out, as they knew I had been involved with a women's spiritual conference in Seattle. After some initial discussion, we contacted Kris Steinnes, from Women of Wisdom and created a California connection.

Kris was helpful in her consults as we had many challenges in organizing the first California WOW conference. It was the spring of 2001 and with optimism and joy we decided it would be easy to put together an event by October. We had no money, no speakers and no location but we did have passion and we drew together a dozen other women for what became known as the "steering committee". Having no funding we asked steering committee members and "like minded women" to contribute whatever they could to get us started.

We began, through consensus, to design a statement expressing the conference's intent, which is "empowering the dreams and spirit of women." Our mission and vision is to impact and heal the world through educating, encouraging and uniting–by sharing woman to woman. This conference is a venue where all can respect, honor and embrace women's individuality and oneness.

That first year we had only one paid keynote speaker and the other two keynotes were volunteers. We decided on seriously reduced prices for elders and teens. We also had a translator and convener for Hispanic women. (We worked hard to include them in any way possible as their community inside of Big Bear was beginning to expand.)

We sought donations and created giveaway gift bags for every attendee. Since that first year, we have come to include a raffle of donated items to help cover costs. We designated a networking table where other events could be advertised and we printed a program of all the events happening that weekend in the area. We recruited local vendors to sell their wares at the conference site in what turned out to be an exceptionally cold courtyard. Frost bitten, the vendors and their wares were moved into the main hall, creating a wall-to-wall audience. A wonderful artist donated a painting for the cover of the flyer in exchange for vending and free advertisement. Since then, we have had a local gallery sponsor an art contest for our cover.

New to the concept of a "women's only" gathering, men were also invited to this first conference and asked to contribute. And they did.

Now all this went smoothly and with great ease until I, as a sort of "go to" person, left town to visit family out-of-state! Things promptly went sideways. The computer work for the flyer didn't happen as the woman who volunteered to do it quit. Although technologically challenged, I completed the flyer in my own inimitable style. Remarkably, it went out as scheduled, and our women's wellness weekend was widely advertised as planned.

That first conference is an amazing memory. Kris, who could not attend the conference, flew down to Big Bear, to meet with the committee and celebrate in advance, our organization and success. Our webmaster, Radha Khalsa, not only got us a web site but also linked us to the Seattle Women of Wisdom site. So the first "Women of Wellness" weekend was convened. The speakers addressed a full house replete with video cameras,

cameras of all varieties recoding the event, a male musician, male furniture movers, women dressed in goddess regalia, as well as jeans, and children of all ages coming in and out of the conference center.

We decided that our next Women of Wisdom Conference would be "women only", with paid keynotes, and a new location, (which didn't work and for the last five years we have been in our original setting). We planned to get professional help with the flier and have a separate inside area set aside for vendors. We also developed a shared leadership on the steering committee. Women who were on the committee volunteered to take on a task, which if they couldn't complete, would notify the committee and another woman would volunteer to pick up that loose end.

My task was to set a date for the planning and evaluation meetings. The committee generated the agenda and the committee through consensus, chose the theme, keynotes, workshop leaders, and set the schedule and prices.

We just completed our seventh conference. This is first conference Kris has been able to attend. It has been an amazing journey. We have seen teens so influenced by women's role modeling that they have chosen careers to carry on service work. We have seen elders honored, indigenous traditions upheld in, honoring the land the conference is held on, and musicians begin or expand their musical careers by writing and performing theme songs for our conference.

We have seen committee members come and go and return again. We have witnessed three to four generations in certain families choose to attend together and many of us have had the rewarding experience of being able to offer the conference as a viable reason to invite our female friends to attend and as an added bonus enjoy the great wondrous outdoors of Big Bear. We have completed seven successful conferences, in spite of being on standby evacuation due to forest fires, road closures due to mudslides or snowy and icy conditions.

And most of all, designing, planning and manifesting the conference each year has given us a venue to come together as sisters, to learn from one another, and give the gift of spiritual well being to each other and our greater community.

Additional comments from Kris:

It was a beautiful experience for me to attend the seventh annual WOW gathering in Big Bear Lake and witness their wonderful community. The weekend had been postponed by one month due to the California fires and then when we did meet, we had to deal with road closures due to landslides from a heavy rain fall the first day and snow the second day, so if you didn't have chains you were turned away. Regardless, those who could make it laughed, shared stories, danced and sang all weekend. Healing occurs everywhere women gather, and we experienced that this weekend as well. I was gifted with beautiful pleated cloth wings that draped from a sparkling neck choker from one of the organizers, Dr. Robin Bradley, and we both shed tears as she expressed her sincere gratitude for what Women of Wisdom had given the women in that community for the past seven years. The retreat was a successful celebration of the Divine Feminine and we returned home with renewed faith in the power of women. I'm so grateful that Chandra called me to assist them to start this Women of Wisdom extension in California. They've done a remarkable job in furthering our mission of empowering the dreams and spirit of women.

The Power of Stories:

My Spiral Journey

Impressions Photography ©2007

Kris Steinnes
Founder, Women of Wisdom, author,
WOW Council Member
www.wisewomanpublishing.com

a talk with Kris Steinnes

I imagine my own spiritual journey prepared me to enter into this ancient and current circle. Unknown and mysterious to me, something led me here.

I was seeking; there was a hunger in me for something, and I really didn't know what it was. There were signs, and one sign led to another, until the path was revealed and I could step into that new picture of my life. It was up to me to take the steps and trust that they would lead me in the direction that would answer my heart's desire.

My awareness of this story perhaps began as I sat in the Seattle Unity Church sanctuary one Wednesday evening. I watched the program director walk up the side aisle and a voice in my head said I would have her job someday. My head turned as if to ask, "Who said that?"

I heard another message on my spiral journey at a workshop led by Victoria Castle, author of *The Trance of Scarcity*, where we were to write our mission for this lifetime. The words fell on to

artwork
Blue Lady
Jenn
Richards
©2007

> "There was a deep knowing and truth in the voice that spoke to me.
>
> —Kris

the paper–"to bring people together." Where did this come from? Certainly, I thought, not from my current life in the clothing design business. Looking back now I can see it was part of my training that prepared me for this path.

The spiral continued to spin as I attended the Unity regional retreat at Crystal Mountain Resort around 1990. Danaan Parry, founder of Earth Stewards and Peace Trees Vietnam, led amazing workshop exercises. I will never forget the profound influence he had on me during one particular exercise. We were blindfolded in a crowded room with 500 people and we were to walk around, touching each other, navigating between all the chairs. After a while we were instructed to pair up with someone, still wearing our blindfolds. As we felt around for someone's hands or arms, I found myself standing in front of a tall man who I could feel wore a sweatshirt with ribs on his upper arms. We were to state our purpose in life to the other person and the other person was to speak that back to us, as if we were already living our purpose. Again I stated that I was to bring people together. After the exercise we were told to leave that person and go somewhere else, before taking our blindfolds off.

I was speechless and quite shaken by what had occurred. I had to sit for ten minutes to let the message sink in. Not seeing this person left me with the feeling that it was not a human voice–my eyes and mind could not censor the message. It was as if a divine voice was speaking to me. And that had a huge impact on me. I didn't say, "No you don't know me, who are you?"—Which would confirm the old messages that I'm not significant, allowing my doubts to rise and ask, "Who am I to do this?" That didn't happen this time. The voice came from somewhere else. There was a deep knowing and truth in the voice that spoke to me.

Could these thoughts and events be seeds planted in my unconscious mind to lead me to my destiny, unknown to me? The seed was growing, but still underground. It didn't know what kind of plant I was yet, but now that I can look back I can see a plan unfolding. A destiny. I remember years before having a fleeting thought cross through my mind–that I was to do something important when I reached my fifties. Even though I didn't know what that was, it was an intuitive awareness about what my future would hold in another twenty to thirty years.

A profound turning point in April of 1992 led me deeper to my destiny. Driving home late at night from Seattle Unity Church, I felt a crystal clear moment, as if time stopped, and a vision came to me to bring women spiritual leaders to speak at Seattle Unity Church. That clear vision, which has always felt like a divine idea, immediately developed in my mind as a picture of creating a week-long conference, where women could meet these amazing spiritual leaders in a setting where community could be experienced.

One month before, I had read the book *The Feminine Face of God* by Patricia Hopkins and Sherry Anderson. I wanted to meet the spiritual women they wrote about and be entranced

artwork

The Seventh Chakra

Robin Maynard-Dobbs

©2000

with their stories. I didn't realize that the stage had been set even before that drive. For two weeks in a row, a woman in a healing group I was participating in told me, "You need to be an advocate for women."

What was she seeing? I had no idea. It sounded political, like burning your bra or marching with signs in a women's rally, something I would not likely do. It took me time to realize that these activities were all related. They were pointing me towards my purpose, which continues to grow to this day, known and still unknown; the mystery continues to unfold.

Who was speaking to me? Where did these ideas come from? I don't know—perhaps from my Girl Scout years, my camp counselor experience where I loved being in a circle, sitting around a campfire, feeling the community spirit of women. It may have come from my higher self, reminding me of my mission that I was sent here to do.

I can't say for sure. What's important is that I paid attention. It took many years for this mission to unfold and reveal itself in life. So during those specific events that I've shared, there was no form yet of what that was to be. The next few years there were many baby steps. I gradually found my path, as I continued to live and experience my lessons. The path can be rocky and it can be exciting as it unfolds. Somewhere I had learned to trust and allow myself to be in the process, however painful it may be at times.

My journey is not unlike the journey of Women of Wisdom, and that story is reflected in this book. It's the journey of women seeking their place in history at this important time of the world's evolution. It's a revolution of women claiming their power, their leadership, their voice and their rights to equally participate in our evolution. My story is one of many taking this journey. I have been fed and nourished by this organization, the people who are a part of it, the people who have contributed so much to the community, and to all the women leaders/authors who bring their wisdom to share and empower us. As I grow, along with all the other women, the organization matures; as the organization grows, I mature. It's a circle, one that continues to evolve.

Veronica Appolonia ©2003
Art: *Elk–Sisterhood*, Kris Steinnes ©1996

Stand Strong

Don't let them steal your power,
Don't let them take it away.
Don't hand it to them on a silver plate,
'Cause if you do you'll pay.

You'll wilt like a hothouse flower.
Your energy will drain away.
Doubt will get a grip on you
So, listen to what I say.

Know your mind and speak it,
And again until they hear.
Let your beliefs be your own.
Don't bow to force or fear.

Just stand strong and be grounded,
But let your spirit fly.
And if anyone tries to put you down,
Well, you just tell them goodbye.
Yeah, you just wave to them bye, bye
'Cause your Spirit has got to fly.

Don't let them steal your power,
Don't let them take it away.
Don't hand it to them on a silver plate,
'Cause if you do you'll pay.

Just, stand strong in your power
And to yourself be true.
You're the one who knows you best
'Cause there's no one quite like you
So, to yourself be true.

You want to stand strong every day.
You want to stand strong in every way.

It is in our unknowing that our freedom lies.

freedom
freedom
freedom
freedom
freedom
freedom

freedom
freedom

Photo, Richard Rowe

CHAPTER 7

Frances Moore Lappé

Biography

Frances Moore Lappé is the author of sixteen books, including *Diet for a Small Planet*, her new book *Getting a Grip: Clarity, Creativity, and Courage in a World Gone Mad*, *Democracy's Edge*, and *Hope's Edge: The Next Diet for a Small Planet*. She has received seventeen honorary doctorates, and was the fourth American to receive the coveted Right Livelihood Award. Frances cofounded two national organizations focused on food and the roots of democracy: Food First, the California-based Institute for Food and Development Policy, and the Center for Living Democracy, a ten-year initiative promoting democracy as a way of life.

Reflections Today

I was delighted to participate in the Women of Wisdom conference in 2003. Since then, I've continued to develop and articulate my understanding that it is the premise of scarcity— of both goods and goodness—that drags human beings into a spiral of disempowerment and destruction. My most recent work, *Getting a Grip: Clarity, Creativity & Courage in a World Gone Mad*, explains this view and emphasizes the human capacity to remake the frame through which we see the world— before it's too late! To do so, we have to rethink the meanings of democracy, fear, and even evil itself. Growing up as a girl in the south in the 1950s, I learned that power is what others have and that fear was a signal to stop. I sense my experience has been shared by many women, and that remaking our relationship with both power and with fear is key to creating the world worthy of our moral capacities. I hope this presentation can help my readers in this process.

–Frances Moore Lappé

artwork

Eve the Gardener

Joanna Powell Colbert ©1994

Rethinking Our Mental Map:
Stories from the Edge of Hope

a talk with Frances Moore Lappé

> You can see right through into new possibilities.
>
> —Frances

I know that every generation feels they live in an extraordinary time, but I really think it's true for us. We are the first generation to recognize that our planet is on a death march. At the same time, we know that not one of us would choose this decline. No one gets up in the morning and says, "Yes, I want to make sure that another child dies of hunger today." Yet thirty thousand children are dying of hunger and hunger-related diseases. No one says, "On my to-do list I'm going to add my contribution to global warming," or "I think it's just wonderful that we've created a world community in which the number of people who can sit in this auditorium control more than half the wealth in all the world."

It's very bewildering and very confusing to see our planet in decline and yet know that even the most callous among us would not make these choices.

So how can this be? How can we possibly understand this?

This is what I've been struggling with since my twenties, when I began writing *Diet for a Small Planet*. I've come to see that there's only one thing powerful enough to create this world that none of us feel that we're choosing. That one thing is the power of ideas.

In *The Anatomy of Human Destructiveness*, Erich Fromm writes, "It is man's humanity that makes him so inhuman." He explains that humanity's unique capacity to construct ideas about reality—to which we then conform—determines who we think we are as human beings, and therefore what we believe is possible. He called these ideas our "frames of orientation."

Fromm says that as human beings, we cannot operate in a void of meaning. It is our nature to seek meaning. That is all well and good if our frames of orientation, or what I call our "maps of the mind," are life serving. But what happens if you and I happen to be alive when the dominant mental map is life destroying? When the dominant mental map puts us on a death march and creates this world that none of us would choose as individuals? That is the nature of the era in which we live.

In order to break free from the mental maps that threaten our world, I believe we have to bring them into consciousness and name them. Naming has power. So we can ask, "What are the dominant thought traps that we carry around in our heads, that we breathe like an invisible ether?" One thought trap I call the "scarcity scare." This is the notion that there is just not enough, and that we're not enough: that there's not enough love, not enough jobs, not enough food. This message comes to us in image after image and word after word so that we don't even know that we're holding it in our heads.

This very first thought trap has gripped our consciousness for several hundred years—that there is not enough land and not enough water. The scarcity scare is the premise of the dominant mental map.

Ironically, when I started on this quest in my twenties I learned that the scarcity scare ends up creating scarcity. We end up creating what we most fear. I think this is a deep spiritual truth, and it is very real in the world today.

The wake-up call for me was when I was sitting in the University of California Berkeley library reading newspaper headlines that were saying we would run out of food, that famine was inevitable, and some people just had to be thrown off the lifeboat in order that the rest of us could eat. But I kept researching, and I learned that there was more than enough food in the world to make us all chubby! What was going on? This is what I call one of the moments of dissonance, when the world kind of cracks apart and you can see right through into new possibilities.

Well, I began to understand that what was going on was that the people who needed to eat food directly from the Earth were too poor to create a market demand for the food they grew, and so more and more of it was going into livestock. In my lifetime we've come up with this feedlot system, which feeds thousands of pounds of grain to livestock that didn't evolve to eat grain. They evolved to eat grass, and so they get fat in these feedlots, and they get pumped full of antibiotics, as many of you know. Nonetheless, in the US it takes sixteen pounds of grain and soy to shrink into one pound of beef. And we say we're running out of food!

We are creating scarcity out of abundance. It is simply a symptom of an economic system based on the principle of scarcity. The system drives people out of the market, and continues to pump out the grain, and then the price falls, and it makes economic sense to feed it to livestock, which returns only a fraction to us in the form of meat.

We have also devised the perfect system for getting rid of a lot of water, as it takes from 2,000 to 10,000 gallons of water to produce a one-pound steak. Somebody once calculated that the amount of water that it takes to produce a steer would float a Navy destroyer. Just visualize that. This is a world in which we're being told that water is becoming more and more scarce. So I began to see that the first thought trap of the dominant map is the creation of scarcity. This premise of scarcity then creates scarcity itself.

I now want to move to the second thought trap of the dominant mental map, which I call "thank our selfish genes," a notion that we are nothing but encapsulated egos in a competitive struggle for material consumption. Thomas Hobbes states it in the 17th century as *homo homini lupus*—"we are to each other as wolves." Thomas Hobbes did not have knowledge about the social nature of wolves, and so he really thought that we are at each other's throats.

Over the centuries we have absorbed the notion that we are nothing but these encapsulated egos fighting it out and competing for material consumption. We are essentially accumulators. So this shabby caricature of ourselves leads to the belief that we have to turn over our fate to the impersonal force of the market. The market will determine outcomes, because we, these encapsulated selfish little egos, can't possibly deliberate with one another over what is good for all of us.

This thought trap is essential in understanding how we got to the place on this planet where we can't even recognize it as ours. We view ourselves this way in image after image. We get bombarded every day by images telling us that we are nothing but accumulators, always wanting more.

I remember seeing a photograph of a multimillionaire on the front page of the New York Times' business section. The man was looking absolutely morose. The story explained that he was so upset because there are now billionaires barely out of braces, and he is only a multimillionaire. Now, the story is not communicating that this man is in need of immediate psychiatric attention—he's just your normal guy, your normal person. He just wants more. So this message comes at us not just through advertising—it's through everything.

I want to tell one anecdote from the organization Heifer International, which does a lot of work with teenagers. They simulated a little Third World village so teenagers could spend the night in these very simple conditions without many material things, and would have to share resources. They told me that since the TV show Survivor has been on, the children's behavior has been altered by the show's images of almost cutthroat competition. Isn't it interesting how these images seep into us?

The notion that this is what we are convinces us that we cannot do better than to turn our fate over to the market; that we have to do this dog-eat-dog activity in the marketplace. That leads us to believe that there is only one kind of market, the market that we have now, which is premised on the single driving force of highest return to existing wealth.

If you set up your entire system on the premise of highest return to existing wealth, which is what we have today, and then believe that you're going to have an outcome that is beneficial to the community and to the Earth, you're deluding yourself.

There are many different ways to build a market, but if it's based on the highest return to existing wealth, naturally wealth will accumulate in fewer and fewer hands. So today, 1,000 corporations control seventy-seven percent of the US economy. For example, in the food industry, ten corporations, on whose boards sit one hundred thirty-seven people, control almost half of our food choices. It's staggering, and it's invisible because of the proliferation of brands and the way we have mythologized the market. We see Maxwell House coffee, Altoid mints, Miller's beer, Post Raisin Bran. Do you know what corporation that is? Phillip Morris. How many of us know that we're supporting Phillip Morris when we're making choices to buy these products?

So there's a tremendous amount of cloaking by the mystique of the free market and the hidden concentration of wealth and power that follows from this particular configuration. We can't see the actual governance going on in our world today. The power is held less by elected governments and political bodies, and more by unelected economic bureaucracies.

Now I know that this could sound pretty radical. If I went out on the street corner and started preaching this, people would say, "Boy, that's pretty radical." But I want to remind you that it was Thomas Jefferson who began to warn us against economic monopolies. In fact, I just learned recently that Thomas Jefferson wanted two more pieces to the Bill of Rights—he wanted a prohibition against monopolies, and a prohibition against standing armies. What a different world it would have been if Jefferson had had his way.

Even in my parents' generation, the idea of economic democracy was more up for discussion. In Franklin Roosevelt's 1936 presidential nomination acceptance speech, he made it clear that political democracy would lose its meaning without economic democracy, without embedding our political rights in economic rights. He talked about an economic tyranny. He called not just for equal opportunity at the polling place, but equal opportunity in the marketplace. Can you imagine a presidential candidate today talking about economic rights, about economic tyranny, about monopolies of power?

I think it's important to fortify ourselves, to embolden ourselves, and to recognize how quickly the conversation has shut out the essential truths that keep us moving toward this world that none of us would choose. We have to get better and better at naming them. As historian Lawrence Goodwyn put it: "We have a language of Marxism, and we have a language of Capitalism, but we have no language of Democracy."

This notion that we are nothing but these selfish little egos and individual cells ends up meaning that we have to turn over our

fate to economic giants, who have no transparency and no
accountability to the common welfare. It also means that we
acquiesce, we go along with more and more transformation of
life's essential resources and life itself into commodities—from
farmers' seeds, to now the most recent phenomenon, water. I
walked into the train station in Boston a couple of weeks ago
and I asked for tap water, and they said, "What's that?" We are
now paying more for water than we are for gasoline (in
2003). Think about it. It's how we live. So we acquiesce, which
violates our deepest sensibilities, to pay for that which is
necessary to life itself.

artwork

*Sacred
Rose*

Nancy
Bright
©2003

" A new mental map is breaking through that affirms and acknowledges not just the capacity, but the deep need of human beings to connect in real community.

—Francis

In order to understand the world today, a world on the brink of war, perhaps, we need to understand that the people who are driving us to war come out of this corporate world in which it is presumed that human beings do not have the capacity to come together to deliberate. Unaccountability is the norm in the corporate structures, where they've been working all of their lives, and lack of transparency is also a given. Their expertise is in selling, not in deliberation or reasoning with others. So that is what is happening—we have been sold.

Do you know that polls (in 2003) show that most Americans believe that Saddam Hussein was behind 9/11? This suggests that a tremendous amount of mind control has made that association, even though there is no proof. And we have been sold fear. It is no surprise to me that the emotional plague of the world today is fear–fear for our safety, and fear of scarcity. More and more fear.

Now the picture that I've just painted is accurate, but at the same time completely inaccurate. That is the second challenge of the world in which we live. Objectively speaking, every measure of our needs, our planet's survival, and the survival of our species and others, is on a downward cycle. Yet at the very same time, something extraordinary is emerging in every continent and in most communities. Something extraordinary is cracking through this dominant map, and fundamentally replacing it with something that is life serving.

Both statements are true: we live in a world in which, in one sense, we are on a death march, and at the same time a new mental map is breaking through that affirms and acknowledges not just the capacity, but the deep need of human beings to connect in real community, and to affect that which is beyond their own survival.

These two needs are suppressed and denied by the dominant mental map, and this denial is a reason for so much depression in the world. The World Health Organization now says that depression is the fourth leading cause of loss of productive life in the world today, and will soon be the second leading cause. My interpretation is that the dominant mental map denies these deep needs for connection, but they are expressed in what is breaking through. As my daughter Anna and I traveled around the world researching our book, *Hope's Edge*, we met people on

CD: *Gaia Rocks*, Shawna Carol
©*2005 Pagan People's Music*

Bless Our Planet

Bless your blue green oceans,
Bless your endless skies,
Your streams and your valleys,
Your mountains so high.
Bless your Gods and Goddesses,
Buddhist, Sikh and Jain.
Jesus, Allah, Yemaya
We praise your many names.

Bless your vibrant cities,
Bless your sacred ground,
Your hillsides and your forests,
And bless your tiny towns.
Bless the winged ones that fly,
Bless the horse and bear,
The elephant, the dolphin,
The cricket and the hare.

We speak a thousand languages,
We speak with the same tongue.
Oh, bless our planet under one sky
And all the people on it.
We all laugh and we all cry.
Oh, bless our planet,
Place of our birth
We are all one family
We're children of the Earth.

five continents who were defying, denying, and putting lies to the dominant mental map—not just with their words but with their actions.

So I want to jump with you to a scene from Brazil, one of the countries that we visited. Brazil has one of the most extreme income concentrations of any society in the world. In the rural areas, one percent of the population controls almost half of the land, and that one percent lets most of the land lay idle while millions go hungry and landless. About two months ago, in 2002, Brazil elected a new president, Lula, who made a pledge that he will end hunger in Brazil. The pledge is for zero hunger in a country in which twenty to fifty million people go hungry, despite being one of the top three agricultural exporters in the world.

A few weeks ago I was in Brazil for the World Social Forum. Imagine standing in a stadium with maybe seventy thousand people singing this man's name, Lula, as he declared that his life's mission will be met if, at the end of his term, every Brazilian has three meals a day. People were weeping, people were cheering, people were singing.

Years ago I could not possibly have predicted that this man, Lula, would be elected. I was so touched by one flyer in particular that was handed to me: "Make like Lula. Participate! This is a story we're writing together." Isn't that wonderful?

While I was in Porto Allegre in southern Brazil I went out to a neighborhood that takes part in participatory budgeting. In the neighborhoods of eighty cities in Brazil, people come together and decide how major capital expenditures will be made. This process in Porto Allegre, which is a very major city in Brazil, has meant new schools, better sanitation, community gardens, new roads in the poor areas, health clinics and all sorts of improvements that had never been made in those poor communities before. It was an extraordinary experience to be in this large community building that was built as a result of this participatory process. They were so proud of this.

I think you'll appreciate this if I just paint one scene where their teenagers came and danced for us—this gaucho dance with the big boots and the long skirts. What struck me were the young men, the teenage boys. They all made eye contact with the girls, they made eye contact with the audience, they were so proud of their costumes and their community. When you think of teenage boys here—so disaffected, needing to be so cool—they wouldn't possibly be in this multigenerational dance. Yet in Brazil, they were so proud, and so energized, and so beautiful. It was a moment I shall never forget.

Towards the end of my time there I saw my old buddy Joe Collins, who cofounded Food First with me, and he said, "Frankie, I just bought you a T-shirt." In Brazilian, the shirt says, "Hope triumphs over fear." That is the slogan of the Workers Party that elected Lula.

There was another T-shirt I saw while I was there that was so simple. It just said, "*Caro un Brazil decente: Lula presidente*": "I want a decent Brazil: elect Lula." Very simple—it's not decent

artwork

Women of Wisdom Art Series

Deborah Koff-Chapin ©2006

> When people know that they're responsible and can see the ripple effect of their choices, they will not want to hurt one another.
>
> —Frances

for people to go hungry. I just want to have a decent country. So we'll see. There are many, many obstacles that this new government is facing, but just imagine being in a country that is so hopeful that they could elect not a millionaire, not an oil tycoon, but a working man. A union organizer is now the president of one of the largest countries in our hemisphere. It can happen.

Anna and I were really interested in going to Brazil for many reasons, but particularly because since I began my work thirty years ago, I would have never expected a genuine land reform to emerge there. This is the country where every attempt at land reform had been snuffed out by killing the peasants. Now, land reform has settled a quarter of a million families on over seventeen million acres of land in the last twenty years, and has taken advantage of a law in the constitution of Brazil that says it is the duty of the government to make sure that land is being put to a social purpose, and to redistribute it if it is not. So in Brazil we witnessed people coming together, getting land for the first time, and creating community.

Then, as we sat and talked with them they told us, "Well, we thought it was all about land. " That was their entry point, getting land. But they continued, "We realized that that was only the beginning. We then had to figure out: What do we want to grow? How do we want to grow it? What do we want to teach our children? What kind of schools do we want, what kind of rules?"

All of these questions brought them back to the fundamental issue of values. They began to see that they wanted to use the market, but not be used by it. So it was very interesting to us that they were not saying they were anti-market, but they were saying that economic gain must be reinvested back into the community.

For example, they said they were creating the first organic seed line in Brazil, the Landless Workers Movement, or MST, the acronym for its name in Portuguese. We asked, "Are you going organic because you yourselves were poisoned by pesticides when you were farm workers?" They looked at us and said, "Well, yeah, that's one reason. Do you think we would go through all this trouble and risk our lives?" A thousand of them had been killed over the last twenty years in the effort to gain land and build new communities. Then they added, "Do you think we would go through all this and then produce something that might harm the consumer?"

It struck us: when people know that they're responsible and can see the ripple effect of their choices they will not want to hurt one another. Whereas in our society, the farmer uses the pesticides and then says, "Oh, it's none of my business what happens to the consumer or the farm worker." It was such a different consciousness in the MST because they had empowered themselves to be decision makers, to know that they were in charge.

They also decided to create school curriculum to revalue rural life. Instead of using the government created textbooks, they created textbooks that used the corn growing process as a way to teach children about science and biology, so that the children would begin to revalue rural life.

We were also moved by an experience in a seminar with leaders from communities from Southern Brazil organizing a meeting with leaders from all over Brazil. Their goal was to make sure that the meeting would be half female and half male. We will never forget the moment when a young man raised his hand and said, "Yes, I think we need more women in the movement, because the great thing about women is that they're not afraid to ask questions." And then he started laughing, and he said, "Okay, ladies, if the men beat up on me for saying this, you've got to come out and protect me."

Now I want to jump way across the world to another example. Anna and I went to Kenya to visit the Greenbelt Movement, which was started by Wangari Maathai in 1977. Wangari Maathai is the first female PhD in the biological sciences in East Africa. On Earth Day in 1977, Wangari planted seven trees to honor seven women environmentalists in Kenya. As she was seeing the deserts encroach, seeing President Moi sell off or give away more and more of the forest to his cronies, she said, "The only way we can fight the desert in Kenya is if village women all over the country begin to plant trees. We need thousands of nurseries, and we need tens of thousands of women to plant trees."

So she went to the government forestry service and said, "This is my plan; this is obvious. Village women have to become the tree planters." And the government foresters said, "What? Village women planting trees? No, no, no. It takes foresters to plant trees." That was twenty million trees ago, all planted by unschooled village women. Through the Greenbelt Movement, African women have created six thousand village nurseries. So the lives of women have been changed, because they used to travel every day, every week at least, to gather firewood, and now they are growing their own. There are many other benefits to the environment, and of course to the soil.

And trees were only the first point. Women realized that they could take charge, because trees had always been their husband's domain. As they realized that they could take responsibility and be successful, and gain that piece of control, they began to look at other aspects of their lives and their villages. They realized in the case of growing coffee that colonialism had put them on a treadmill of export agriculture. They were told, "If you grow coffee you can earn an income and import the food you need." Well, that's what was told to many countries, and so there's now a market glut of coffee; coffee prices are the lowest they have been in a hundred years. Of course you wouldn't know that if you stand in the coffee line, but it's true.

So we talked to these villagers and they said, "We've worked all year. We've worked all year to grow all this coffee and we've made zero profit." So they began to reclaim their traditional food practices using seeds and plants that were drought resistant, because drought is terrible there. And they began to realize and revalue what their culture had always had: very ingenious ways of sustaining themselves and protecting against drought. I'll never forget as we were leaving one village, an elder, Lea Kitsomo, grabbed my arm, and she said, "When you go home to your people, you tell them that we have lost our food traditions, but we are gaining them back."

In Kenya we experienced this sense of possibility, the entry point where a new vision can emerge, and change can take hold. We all need this one point where we can see ourselves as effective in an area where we didn't believe in possibility before. In the case of the Greenbelt women, it was planting trees. And planting trees caused a rippling effect, changing many things locally and globally.

Poem

Strong Heart

It is the fragile life force of the small things that matter

This is the life force that holds our world together

It takes a strong heart to rebuild, reseed, and replant

One tree at a time,
One plant at a time,
One vision at a time.

It takes vigilance to know what is being lost,

What is already gone,

That we never knew.

It takes a strong heart to fight for these things.

As we traveled around the world it became clear to us that governments that have become delegitimized have lost credibility. They are more and more becoming simply mouthpieces for the invisible economic bureaucracies called corporations. Civilian movements are rising on every continent and in every country, and linking with one another and supporting one another. This is the invisible hope cracking through the dominant mental map.

What is our doubt? What keeps us trapped in fear? Our culture tells us that of course we can't trust the power of love, the desire for cooperation. So I was just tickled to recently read studies from Emory University in Atlanta, Georgia, where scientists had examined the MRI pictures of people participating in the prisoner's dilemma simulation game. This game tests whether "partners in crime" will trust each other to remain loyal, or betray each other for personal gain. The scientists discovered that when people were cooperating, when people were working together, that pleasure centers in the brain lit up! These are the same parts that light up when we eat chocolate. The scientists said, "Wow, this is really surprising. We're wired to cooperate." Of course we couldn't have made it to this point as a species if we weren't fundamentally cooperators. I just love it that scientists are catching on.

So really, what are we talking about? We are talking about possibility and about hope. We are talking about how to have hope in this unprecedented, scary time. I have already hinted at this message in several ways. When we were writing the book my daughter Anna said to me, "You know, if you had predicted any of the things that we're writing about now, if you had predicted them thirty years ago when you were my age, people would have considered you an absolute naive idealist. Nobody would have imagined land reform in Brazil and the Greenbelt Movement in Kenya. Nobody would have believed you." We had to admit that we were humbled and surprised when Lula won in Brazil and Wangari won in Kenya.

So it was a message we had to incorporate one more time— we don't know what's possible. And that's our freedom. It is in our unknowing that our freedom lies. Because you see, when we acknowledge that we can't know what's possible, then we are truly free to choose the world we want. We can be open to all possibilities.

We have to say that we don't know. This is what I'm
suggesting—that we stop trying to seek hope in evidence, that
we stop trying to seek hope in some proof that love will triumph
over fear, that we stop seeking hope, and instead we become
hope. Whenever I say that, I am reminded of the T-shirt that is
worn by all the Kenyan women in the Greenbelt movement. It
is so simple. I think it's what you all are about. It just says, "As
for me, I have made a choice."

> We all need this one point where we
> can see ourselves as effective.
>
> —Francis

artwork
Sky Goddess
Montserrat
©2000

Empower Your Self

explore your dreams and spirit...

1   What are your dominant thought traps?

2   In what situations do you buy into the fear of scarcity?

3   What makes you feel competitive?

4   How do you contribute to the current market system of over accumulation?

5   What is your vision for a new world that supports life?

6   How can you reinvest back into your community, to the world?

7   What are you hopeful about?

> "When we dance a circle with our arms around each other, we're creating wholeness.

we're creating wholeness
we're creating wholeness
we're creating wholeness
we're creating wholeness
we're creating wholeness
we're creating wholeness

Seven Sisters, Diana Denslow ©1998

we're creating...
we're creating wholene
we're creating wholene
we're creating wholene
we're creating wholen

Photo, Liisa Korpela

CHAPTER 8

Brooke Medicine-Eagle
and Nicki Scully

Biography

Brooke Medicine-Eagle is a Native American Metis, an Earth-wisdom teacher and catalyst for healing; a visionary, sacred ecologist, harmonist and recording artist. Based at Earth Heart Sanctuary in Montana, her Beauty Way awakens physical and spiritual health through private sessions, retreats, and women's mystery teachings, and creates a sustainable lifeway model. Her dedication is bringing forward the ancient truths for living a fully human life in harmony with All Our Relations as we approach the crossroads into the Golden Age. She is the author of *Buffalo Woman Comes Singing*, a spiritual autobiography, and *The Last Ghost Dance*, a global, visionary view of Earth magic and ascending into our greater humanity.

She invites us to remember that our power and magic lie in Oneness.

—Brooke

Nicki Scully is an acclaimed teacher of metaphysics, Alchemical Healing, and the Egyptian Mysteries. Her books *Alchemical Healing: A Guide to Spiritual, Physical, and Transformation Medicine*, and *Power Animal Meditations: Shamanic Journeys with your Spirit Allies* have become classics in their fields, and her CDs are at the leading edge of the guided journey experience. Her newest book, *Shamanic Mysteries of Egypt: Awakening the Healing Power of the Heart*, is coauthored with Linda Star Wolf and is an inner guide to the mystery teachings of ancient Egypt.

Reflections Today

We are in an intense time of crises and change, and I have been shown that women will lead the world into a new and golden time. Our charge as women is the nurturing and renewing of life, and this is accomplished through good relationship. Working through circles, through the heart, through loving connection, and through empowered ceremony, we walk a new and beautiful way into the world.

The ceremony I offer here is inspired by the words of White Buffalo Calf Pipe Woman, who came bringing a message of Oneness and Holiness to all people. She invites us to remember that our power and magic lie in Oneness, in coming together in unity with love in our hearts.

Working with Nicki in this ceremony is a demonstration of putting our hearts and minds together in a good way, and that powerful women can join together to make a powerful and positive difference in the world. Not only can we make that difference, but in this time of social, ecological and spiritual crises, we MUST!

–Brooke Medicine-Eagle

As an alchemist, I strive to utilize the raw materials given in every situation as the prime material, the grist for the alchemical mill. It is an opportunity to transform whatever is the "matter" into the alchemical gold, or universal medicine that is the result of the alchemy at hand. Working with Brooke provides a delightful opportunity to mix our medicines and combine our thoughts, visions and ideas to create something new and unique. May our deep heart connection and the love we feel for one another be reflected in this sharing of our distinct, yet parallel, paths, and may it inspire a new level of commitment to sisterhood, and to the community of women that radiate out from this WOW gathering.

–Nicki Scully

A Call to Community:
We Are All Relations

a ceremonial sharing with

Brooke Medicine-Eagle and Nicki Scully

Brooke:

I've been told that one of my assignments is to bring people together to learn how to do ceremony again. Native and tribal people who have lived together in communities have understood how to come together—they know who brings what and who handles which aspect of the whole experience. It comes together with practiced ease and it's not a big production; it's just life. Part of our challenge is that most of us haven't had that background, and so we're at the level of learning and practice. I think we've been practicing a good long time, and now is the time for us to put our spirits into action through ceremony.

Be with us as we say a prayer to begin. My sense of prayer is always to call on the highest and finest that you can bring in— we need all the help we can get.

Oh Creator, you who live within and around us, who create

the holiness of which we are a part; we give thanks for our

lives on this good and beautiful day. We give thanks for your

presence within us, and for our presence here on this sweet,

sweet Earth—we who are meant to walk across this bridge

into a golden and enlightened time. And so we give thanks

for the beauty, the richness and the magnificence you have

put inside us, which we sometimes forget. Help us to

remember it and to bring it forth in incredible, magnificent,
joyful and graceful power, that we might do the job we
came to do, to fulfill the charge that we were given: to
transform this beautiful planet, to renew her, and to bring
life, aliveness, beauty, wholeness and sweetness back into
the realms of our lives; to bring ourselves together in joy
and sweetness. So Creator, for this day, for this time, for
this power, for this beauty, we give great thanks. For All
My Relations.

I asked White Buffalo Calf Pipe Woman to help me get a deeper
sense of community—to truly understand about deep sharing
and being there for each other, and about the empowerment of
Oneness in any way I could understand it. Instead of giving me
the talk I thought she'd help me write, she gave me an immediate
need to meet in my community, as someone was ill.

So I was offered an interesting choice: to talk about community,
or to walk my talk in my community and to be there for those
folks. I chose to put my head, heart and hands into nurturing,
supporting and being there for them. That was a wonderful
opportunity, and I think the same choice is what we all have in
front of us: to understand how to not just talk about it, but to
actually be with each other in a common unity.

As I began to meditate on the importance of community, one
thing that came to the front is being there for each other. I don't
know how many of you experience feeling lonely or separate,
like there's no one to support you, feeling that kind of anxiety.
We're a human family, which is an extended family. Without
that we really feel very, very lost. So what coming together in
community is about is nurturing each other, helping each other,
and giving emotional support. It's about helping each other build
our homes, aid the ailing, work with the children and the elders,
and be there for them.

All of those things are very simple, everyday things, and yet
that's what community is about, and that's what I feel will give

us something different than the kind of terror and insecurity that the big game out there is playing and trying to get us involved in. It's being there for each other that gives us the place to stand in the world. We need to feel that we are truly there for each other.

When we come together in community, the quality of our lives will multiply exponentially. Take a moment just to think how your quality of life has been enriched by this women's community, how you've been uplifted by it. Who's been there for you that you might not have met if you hadn't been in this community of women?

It's not about heroes; it is about how each of us shows up as authentic individuals.

—Nicki

Being together is so very powerful. For example, I think about how much money we pay for insurance to big corporations, which takes it out of our communities, out of our reach, out of the realm of our true benefit. I believe that some of the businesswomen in this community could form a bank, and gather this community's resources and money. If you put as much money into that bank every month as you put into insurance and invested it wisely, it could be used to help anyone in real need. You would begin to build a kind of security and love and support for each other that would be remarkable. It would change your lives remarkably to empower yourselves in that kind of way.

Nicki:

We all know something about community because we've had to be part of some kind of community just to sustain ourselves. The indigenous tribes who inhabited this country before we got here had a complex interactive community system within which people flourished. The first pioneers who settled here from Europe were totally dependent on one another as they struggled to survive in a patriarchal system that restricted women's contributions to the rigid strictures of acceptable family roles. As the country grew and individuals began to spread out and separate, women moved beyond the limitations of the prevailing puritan culture into assertive positions, eventually becoming shakers and movers in virtually every aspect of the culture. We've arrived as new pioneers at a unique time right now where this global community is being birthed, and we're a part of it. It's like no other time ever on the planet, where we have access to each other around the world. The opportunities are unprecedented, and our choices are wide ranging, yet crucial.

This conscious community here in Seattle is a node of that larger, wider community, and as we come to maturation and understand what that means, it changes everything. As we retain the strength of each individual within the community, honor the diversity, welcome and realize the unique gift each person brings, it strengthens the community.

The time of the charismatic leaders like John Wayne is over. It's not about heroes; it is about how each of us shows up as authentic individuals; it's about how we inform and empower each other, how we watch each other's backs, and how we support each other as we move forward. Conscious community honors and utilizes the unique gifts of its members, and those of us with resources and capabilities can utilize them to, as Brooke said, bring true benefit to both our own and the larger community. There are so many sources of inspiration in the world right now to help us, and with our connections and awareness of all these other movements we really do have a network that can make a difference and move us forward as a community. What it takes is for each of us to develop and honor our commitment to support each other in community. Once we understand, recognize, and honor that commitment with every walk and every talk, then we will live in a state of permanent dedication to the whole of being and the whole of creation. That is one of the main goals of conscious community.

Brooke:

So a second thing that came to me when I thought about the importance of community is something that's in our attention right now, and that is the better serving of our world and All Our Relations. When I asked White Buffalo Calf Pipe Woman when this new time is coming, she said, "When you are caring and sharing, cooperating and unifying, and doing all of those things that bring you together in cooperation—whenever you're doing that, in any moment you're doing that, you are in the new time. And any time you're in division, separation, warring and fighting, you are in the old time, and the old time is going down." So that was really very interesting to me to think about it in that way.

She teaches about holiness being a kind of personal attention, literally a kind of attention. We have an ability to expand our attention and awareness to include the wholeness of things. So holiness isn't a white-haired, white-bearded guy in the sky that we pay attention to at a certain time of the week. Holiness is about recognizing the whole thing, and that's what healing is about—it's about paying attention to the wholeness, to the Oneness of everything.

She has said again and again that our power is found and magnified in unity. That's exactly where it is. Most of us and our own institutions don't have major financial or political clout right now, and as a consequence we have to find our own magic—we have to find true power. Many of us have been waiting until the grants come our way, thinking maybe that's when we'll have enough power and we can act. My experience is that the money we hoped for is not coming our way right now.

> " We have to come together and magnify our power through oneness of intention and action.
> —Brooke

To find the magic and power that we truly have, that the Creator wants us to develop, we have to come together and magnify our power through oneness of intention and action. Certainly in this political climate right now we are being called to work together. The cultural creative researchers talk about how there are thirty-five to forty percent of us that think and feel in a similar manner. If we could put that power together, we could vote in anybody we wanted. It's our hassling, fighting and separating that prevent this.

I was thrilled to see this year's theme: "A Call to Community: We Are the Ones We've Been Waiting For." A long, long time ago a master teacher of mine was talking to a group of us, saying how there were a lot of folks wanting to get into the earthly experience and there weren't even enough bodies! We said, "What's that about?" He replied, "Well, listen. The great, deep, old, finest, and most developed souls in the whole of the universe are literally arm wrestling to get onto Earth right now." It seemed like an odd thing to say, and we said, "Why would that be?" He said, "Basically, we are in an evolutionary time when the energy is having to spin faster and faster—and when it gets spinning fast enough, it will make a quantitative and qualitative leap into a whole new and transformed time."

So what's going on now is an enormous speeding up and multiplication of the energy of things. He said that when you step on to the planet right now, *if you're willing to walk in a positive and powerful manner*, you clean up centuries of karma. The interesting thing is that it's not just the great teachers, the Dalai Lama or other masters, who won the arm wrestling—it's us! It's a really intense time, because we're asked to move out of what the Toltecs called the Bottom of the ninth hell—warring, destruction, division and competition, which is the lowest you can go.

When you see what's going on out there, with children killing each other in schools for example, we are really at the bottom of the pit. So here we are, raised in this old, divisive way, and yet we must be truly amazing beings, because our challenge is to move the whole planet from that into this new, enlightened, loving and cooperative time. *We are the ones.* So it's incredibly exciting—we're the Rainbow Generation that will move us into a new and golden time.

I had a vision. White Buffalo Woman was there, and I was standing right on the edge of a chasm. I saw there was no way that I could get down or jump across it. I noticed that I could smell the sweetness and the flowers wafting over from the other side. The light there was like on a spring morning after it's rained and it's all fresh and shimmery with rainbows—just beautiful! There were children and little animals playing together and people happy—it was truly the golden time.

artwork

Women of Wisdom Art Series

Deborah Koff-Chapin ©2004

I was wondering how I could possibly get across the enormous chasm. And then whoosh! The one I call Rainbow Woman, who I always feel is White Buffalo Woman's energy, appeared beside me. Like the Navajo Kachina, she kept her feet on the ground, and whoosh! Her head and arms went over and bridged that chasm. She became a rainbow of light. She said to me, "The only way you will bridge this chasm is by creating a bridge of light—a rainbow. It's about light. And if you'll notice, a rainbow is made of every color, every shape, every size—in other words, All Our Relations. No one is left behind or left out." So her teaching is about coming together in community, unifying, all of us putting our energies together in common unity; and that's the way we'll get across the enormous chasm of chaos and crisis before us.

Nicki:

What Brooke just said sparked so much in me. One of the Egyptian Goddesses that I work with quite closely is the Goddess Hathor—her name comes from Hat Hor, or "house of Horus, Mother of the Sun." She is the Cow Goddess—not that far off from the buffalo, particularly White Buffalo Calf Pipe Woman in this country; perhaps a cousin. Her milk is the Milky Way. She is the Goddess of love and joy, and of celebration. Brooke's vision reminded me of the first time I took a group to Egypt and visited Hathor's temple in Dendara. One of my really dear friends with me on that journey had a vision in her temple.

It's a similar vision of the community of people on the planet, walking on this good road together. She saw all the generations: the old ones helping the young ones, and all the ways that we helped and supported each other as we traveled on that road. And then that road hit a dark time, a storm of major proportions the likes of which we've probably been moving through for millennia—like that chasm and that dark space that Brooke spoke of. Hathor is closely related to the Goddess Nut, and in that form she overarches the sky and provides that rainbow bridge. The night sky is her body, and we pass through it, much like the sun as it passes through the hours of the night, in the cycles of time. In the vision, she said that the way to the golden age that we seek is through kindness and remembering to help one another. I wonder at the synchronicity of this global community coming together and discovering that we all come from the same place, and in our hearts we all believe and pray for the same things.

> Wake up to the realization of how much impact every breath, every word and every action has.
>
> —Nicki

As a collective we are waking up, and the job of the moment, not only for this individual community, but for the world community, is conscious evolution. We are evolving and changing—that's the name of the game; it's the only constant. But while we're moving inexorably toward an unknown future, many of the several billion minds on this planet are asleep at the wheel, and they don't realize that every thought and desire is actually setting a vector for our future. We are being directed by the collective mind and the choices that we're making. So I feel that waking up to the realization of how much impact every breath, every word, and every action has, is vital to establishing a world community that can support and sustain life.

artwork

Into the Fire

Montserrat

©1998

Brooke:

When I was on Bear Butte in South Dakota at my last major vision quest, I was given a numinous vision. The ancient grandmothers danced down off the mountain in a line of light, and then they danced with my mother, my grandmother—all these swirling women and me. It was a reminder that women are literally the leaders in this process of transformation, charged as we are with good relationship, and positive relating in all its forms. That is a major key in this time right now. So the key to success for the next generations is women. We step forward and lead in this way of communing. While many of the men are leaders in the lines and rows and hierarchies, I believe that women lead in the community of the heart circle, and that's what we're about. That's why it's wonderful to come together in community this way.

The lesson of the Piscean age that we're passing through is about heart, love, good relationship, forgiveness and brother/sisterhood. The cross is not just a Christian symbol. If you think of the human body, the true meaning of the cross is a symbol of the heart. It crosses right here at the heart. In the past, hoping to allay some of the feminine Earth-based messages of Jesus, the church and power structures led us into a false sense of the cross as death and violence, and left out this central quality of the heart. I think the real symbol for that crucifixion experience should have been the empty cave, the rebirth, and that was a little bit too feminine for them.

So the cross points to the human heart. That's where the action is, and that's the whole teaching of the Piscean age. It's literally the test we're going to have if we want to pass through to the Aquarian age—this approaching golden time that will be filled with enormous power. Without moving and acting from the heart, we'll just be using power to do the same destructive and unsustainable things that we're doing now. We need to find a heart-centered place. That's the real key to this chaotic puzzle that we're in.

White Buffalo Woman talked about the Sacred Pipe, and the wholeness and holiness that it represents. She said, "With this pipe we will walk forward into a new time—a golden time, and until the end of time. And I will meet you there if you come on this same path." So that's what our lives are about right now, putting our hearts together to stand at the center in that way.

Poem: Marcia Moonstar ©2007
Art: *Raven Dream*, Denise Kester ©2003

Raven Moon

In the shadows of the dark moon,
winds of destiny are calling you,
Raven Moon, Raven Moon,
You are the messenger of change,
Seeker of wisdom, speaker of truth,
healer of our troubled and wounded past,
giver of fearless courage,
singer of celestial songs,
bringer of magic moments,
diviner of time, star time,
traveler between the worlds with your
Raven wings,
soaring to greater heights,
past the edge of time, into the spirit world.
Where you become the spirit messenger,
The keeper of the great mysteries,
meet the faceless, nameless one,
feel everywhere spirit,
hear the voice of the great spirit speak,
"When we set aside our differences,
Together as rainbow warriors,
We can be the bringers of a new dawn."

Creator agreed that for each of us, our magic, uniqueness, special gifts and purposes are set in our hearts. So what we're to do is to gather that power of Earth and Sky back into the heart. Creator's energy comes through the heart. And if we can open and quiet ourselves enough, that coding, imprint, richness, and uniqueness can be expressed as our rare and unique gift to the world.

Allowing Creator's light to shine through you is the energy that we're moving towards—that's the aliveness, richness, and peace that we want to manifest. So when we dance a circle with our arms around each other we're creating wholeness. It's literally coming from the heart. When we dance, we're extending that energy into an enormous circle of wholeness. When we focus our heartful intent at the center of that circle, then our dance can be enormously powerful. The puzzle begins to come together and makes sense. Each of us contributes our unique gift, and that magnificent symphony of love comes together at the center of our circles.

So the heartbeat is magnified by the drum, and we begin to dance the dances like they did in the past, and use our energy in ceremonial and ritual ways that I call Spirit Dance. It's just a way of saying we come together and dance, we come together and do ceremony. One powerful way we begin to manifest this new time is that we come together in ceremony.

Nicki:

When we come together in ceremony and in community, whatever the ways we come together, we as people are only half of the equation. The other half, the extension of our community, is spirit, and until people recognize that we are just half the equation, we get just half the goodies. In the peyote road they have an altar that is built up gradually in sand, and then it goes back down like a half moon. What you see above ground represents the part of the material world that is visible, the physical component. The rest of the circle, the hidden part, is the spiritual component, and any call to community must include a call to spirit.

It's amazing how the guidance from spirit is so present and is so much a part of what all of us do. So in order to give our community its true spiritual core, we have to include our spiritual guidance. It gives us depth, sincerity and humility to the larger picture, the bigger picture. Once again it brings us back to our

> " So when we dance a circle with our arms around each other we're creating wholeness.
> —Brooke

heart and our connection to the wholeness of our heart.

In our ceremony we are going to open our hearts, honor and convey our commitment to ourselves with an open heart, and extend that to the entire circle that's convened here tonight. In this way, we honor the community that is created, that is already here. We're simply celebrating it, and remembering our dedication and what it takes to keep it alive.

Brooke:

Expressed in the Lakota way, what we're doing tonight is referred to very formally as *Hunkapi*, although we won't do that formal ceremony. That's a very specific ceremony done by traditional people. Yet I said to White Buffalo Calf Pipe Woman, "It seems like things are just shattering—families are separated, communities are broken apart. I'd like to think that that's something positive happening, but what? I feel like everyone is so stressed by that. I just don't understand."

And she said, "What that's about is the breaking apart of the parochial 'we're the only important ones' kind of stuff. It's literally shattering and breaking that old way apart. What we're meant to have is a universal *Hunkapi*; we're meant to take each other as brothers and sisters in the way of *Hunkapi*." When you do a formal ceremony, what you're saying is that "I literally take this person to be my blood family," in a sense. For instance, marriage is a primary *Hunkapi*. You take your partner to be your absolute family, and that is a deep, deep powerful and long lasting vow. So that's not a light thing that you do. She was talking about us remembering and acknowledging each other as true family.

So if your grandmother isn't there, there's another older lady there who can be treated as your grandmother. If your uncle, your kids, and your grandkids aren't around, there are people right there beside you that you need to honor and welcome. There are people of all colors, sizes, shapes and persuasions around you, and they are your family. And since we are here in this particular gathering, this is our family, and to acknowledge and bring that together formally is what we're going to do in this simple, yet profound ceremony tonight.

Black Elk reported White Buffalo Calf Pipe Woman's words, who basically said, "When I take someone as my sister, I take not only this individual person, but I remember through her that I'm a sister with all women. And also the most important part is that I remember that I am one with all things in holiness." So working with that energy to create community, common unity, a stronger bond in this community, and to bring that energy together is what we'll be doing tonight.

Nicki:

This ceremony will also include the component of opening the heart to be able to perceive from that place beyond judgment in absolute presence, and an opening of the hands to access the Universal Life Force energy to assist us in our future creativity as well as the ceremony at hand.

Brooke: "Hunkapi Ceremony"

We'll begin with a prayer:

> *Oh Creator alive within us, Almighty One, Magnificent One, help us to consciously and freely choose this community, this wholeness, this holiness that is ours, that is the truth, this Oneness that is us. Let us consciously and freely choose this in this reality, to become one with each other and all things. Mitakuye oyasin. All My Relations.*

Nicki:

I think it's really good to do this standing. We want to begin by asking you to focus on your heart, and find the eternal flame that lives within your heart. As you bring your heart flame into focus in whatever way you perceive it, feed it with love, for love is the fuel. Now bring your attention deep within the Earth and begin to breathe, drawing your breath from the heart of the Earth, all the way up through the various layers of the Earth. Inhale all the way up from the soles of your feet up through your body to your heart. Let all the good juice, all that intelligence and power from the heart of the Earth, and all the layers and elements of the Earth mix with your heart flame. As you exhale, express it through all the cells of your body and out into the world from your heart. So you breathe up from the heart of the Earth, let it blend with your heart fire, hold it for a second while it blends, and radiate it out into the world with love. Once more, up from the Earth, let it blend with the fire, and exhale it out.

Now keep breathing in this way while I describe the next part of the breath. While you are breathing the Earth breath, intend your next in-breath to also draw from the sky, from a source deep in the cosmos, and pull the breath on your inhale down from the heart of the universe, down through your crown and into your heart. Let this stellar intelligence, power and energy mix with your heart flame and join with the power of Earth, and then exhale from your heart, through all your cells and out into the world with love. So breathing in, pull the breath down from above, let it mix with your heart flame, and express it out. One more time from above. While you are breathing from Earth and Sky, all that power and intelligence that you inhale mixes with the love in your heart flame, and is expressed out into the world. And again. This heart breath works like a bellows. It increases and intensifies your heart flame. Stay focused on your heart flame as you continue to breathe the heart breath. Soon your heart flame connects with the heart flames of the people on either side of you. As we continue breathing together, your heart flame connects with all the other heart flames in this sanctuary. Together we create a huge glow, a light that radiates throughout Seattle and beyond.

As you focus within your heart flame, you will perceive a tiny seed of light within the heart of your heart flame. With each breath, it seems as though that seed of light begins to take shape. It turns into the bud of a flower. As you continue to breathe the heart breath, the petals begin to unfurl from this flower bud. For many of you that flower will be a lotus, and as the petals unfurl, your breath is like the rays of sunshine touching the flower in your heart. As the love continues to generate through your heart, the petals open, and the lotus releases an exquisite fragrance.

As you continue to breathe, that fragrance fills the space of your body, and fills the space of this sanctuary. And as you continue to focus on your heart flame, it's as though the vapors of the fragrance of that lotus begin to take form. The form is the embodiment of the emanation of compassion that lives within your heart. On your next breath, notice how it might take the shape of White Buffalo Calf Pipe Woman, or Kuan Yin, or Mary, or Hathor, or Sekhmet, or any of the Goddesses or bodhisattvas of compassion that dwell within your heart, ready to come alive.

On your next breath, as you feel the energies of Earth and Sky come together in your heart, it's as though that manifested being transmits back to you the energy—the power of love and compassion. As you exhale it pulses throughout your body, filling every cell of your being with loving, compassionate light. Inhale from above and below to your heart and, feel it blend with the compassionate being at your core. Hold your hands up, with your palms facing forward. As you exhale this time, the energy moves out and runs down your arms and into your hands, and you feel the light come pouring off the palms of your hands. Take another deep heart breath and feel that current of life force strengthen as it radiates throughout your body, and pours out from your heart and your hands and your fingertips. Now bring your hands together over your heart, and feel that energy circulate back within you. As you're pouring that loving energy back in through you and circulating it, remember your dedication, your commitment to life and community.

> Remember your dedication,
>   your commitment to life and to community.
>
> —Nicki

Brooke:

As you continue to breathe and carry that energy, this connection in community will be very simple. We have this wonderful energy in our hands, and so we're going to turn to one another, place our left hands on each other's hearts, look into each other's eyes, and make that really clear connection. And to honor your sister you're going to say to her, "My sister, my friend, All My Relations," and she will repeat that back to you. So find the people you'd like to connect with in this way and make a special bond with them. We'll just sing and allow you to move around, remembering, "My brother, my friend, All My Relations; my sister, my friend, All My Relations." So go ahead and make this commitment to each other, and then we will come together and make it to the whole community.

[pause for ceremony]

Brooke:

Now if you'll turn your attention to the front we'll say this together, remembering that we say it not only to each other as individuals, but to all our sisters and brothers, and to the wholeness and holiness that is around us.

My sister, my friend, All My Relations.

My brother, my friend, All My Relations.

Mitakuye oyasin, All My Relations.

We're going to say a prayer together to complete. Let's focus our attention on our heart breath, our own breath, and give thanks for this moment:

Creator, I thank you for my life.

Creator, I thank you for my loved ones.

Creator, I thank you with all my heart

for this loving and supportive community.

May we use the power of this common unity

in service to All Our Relations. Ho! Yi aaaa!

artwork

Women of Wisdom Art Series

Deborah Koff-Chapin
©2006

Empower Your Self

explore your dreams and spirit...

1   When you have to make a choice between work and
     family, do you walk your talk?

2   Where in your life do you have people to support you?
     When do you feel separate and isolated?

3   How can you show up as an authentic person and/
     or a leader?

4   What are you waiting for to take action?

5   When do you separate yourself from your community?

6   Who is your true family?

7   What does the flower in your heart represent in
     the meditation?

_____

_____

_____

_____

_____

_____

_____

New people come to sit around the fire
and stir the pot.

and stir the pot
and stir the pot
and stir the pot
and stir the pot
and stir the pot

Strewing Mercy, Suzanne Cheryl Gardner ©2003

and stir the pot
and stir the pot

CHAPTER 9

The Creative Cauldron at Women of Wisdom

The Creative Cauldron
at Women of Wisdom

introduction by Kris Steinnes

Throughout the years, Women of Wisdom–the organization and the conference–has been a creative cauldron. New people come to sit around the fire and stir the pot, new ingredients and spices are thrown into the brew, the hunger changes and the nourishment evolves (along with the indigestion!). The organization, the conference, the participants, and the presenters all influence each other to create a new experience year after year. It has to be this way–how can a celebration of the Divine Feminine remain static?

Chaos is as much a divine trait as clarity, and at WOW chaos is allowed–even invited–into the celebration. With chaos comes mystery, the unknown, creativity and new life–all different colored cloaks from Her closet, different ways to see and know Her beauty and also her furor!

This chapter reflects the creative forces at work at WOW, and lifts the veil a bit into what can be experienced through this celebration of the Divine Feminine. We include contributions from artists and organizers who have come to WOW to offer their skills and their gifts, and we share their experiences of being touched and how in turn they have touched so many others.

The way these women have contributed, and the ways their contributions have evolved, reflects the Divine Feminine at work and play. One thing leads to another–one thought or feeling gives rise to the next. One artist comes to the event with an idea to provide crafts that celebrates the Goddess, so–aha–we have a Goddess Market. One participant at the Goddess Market has an interest in oracles, so–aha!–she creates a Temple of Healing and a Temple of Oracles where women can receive healings and oracle readings. A committee member who loves to sing brings a choral arrangement to the stage, which inspires others to expand the arrangement into a theater piece, which later turns into a theater piece where the whole audience participates. Aha! –ritual theater arrives at WOW.

WOW has encouraged this way of creating, for it allows organizers and the audience to be truly present as who we are, contributing to the whole. In this atmosphere of acceptance, freedom, and creativity, we can be ourselves. And only as ourselves, can we truly offer our love and our power to Her who, in turn, helps us contribute more fully to the world.

Words are powerful and profound. But so are images, colors, movement, and light. This book would not be complete without a sampling of experiences from this dimension of the conference. So, please join us as these artists evoke the colors and forms and sounds of the Goddess and the ways in which she works for us and through us!

artwork
Mermaid
Sue Coccia
©1999

The Creative Cauldron:

Interpretive Conference Art at Women

of Wisdom by Deborah Koff-Chapin

introduction by Kris Steinnes

As the song enters my heart it inspires the impulse to draw.

—Deborah

Visual art has always had a strong presence at WOW—from artists selling paintings, jewelry, totems, and sculpture at the Goddess Market, to Deborah Koff-Chapin, a visionary painter from Whidbey Island, painting at the conference and donating her paintings to our silent auction.

Since 1995, Deborah has been a witness and an interpreter at WOW conferences. Often hidden from view, this petite woman would sit silently in the corner of the room, painting her vision of the events, and her beautiful offerings are profound expressions of all of our experience. We were blessed by her generosity to donate her time and talent towards our endeavors.

Deborah Koff-Chapin
Conference Interpretive Artist
www.touchdrawing.com.

a talk with Deborah Koff-Chapin

Each year at the opening night of the Women of Wisdom Conference in Seattle, I carry my drawing materials to the front of the lecture hall. It is usually a slow progress. There are so many beloved friends to hug, and I have not seen some of them since the previous year's conference. I sense the anticipation in the air, and feel so glad to be there. It feels as if Women of Wisdom exists in a timeless realm of its own. In this magical space, we generate a field of inspiration that transforms lives and reverberates throughout the region.

I arrive at the front of the left aisle and set up my portable art studio—a milk crate for my table and a floor cushion for my seat. I lay my drawing board on top of the crate and roll a smooth layer of paint onto the surface. Next I place a sheet of paper on top of the wet paint. A stack of paper sits ready for me on the floor. I ready myself for the intense focus of listening and drawing.

When the conference opens and the singing begins, I feel a rising joy. As the song enters my heart it inspires the impulse to draw. I see the hint of an image or shape in my mind, and respond to this impulse with the movement of my fingertips on the paper. Wherever I touch, the pressure creates impressions through contact with the wet paint on the underside. Through the translucent paper I can see a light version of what is taking form. I continue drawing until the image feels complete. As I peel the paper off the board, I see the completed image on the underside of the page. I glance at it quickly, and then lay it aside. Again I

artwork

Women of Wisdom Art Series

Deborah Koff-Chapin ©2003

smooth the paint on the drawing board and put another sheet. I wait, listening to what is happening on stage and in my heart. When I feel the next impulse. I dive into drawing once again.

When the keynote presenter takes the podium, I am warmed up and ready to submerge myself in the flow of their words, and the feelings and images they evoke. As the speaker moves deeper into their presentation, I expand into deeper listening and drawing. Their thoughts pass through me and take form on the page. I am in high gear as the energy builds. The images come in faster and clearer. At times I begin drawing an image that doesn't seem to line up with what the presenter is saying, only to find that they begin speaking about something that relates to the image once it is underway. It becomes a dance between the thoughts of the presenter and my own intuition. This is truly creative listening.

> *A way to honor each other and honor the spirit of the gathering.*
>
> *—Kris*

Over the years, I have had the honor of drawing for many of the great women authors, musicians and leaders of our time at the Women of Wisdom Conferences. It is a blessing to translate their thoughts and energies into images. Each year we sell a few drawings to benefit women's shelters and the WOW Foundation, but there are plenty left, tucked away in my drawing files.

It is interesting to note that at the same time Kris started working on this book, I had the impulse to dig through those files and see how many drawings I could locate. I found WOW touch drawings for every year going back to 1995 (except 2005, when I was sick). These pieces now form a retrospective of WOW drawings on my web-site. Looking at them again, it was tremendously satisfying to see the body of work that had developed over the years. Several of the drawings have been selected for this book. I hope they transmit some of the vision that inspired them.

The Creative Cauldron:
Ceremonial Expression at Women of Wisdom

introduction by Kris Steinnes

From the beginning, everyone connected to WOW intuitively understood that when women gather, we want a way to honor each other and honor the spirit of the gathering, so ceremonies were woven into our format early on. Ceremonies draw us together, center us, provide a way for understanding why we're here and focus our attention on what we want to accomplish. Ceremony allows us to go deep within, individually and with the group.

Each year the conference committee planned these ceremonies, keeping in mind the annual theme. But while they changed year to year, there developed a consistency that women appreciated and enjoyed, and many women just came to the conference opening to be part of the ceremony, even though they weren't staying beyond that evening. At the Opening Ceremonies in 2004 committee members spoke the poem included here: "Invocation to Women of Mother Earth" for the theme, *A Call to Community! We Are the One's We've Been Waiting For.*

Rev. Judith Laxer joined the conference planning committee in 1996 and soon became involved in planning our ceremonies, and by the year 1999 she became our Ceremonial Director. Her experience at leading ceremonial rituals and working with other women to bring an inspiration to our openings and closings has been a blessing for all involved.

artwork

*Butterfly
Crop Circle*

Lydia Ruyle
©2007

Rev. Rosa Redtail and Rev. Judith Laxer
©2004 WOW Opening Ceremonies

Invocation to Women of Mother Earth

Invocation to Women
Women one and all
Hear Her voice
Heed her call
Mother Earth awakens you to power
We call upon your wisdom.

She who lives in jungles deep
Who knows the healing secrets of the plants
Women of South America
We call upon your wisdom.

She who hears the pleas of the poor
Who feeds and comforts the hungry
Women of Central America
We call upon your wisdom.

She who cares for those with A.I.D.S.
Who seeks fair pricing for medicine
Women of Africa
We call upon your wisdom.

She who walks on mountains high
Who knows the oneness of creation
Women of Tibet
We call upon your wisdom.

She who kneels to aid the birth
Who embraces the cry of new hope
Women of Asia
We call upon your wisdom.

She who stand firm in the darkest hour
Who has courage in times of oppression
Women of China
We call upon your wisdom.

She who holds the hand of the dying
Who guards the doorway of their passing
Women of Eastern Europe
We call upon your wisdom.

She who sings her babes to sleep
Who covers them with loving prayers

Women of Western Europe
We call upon your wisdom.

She who organizes labor unions
Who protests for equal pay for women
Women of Russia
We call upon your wisdom.

She who authors laws of peace and reason
Who demands justice and equal rights
Women of India
We call upon your wisdom.

She who carries water to those who thirst
Who knows the living waters of life
Women of Australia
We call upon your wisdom.

She who guides the children's hand
Who teaches a vision of a compassionate world
Women of Canada
We call upon your wisdom.

She who sustains on nature's bounty
Who cherishes her interdependence
Women of the Islands
We call upon your wisdom.

She who watches the night sky
Who knows the pain of war and the price of peace
Women of Middle East
We call upon your wisdom.

She who marches in peaceful protest
Who says no to war and yes to peace
Women of the United States
We call upon your wisdom.

She who is here tonight holding this sacred container
Who envision and lead us into a New Age of Peace
Our own Women of Wisdom
Mother Earth awakens you to power
Mother Earth awakens you to power
Mother Earth awakens you to power
Be here now
Blessed be!

The Creative Cauldron:

Ceremonial Bliss!

Rev. Judith Laxer
WOW Ceremonial Director
and past board president.
Founder & Minister, Gaia's Temple
www.gaiastemple.org

Photo. Colette Hinkle ©2007

a talk with Rev. Judith Laxer

> *The energy is real and creates a sense of safety, purpose and cohesiveness.*
>
> —Judith

The buzz of energy was palpable as we stood waiting in the hallway. When the doors finally opened, we walked into the darkened fellowship hall of Seattle Unity Church. Two rows of women holding lit candles formed a pathway into the sacred space. As we entered in this processional, the women sang, "Remember, remember, remember who you are!"

A salty wave of spontaneous emotion rose in me and spilled out from my eyes. I didn't know why this meant so much to me, because I didn't feel that I had forgotten who I was. But there was something so beautiful, so important, so ancient in being sung to by women I didn't even know. This was my first impression of Women of Wisdom. And I was hooked!

Thereafter, I would not miss a single conference. WOW grew rapidly and a huge community of women artists, teachers, and participants emerged. The February Conference became the highlight of my year. I quickly became involved in many of its aspects: directing and performing in ritual theatre, teaching workshops, reading tarot cards in the Healing Temple, and serving two years as Board president for the organization. But I was most enthralled with helping to create the opening and closing ceremonies. In 1999, a shift in leadership occurred due to our growth, changing dynamics and the need to share the load and I stepped up to become the Ceremonial Director for Women of Wisdom and would remain so until 2006. This was my thing! I have an extensive background in the performing arts, specifically musical theatre, and when my spirituality became a priority in my life and led me to become a Priestess, my former training dovetailed perfectly with the ceremonial needs of the Conference. Ritual is theatre, after all!

Opening and closing ceremonies are important for any event, but especially for a woman's spirituality conference. The energy created ceremonially holds the intention of the gathering. This energy is real and creates a sense of safety, purpose and cohesiveness. The ritual aspects of ceremonies (the parts that are repeated over and over) provide a sense of comfort and familiarity. The opening ceremony sets intention, raises energy and awareness and welcomes the community. The closing ceremony brings a chance to acknowledge the effect the event has had, and provides closure for the participants.

WOW conferences attract women from many different walks of life, backgrounds, and spiritual paths. It was important to embrace this diversity and make everyone feel welcome. There were several things I knew would help to create great ceremonies: The women would process into the space with music accompanying their journey, (I remembered the powerful effect that had had for me) and the ceremonies would happen in circle.

artwork

11 of 12

Diana
Denslow
©2001

The circle model is feminine in nature—everyone a part of the whole, each woman able to look around and see all the others standing with her. Elemental energies would be invoked —sometimes five, sometimes seven, following Earth based spiritual traditions. A ritual gesture would demonstrate the message in the conference theme. The conference committee would be featured, and all volunteers acknowledged. And the ceremony would end with a spiral dance that would unwind into the opening night presentation, kicking off the week.

As soon as the conference committee had determined the theme, I would put out the call in the WOW community to anyone who wanted to join the ceremonial team and our brainstorming would begin. Creating these ceremonies together was fun and fulfilling. It is important work, and the women who joined the teams over the years were big hearted, talented and dedicated. There were growing pains, to be sure, as we explored leadership dynamics and practiced our communication skills in circle. But these were minimal, and the results of our work were well worth our efforts.

I can recall many moments of pure magick in both the planning and the enactment of these ceremonies over the years. Two in particular stand out for me as I write this.

The first happened at our Tenth annual conference. We had come a long way, and felt proud of offering ten years of women's empowerment to our community. During the opening ceremony we used a song that women's circles have sung for many years:

"Woman am I, Spirit am I, I am the infinite within my soul. I have no beginning and I have no end. All this I know!"

Everyone softly sang this over and over while committee members took turns coming to the microphone to read the names of all the women who had participated in the conference for the first ten years: presenters, volunteers, performers, artists, office staff…everyone! The list went on for some time, and as they spoke the names into the circle, the room began to thicken with love and gratitude for all of them, for all of us. When we sang Shawna Carol's "Carried by the Love of My Sisters!" during the spiral dance that night, many women couldn't sing for the tears caught in their throats.

The second of these two magickal moments occurred at the

Conference in 2006. For the theme, "Return to the Well," Kathy McKeever created a magnificent "well" on the main altar, covered in moss and fern and encircled with stone. At the closing ceremony, we invited women to come up to the well and fill their jars with the holy water that had been added to and blessed all week. I felt lucky, honored, my senses heightened with gratitude for our freedom to gather in a circle of our own design. The sight of these women, all of them beautiful, returning to and dipping their ladle into our collective well to take their rightful replenishment was a magnificent sight I will never forget.

Working with the powerful, visionary, and talented women in this organization has afforded me the opportunity to express my creativity and hone my leadership skills. Not to mention make some lifelong friends! In Women of Wisdom, our common ground is our passion for growth and learning; experienced in the sacred space we create together. I cherish these experiences of growth and community that I have shared with those I have come to love so dearly.

> I felt lucky, honored and acutely aware of and grateful for our freedom to gather in a circle of our own design.
>
> —Judith

artwork

Women of Wisdom Art Series

Deborah Koff-Chapin ©2004

The Creative Cauldron:
Musical Expression at Women of Wisdom

introduction by Kris Steinnes

Since its inception, the evening program is one aspect of the conference that has been especially open to and influenced by creative forces. Inspired by the gifts brought by our keynote presenters, and by the evolving interests of our audiences, the WOW evening event has grown and changed. In our second year we started to bring women singers to our stage. We first invited Libby Roderick, and Libby was followed by well-known artists in the women's music movement such as Holly Near, Cris Williamson, Ferron, Betsy Rose, Lisa Thiel, Susan Osborn, Rhiannon, Jennifer Berezon and Jamie Seiber. During one particular conference we created an informal choir of committee members, led by our music directors. Members sang back up to Marita Berg's "Stories" and sang "Pray Like a Woman" with Lorraine Bayes.

Marita Berg was our first Musical Director and she led our music for the first five years. She began the first conferences by leading the audience in women's chants. The songs hit just the right note for the beginning of the conference—creating an atmosphere of excitement and attunement that ushered in the rest of the program. One gift that Marita gave us was the song "Stories." The idea of sharing women's stories has been an important thread weaving through our conference week.

Lorraine Bayes became WOW's Musical Director in 1998, and ever since has been instrumental in building the music program. She has skillfully and intuitively taken themes of the conferences along with the essence of the keynote speakers into account when choosing music. Over the years, the evening program has grown to include dancers, poets and one year even a fire dancer!

Lorraine, herself, has been a key performer in our theater

When I Hear Music words and music by
Libby Roderick. CD: *If You see a Dream*
©Libby Roderick Music, 1988.

When I Hear Music

Women make music, women make love
Women make babies, women make visions of
Women make peaceful world, women make dreams
Women make music, music, music, music…

When I hear music, music sets my heart on fire
The magic soars upon the wind, it fills me with desire
When I hear music, music makes it all worthwhile
The sorrow bursts into a song and I remember.

Women make progress, women make change
Women make trouble, women make men rearrange
Women make dancing, women make do
Women make music, music, music, music…

When I hear music, music sets my heart on fire
The magic soars upon the wind, it fills me with desire
When I hear music, music makes it all worthwhile
The sorrow bursts into a song and I remember.

That women's arms hold up half the sky
That women's voices sing out half the song
That if this world is ever going to ring with hope
That we must make a right to more than half the wrong.

Women make clothing, women make steel
Women make nations, women make visions real
Women make healing, women make time,
Women make music, music, music, music…

When I hear music, music…

productions, and co-produced the Women of Wisdom CD. Lorraine's diverse musical abilities have enhanced all of our experience over the years.

I have a particularly fond memory of Lorraine coming to me one year, expressing her desire to create a song using themes from each year's conference. When she sat on the floor of my office singing the song for the first time, I cried at how beautiful the song was, and how deeply and accurately she reflected who we are.

" The music flowed, cleansed and nourished our bodies and souls.

—Lorraine

The Creative Cauldron:

Music Through the Years of Women of Wisdom

Photo, James A. Nelson ©2007

Lorraine Bayes
WOW Music Director 1998-2004
National award winning singer,
songwriter and recording artist.
www.tickletunetyphoon.com

a talk with Lorraine Bayes

"Women of Wisdom, Women of Wisdom
Rise and Shine Sisterkind
Spirit of Woman, Rise and Shine.

—Lorraine

I open with the lyrics from the "Women of Wisdom Song" because the words ring so true! Through the years, a tapestry of beautiful, musical artistry and inspirational, true-life stories has been so generously offered and shared. With creative honesty, courage, and joy, the spirit of music and song gracefully wove itself into the WOW community as an integral part of remembering and reclaiming many ancient teachings and eternal ways of the Divine Feminine and the Mother of Us All. "Mother, we are healing" repeatedly resonated through all of us, as we gradually opened to living in our wholeness and holiness, connecting and honoring the circles of our lives.

artwork

Women of
Wisdom
Art Series

Deborah
Koff-Chapin
©2003

> *We listen to and witness the voices, sounds, music and stories of women who sing for life.*
>
> —Lorraine

With a devoted sense of sisterhood, the power of cocreation, the spirit of beauty and our strong love, the WOW music force grew and brought to fruition many life-transforming and life-supporting musical moments. The music flowed, cleansed and nourished our bodies and souls, through radiant ceremony and concert celebrations, and profound, original ritual theatre productions.

In the early years, Marita Berg, the first music director for Women of Wisdom, Simone LaDrumma, well-loved drummer/performer, and I molded the creative muse with the primal power of the women's drumming ensemble, *Ladies Don't Drum*. I experience a visceral delight in remembering the large sanctuary floor of the Seattle Unity Church rockin' and rollin' with the ecstatic joy of dance and rhythm—people jumping alive with Spirit. Music, through its eternal universal language, brought together men, women, and the generations of ages, and assisted WOW in expressing and presenting cultural diversity.

Music also formed an integral role in the opening and closing ceremonies at the WOW conferences. Guided and directed by Rev. Judith Laxer, these ritual gatherings created sacred space and a container of inclusiveness and belonging—always acknowledging the circle of all directions and elemental powers, and always dancing the spiral, often singing, "Carried by the love of my sisters, I'm carried by the love of my sisters," a beloved song by Shawna Carol.

Another beloved song, my anthem of praise "Pray Like A Woman," was proudly shared by a small group of women at one of the closing conference banquets and Goddess Talent Shows. After listening to each other's healing stories from a WOW workshop, "Beautiful Breast Care," presented by Sally King, we all stood in self-affirming love and invited all the women to stand, hold up their breasts and sing in health and unity: "Pray, pray like a woman." It was a divine moment, and blended flamboyantly with the humor of Madame Judishka, our wildly funny mistress of ceremonies, encouraging many women to step up, show their beauty and hidden talents.

These delightful enactments of sacred play and archetypal adornments culminated in the creation of a Goddess Ball. Here the many guises and expressions of the Goddess were set free to come out and blossom in myriad colorful regalia. What a total

CD: *In All Her Fullness,* Lorraine Bayes ©1999
Art: *Sisterhood,* Montserrat ©1999

Pray Like a Woman

Pray ~ pray like a woman Pray ~ pray like a woman
Everyday ~ Hey! Hey! Pray like a woman
In every way ~ Pray like a woman

From the breast of the Mother
To the blood of our birth
From the song of pleasure
To the lovers of the Earth

In the hour of our longing
Each flowering start
In our tears and our laughter
Grow the gardens of the Heart

Pray ~ Pray like a woman
Pray ~ Pray like a woman
Everyday ~ Hey! Hey! Pray like a woman
In everyway ~ Pray like a woman

In the Body of the Goddess we shall dance and sing
In the Body of the Goddess love is circling ~ circling
Everything ~ Spread your wings!

Pray ~ Pray Like A Woman ~~~ Pray ~ Pray Like A Woman!

Feeling as though we were coming home.

—Kris

joy! These musical events, always accompanied with community song and drum, composed energetic bridges, linking all parts of the WOW conference together: connecting the participants and presenters, the artists and vendors, the healers and medicine women; and inviting all to share in food, fun and friendship!

Often the roles and responsibilities of being the music director were truly an experience of being a midwife. Each unique creative birth required constant resourcefulness, tireless patience and many dedicated, multitalented beings to put together the grand, spiritually inspired performances. *The Goddess Chant*, a musical theatre production with music and recording by Shawna Carol, brought together musicians and drummers, a choir, a tribe of belly dancers, and other solo artists, who helped fulfill the dream of this original, seminal work. Attracted and drawn to this performance was an exceptional conductor and gifted composer, Pamela Gerke, who put all the parts together, uniting the highly skilled singer-songwriters with the passionate newcomers who were so thrilled to join in this celebration to honor the Great Mother Goddess.

A field of resonate beauty remained from *The Goddess Chant*, and a new door opened to more amazing musical, ritual theater productions. WOW conferences continued to be graced with wonderful music and magick through Pamela Gerke's epic, *Temple Dreams: an original Herstory of the Goddess*; and *The Elemental Journey of Venus*, collaboratively written by many WOW performers, featuring original women's stories and songs that illuminated an astrological narration and interpretation of the five-pointed star path of Venus.

All the generative seeds of this beautiful music took root to create the magnanimous spirit singers in the Sacred Fire Choir. This enchanted group has thrived and served Women of Wisdom for years, giving their song in the Beauty Way.

To honor WOW's ten-year anniversary, a compilation of songs and music by legendary women musicians was recorded and documented on the *Women of Wisdom Collection* CD. Here, we listen to and witness the voices, sounds, music and stories of women who sing for life—creative women who walk our sacred Earth with open, full hearts, as peaceful warriors, teachers, healers and visionaries..

The Creative Cauldron:
Theater at Women of Wisdom

introduction by Kris Steinnes

As Lorraine indicated above, in 2000, WOW celebrated with our first ritual theater performance of Shawna Carol's *Goddess Chant*. We had always praised the Divine Feminine through art, dance and music, but now we could experience Her presence through ritual performances in which everyone–including the audience–participated.

Goddess Chant and subsequent performances were alive, and created a sacred atmosphere of participation, cocreation, and unity. At several performances, an archway with boughs of cedar was made and people were blessed as they entered the sanctuary. During one performance, the audience raised their arms with candles, shining the light into the room. We were often moved to tears during this experience–remembering these rites of ancient times and feeling as though we were coming home.

Here, we will follow this evolution toward ritual theater from the beginning. First, we will hear from Susan Chiat, who was attending a WOW workshop when the idea came to her to produce *Goddess Chant* for a WOW evening program. Then we will hear from Shawna Carol, the initial creator of *Goddess Chant*, which had so inspired Susan. She will describe how she came to work on the piece for a West Coast WOW performance. Finally Pamela Gerke will share her story of how she and other artists developed the annual WOW theater performances and launched the Sacred Fire Choir, which came to the WOW stage in 2001.

All three of these women have been key players in our gatherings. Susan Chiat offered her organizational and event planning expertise, and led the board for the Women of Wisdom Foundation's first three years. Shawna Carol has blessed us with

artwork

Spirit of Singing Hill–WOW CD Cover Art

Deborah Koff-Chapin
©2000

performing her songs on our stage for several years, and Pamela Gerke inspires us with theater performances, several which were her original compositions, and by leading the Sacred Fire Choir.

I experienced the music's potential for healing in a group.

—Susan

The Creative Cauldron:

Bringing *Goddess Chant* to WOW

Susan Chiat
WOW member since 1996,
Past conference committee member
and past Board President of
Women of Wisdom
www.seattlehealingarts.com

a talk with Susan Chiat

At the 1999 Women of Wisdom Conference I attended "The Cauldron of Creativity," a daylong workshop presented by Starhawk, author, teacher, ritualist, and political activist. The day included powerful rituals, drumming, chanting, and energy work, and I dove deeply, drinking nourishment and inspiration from the experience. At one point over a hundred women surrounded me in a circle of support. Among these women was my best friend, composer and sound healer Shawna Carol.

The year before, I had attended Shawna's CD release concert for *Goddess Chant*, a series of beautiful, uplifting, and poignant songs she wrote dedicated to the Divine Feminine. I was already intimately familiar with the music, but at the live concert, which included a choir, band, dancers, and a ritual theater piece, I experienced the music's potential for healing in a group. I knew for certain that *Goddess Chant* would make a wonderful addition to the Women of Wisdom community, and hoped we could bring it to Seattle sometime in the future. This seed, planted in my subconscious, finally sprouted one year later at Starhawk's workshop.

At the end of her workshop Starhawk challenged the women in

artwork
Women of
Wisdom
Art Series
Deborah
Koff-Chapin
©1999

the group to make a commitment to our creativity. Without thinking, I rose up in the circle and announced, "I am going to produce *Goddess Chant* at next year's Women of Wisdom Conference." Of course, only Shawna and I even knew what *Goddess Chant* was. But that didn't matter. My words had been spoken in a sacred circle of power. And thus the creative production of *Goddess Chant* began.

Throughout the production process for *Goddess Chant* in Seattle, I felt an invisible hand effortlessly guiding me. Of course, I had a lot to do to make the concert happen. Most importantly, I had to present the idea to the WOW conference steering committee and gain their support. I knew that original music from female artists had always formed a strong component at the WOW conferences, yet concerts were not always well attended when artists were showcased on their own. I was determined to help change this and felt strongly that *Goddess Chant* would succeed.

During a break at the spring conference planning session, I surreptitiously put *The Goddess Chant* CD in the stereo. Inspired by the words of the song, "I am the Goddess," which declare:

"I am the Goddess, I am the Mother. All acts of love and pleasure are my ritual."

All the women started dancing around the room. Then they asked each other, "Who is this? What CD is this?" Smiling sweetly, I answered them, saying, "This is *Goddess Chant*, and I want to produce it as a ritual theater concert at WOW next year." They all responded enthusiastically. After all, once they heard the music, how could they refuse?

Buoyed by the steering committee's response, I felt energized to move forward, but wasn't sure about the next step. While I had produced hundreds of events over the past decade as the Program Director of Interface, Boston's premier holistic center, I had never put together this type of event before. So I prayed and stayed relaxed and open. Then in the early fall I put an ad in the WOW newsletter seeking choir members. Within days after the newsletter's publication, I knew the Goddess had answered my prayers when a woman named Pamela Gerke called me and said, "I'd like to be in your choir; and by the way, I'm a conductor." As soon as I learned that Pam had conducted the

Seattle Women's Ensemble and was more than capable to guide the choir, I hired her on the spot. And in working with her in the next few months, I knew without a doubt that she had definitely been Goddess-sent!

Judith Laxer also heard the call and joined our team, working with the dancers and creating and leading us as director in *Goddess Chant*'s ritual theater component. Many other wonderful women shared their passion, talents, and energy, for which I felt very grateful. It was truly a collective effort.

Besides the important artistic aspect of *Goddess Chant*, I also wanted the event to succeed financially. To this aim, we did some extra marketing to spread the word. I also regularly visualized a sell-out crowd. Imagine my excitement when on opening night, right before the concert began, I peeked through the stage curtain and saw a packed house!

But it brought me even more joy to see the audience's reaction as they stood up dancing and singing with the choir; crying, laughing, and inspired by this wonderful musical piece that honors the Divine Feminine and celebrates the creator as the Goddess. It was a tremendously healing night for everyone present and an absolutely smashing success!

artwork

Women of Wisdom Art Series

Deborah Koff-Chapin
©2000

The Creative Cauldron:

The Creation of *Goddess Chant*

Shawna Carol, Singer-songwriter,
composer of "Goddess Chant"
WOW performer, workshop presenter
www.goddesschant.com

a talk with Shawna Carol

> *Affirming our divinity and the divinity in all things.*
>
> —Shawna

In 1986 I was meditating when a fully arranged choral chant came to me. Candlelight filled a darkened church as a large choir sang the pagan ritual blessing, "Blessed Be."

1986 was also the year I read Z Budapest's *The Holy Book of Women's Mysteries*. The book introduced me to the Goddess as a modern living possibility, not just an ancient myth. When I finished the book, I thought it the most revolutionary concept I'd ever encountered. And as I developed my personal relationship to the Goddess, I felt all my old internalized misogyny transform to wholeness. I wanted women everywhere to have this healing I was experiencing.

I began to envision a large mass-like work, which would help us all realize Her. After all, for hundreds of years the sung mass was the way we praised God and made "Him" real. For the next nine years I worked on creating sacred chants to the Goddess, and on the Spring Equinox in 1997, we released the recording with a live performance. Performing the music live gave us the first opportunity to include ritual elements, and the effect on the audience was stunning. I was high for a week.

CD: *The Changer and the Changed,*
words and music by Cris Williamson ©1975
Art: *Standing in Heart Power,*
JoAutumn Brock ©2007

Song of the Soul

"Trying to survive the
strangeness and the dying by
learning to listen to my own
voices, my spiritual Guides."
–Cris

*Open mine eyes that I may see
Glimpses of truth thou hast
for me
Open mine eyes, illumine me
Spirit Divine*

*"Love of my life," I am crying,
I am not dying
   I am dancing
Dancing along in the madness,
there is no sadness
Only a song of the soul*

*And we'll sing this song,
why don't you sing along
And we can sing for a long,
long time
Why don't you sing this song,
why don't you sing along
And we can sing for a long,
long time*

*What do you do for your living?
Are you forgiving, giving shelter?
Follow your heart, love will find
you, truth will
   unbind you
Sing out a song of the soul*

*And we'll sing this song, why
don't you sing along
And we can sing for a long,
long time
Why don't you sing this song,
why don't you sing along
And we can sing for a long,
long time*

*Come to your life like a warrior,
nothin' will bore yer
You can be happy
Let in the light it will heal you,
and you can feel you
And sing out a song of the soul*

*And we'll sing this song,
why don't you sing along
And we can sing for a long,
long time
Why don't you sing this song,
why don't you sing along
And we can sing for a long,
long time*

"When you look into your sister's eyes, praise her.

—Shawna, from her CD, Goddess Chant

The songs in *Goddess Chant* reflect on many themes related to worshipping the Goddess: affirming our divinity and the divinity in all things; the function of ritual and its power to connect us with Spirit; celebrating sacred pleasure; and overcoming the harmful messages of patriarchy as we reclaim our Divine Feminine power. The very essence of *Goddess Chant* is to provide a liturgical experience that calls upon thousands of years of sacred Western music in service of the Goddess.

In 2000, thanks in part to Susan Chiat, *Goddess Chant* received its West Coast premiere at Women of Wisdom. WOW brought together an awesome group of artists with whom I have continued to work for years, and so many other wonderful singers and musicians now known as the Sacred Fire Choir.

I will never forget the opening of the WOW *Goddess Chant*. We performed the invocation "Make Sacred Space," and Judith Laxer, WOW's Ceremonial Director and her Priestesses began calling in the four directions. After the East–the first direction– was called, the Priestess said, "Blessed Be" and five hundred voices answered, "Blessed Be." At that moment we were no longer in a performance. All of us, singers and audience, were in Sacred Ritual together in the name of the Goddess.

We had become one.

The Creative Cauldron:
Theater and Musical Performances

Pamela Gerke
Conductor/composer, Sacred Fire Choir
Producer, "Ignite", Sacred Fire Choir's CD
WOW member, past WOW Council Member
www.sacredfirechoir.org

a talk with Pamela Gerke

With joyful voices, we gather in creative community, honoring Earth, healing through song, and celebrating the Divine Feminine Spirit in all.

In the summer of 1999, I read a WOW newsletter announcement for an upcoming production of a ritual concert called *Goddess Chant*, written by someone named Shawna Carol. I called the phone number and said I was interested in being in the choir; and by the way, if they needed a conductor I could help out. Meanwhile, Susan Chiat, the instigator and producer, had been praying for a conductor for *Goddess Chant*.

I didn't know it then, but I was about to meet my tribe.

When rehearsals for *Goddess Chant* began, I knew some of the choir members from the Seattle Women's Ensemble (which I had conducted from 1992-99), but most of these singers were unfamiliar. Almost seven years later, many of the beautiful *Goddess Chant* choir members have become my dearest friends and artistic collaborators. Women of Wisdom and Shawna Carol's concert brought us together, and for that I will always be grateful.

artwork
Life is But
a Dream
Nancy
Bright
©1998

> "
> It was a
> cool drink
> of nourishing
> water for me.
>
> —Pamela

The Goddess Chant concert was a splendid experience; all the singers looked at me with shining, trusting faces, willing and eager to receive my direction. It was a cool drink of nourishing water for me. Through this production, I met many women who would become important in my life.

In the year after our first *Goddess Chant* concert, members of the performance became a group called the Sacred Fire Choir (I liked the rhyme!). In 2001 we performed my own composition at Women of Wisdom, *Temple Dreams: A Jazz Opera*, together with *Temple Awakenings*, created by Connie Amundson and others. In full costumes, with a cast that included children, a troupe of belly dancers, and some men (as "spear carriers" no less!), *Temple Dreams* crystallizes a moment in herstory when the women of the Temple of the Great Mother realize that the patriarchy is a-comin'. Following that, *Temple Awakenings* tells of the present time, when our memories of the feminine power are reawakened.

The following years brought continued opportunity for creative collaboration and performance at Women of Wisdom. In 2002 Lorraine Bayes and Kris Steinnes produced the WOW Compilation CD, celebrating ten years of music at Women of Wisdom for which Sacred Fire Choir recorded my composition "Poem (To The Elementals)." By that time the choir had fully formed as a large, non-auditioned ensemble, including men, and sang at the Women of Wisdom CD Release Concert with Libby Roderick and Susan Osborn. At the 2003 conference we performed *Welcome to the World*, an original show that follows a soul's incarnation on Earth and the conscious choices she makes. "Earthquakes of Power," a composition on our Sacred Fire CD, *Ignite!* opened the show, asking, "What kind of choices will you make with your human powers of mind, body, emotion and spirit?"

Two years later, in 2005, we created another musical theater piece titled *Goddess Revels: An Elementary Journey with Venus*. In that show, we traced the journey of Venus across the skies and across our hearts, as we learned about love and how to nourish ourselves. It also incorporated personal stories of WOW participants. These stories were interwoven with music, drama and dance and were a visual feast!

CD: *Women of Wisdom*, Pamela Gerke ©2000
Art: *Sacred Feminine*, Suzanne Cheryl
Gardner. ©2005

Poem (to the Elementals)

Dawn, facing East,
on a windswept mountaintop
I am breathing.
Thoughts are beginning:
the circle is cast,
Sacred ground marked
by the eagle
who swoops and glides
over my young head
in clear air.

Noon, facing South,
Sun full force,
I a climbing a volcano!
Fiery eruptions are my passions:
Spirit blood coursing
like hot hat lava
over Earth desert,
moving with will
to heal and destroy.

Twilight, facing West,
I am bathing
in a cool, blue lake
nourished by plenty
of love and courage,
heart replenished,
intuition cleansed
in the watery womb.

Midnight, facing North.
I am stony silence.
A dark cave.
My salty body is ancient wisdom,
crystal jewel reflecting
the pyramid of days,
solid Earth,
secure in the nature
of birth and death.

Air, fire, water, Earth.
Make me whole again
and again.

Beyond time, beyond space,
I have no face
My body disappears
in the center of the wheel.
By Earth, her salty body,
Air, her clear breath,
The waters of her womb,
And the fires of her spirit!

By all above, all below,
and all in the center:
The circle is cast!
Air, fire, water, Earth.
Make me whole again
and again.

Some of our evening presentations began with the Sacred Fire Choir entering the theater down the aisles, dancing through the audience, dressed in colorful costumes, and singing songs such as "Behold There is Magic" by Abbi Spinner McBride. The energy that the choir and ensemble created became a highly anticipated event at Women of Wisdom, and continues to bless audiences each year, whether it's a theater performances, or opening an evening with songs.

artwork

Women of Wisdom Art Series

Deborah Koff-Chapin ©2004

Pamela Gerke ©2007
Art: *Dragon*, Sue Coccia ©2002

We All Come From the Goddess

We all come from the Goddess
and behold, there is magic all around us!
Sanctified by our own names,
we spread our Spirit light in all we do.
We bless our planet and all who live on it
and bring into this moment all the love we can carry,
for we are sensuous and powerful.
We celebrate the wheel of the year
and the feeling music brings!
In gratitude for the love of the Great Mother,
blessed be.

It is women who must
lead the changes in our world...

lead the changes in our world...
lead the changes in our world...
lead the changes in our world...
lead the changes in our world...

Eve, Montserrat ©1994

lead the changes in ou...
changes in our world...

CHAPTER 10

Riane Eisler

Biography

Riane Eisler is the bestselling author of *The Chalice and The Blade: Our History, Our Future, Sacred Pleasure, Tomorrow's Children, The Power of Partnership*, and most recently *The Real Wealth of Nations: Creating a Caring Economics*. Dr. Eisler is a cultural historian and evolutionary theorist, President of the Center for Partnership Studies, cofounder of the Spiritual Alliance to Stop Intimate Violence, and consultant to business and government organizations on applications of the partnership model. She has done pioneering human rights work, expanding the vision of international organizations to include the rights of women and children. She keynotes conferences worldwide and her website is www.rianeeisler.com.

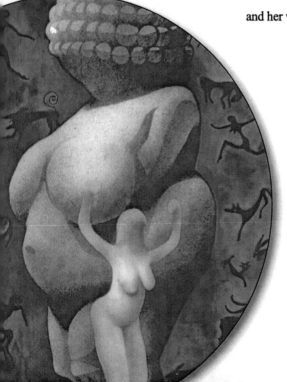

Reflections Today

Speaking at WOW conferences has been a great pleasure for me because of the wonderful women I meet, including the organizers. I speak at many conferences, but speaking to women—sharing with women what I have learned and discovered—is always my greatest delight.

My work over the last thirty years has taken me into many fascinating realms—from the study of archeology and ancient myths to the reexamination of data from sociology, anthropology, political science, and economics. The more I studied, the more I saw that one of the great problems with what we've been taught as knowledge and truth is the absence of women's voices. We must change this if we are to build a better world not only for women but for us all.

I believe that feminine consciousness is today more essential than ever, because it is women who must lead the changes in our world. For me, this consciousness has a spiritual dimension. But it is not spiritual in the conventional sense, because for me, spirituality is putting love into action. We must reclaim our heritage as spiritual leaders. This is our great challenge and opportunity: to join with one another and with enlightened men to build the foundations for a more equitable, peaceful, and joyful world.

–Riane Eisler

artwork

Venus de Willendorf

Robin Maynard-Dobbs
©1995

Spiritual Courage:
Putting Love Into Action

a talk with Riane Eisler

> All of us here are animated by a yearning for something better.
>
> —Riane

If there ever was a time when we need to put love into action, it is now. Take a look at our world—it is so interconnected, not only by technologies of communication and transportation, but also by technologies of destruction. War and terrorism can reach the other end of the world in a matter of minutes. So we really are at an evolutionary turning point. We have to join together to lay the foundations for a peaceful world. And this is what I have so much passion for—not only because of my research, but because I am a mother, and a grandmother.

How are we going to make a difference? How are we really going to heal this world—this world that is so full of suffering; where especially women and children are all too often brutalized? How can we even think of peace as long as that violence continues?

I'm not going to exhort, to preach that people should be kinder and better and more loving; because after all, spiritual people have been doing this for millennia. Instead, we're going to look at how we can create the conditions that will support the kinds of relationships and behaviors we yearn for: relationships of mutual benefit, of mutual respect, of mutual accountability, of nonviolence, of caring. These are the relationships we want, yet they are so different from what we see in so much of the world— top down rankings of men over women, race over race, religion over religion, nation over nation; rankings that have to be backed by fear and force.

When I talk about the conditions that will support better relationships, I'm talking about beliefs and institutions, starting with family, education, and religion; all the way to economics and politics. I am talking about conditions that can sustain what I call "Cultures of Peace." I am talking about systemic change.

Those of you familiar with my work know that I've introduced two new categories for understanding and transforming culture: the dominator model and the partnership model. And I will tell you about these.

But I would like to start on a personal note, because all of us here are animated by a yearning for something better —something more evolved, more spiritual, more caring, more loving. I think all of us have, at some point in our lives, asked whether so much misery, violence and insensitivity are inevitable. For me, asking this question is rooted in the experiences of my childhood.

My Life and Research

I was born in Europe in Vienna, Austria, during a time of a massive regression to the domination model. It was during the Nazi's rise of power in Germany. From one day to the next my world basically collapsed. My parents and I became hunted; hunted with a license to kill.

I am only here by two miracles really. One of them is what I now think of as the spiritual courage of my mother. This miracle took place on *Kristalnacht*, "the night of the broken glass," so named because of all the glass that was broken in Jewish homes, shops and synagogues. This was the first night of official terrorism by the Nazis against the Jews. On this night, a gang of Gestapo men came to drag away my father. But my mother recognized among the Nazis who came to our home, a young man who had worked for our family business. She just got enraged. She said, "How dare you come here! We have been so good to you. And you come here to loot and to take away this man who has been so good to you?"

My mother had the spiritual courage to stand up against injustice out of love. This is not courage to go out and kill the enemy; it is courage rooted in love. She could have been killed. But by a miracle, not only was she not killed, but my father was returned, and we were able to escape. We escaped Europe by a hair's breadth—and this is the second miracle. We were on one of the last ships from Nazi Europe before the *St. Louis*, which carried a thousand Jewish women, men, and children, was turned back from Cuba. These refugees were turned back by the Cuban authorities and by every single nation in the western hemisphere, including the United States. They had to sail back to Europe, where most of them were killed in Nazi concentration camps.

All this led to questions. "Why is there so much cruelty? Is it inevitable, or are there alternatives?" We have been told that this cruelty is human nature; it's in our genes. Of course these theories are updates of the old story of Original Sin. We are evil and we need to be controlled.

This is one of the metamyths that are part of the system of beliefs that support the domination model. And yes, in case you haven't noticed, we're in a period of regression to the domination model. But that does not mean that we cannot move forward.

My analysis of history is not within traditional categories, like capitalist vs. communist, or right vs. left, or religious vs. secular, or East vs. West—categories that don't describe the totality of social systems. My research revealed two underlying configurations of beliefs and social structures; what I called the *partnership* model and the *domination* model. What we can see, going way back into our prehistory, is the underlying tension between those two possibilities for structuring all relations, whether they're parent/child relations, woman/man relations, relations within a tribe or nation, or between different tribes or nations.

But these configurations can only be seen by using a gender holistic lens. The way a society constructs the roles and relations of the female and male halves of humanity is still generally seen as "just a women's issue." But it actually directly affects how every single institution operates. It is, for example, central to whether you have an authoritarian, top-down family, or whether you have a more democratic family. It is central to the systems of beliefs and values that guide not only our personal life options as women and men, but our social policies.

The Importance of Our Primary Human Relations

If we want to build that better future; if we really want a more peaceful world, a world where peace is more than just an interval between wars, we have to go beyond temporary fixes, beyond having another treaty in between wars. We have to go beyond just putting our fingers in the dikes. We just don't have enough fingers, do we? We have to build the foundations for a more just, sustainable, and peaceful world, starting in our primary human relationships. These are the relationships between the female and male halves of humanity, and between them and their sons and daughters.

Why? Because it is in these primary human relationships that people first learn, and continually practice, either respect for human rights or accept human rights violations as normal, even moral.

If those relationships are top-down relationships where violence, fear, abuse and domination are considered natural, people will continue to build political institutions, economic institutions, religious institutions, and technologies that follow the same pattern. Now, this is not a one-way process. It's an interactive process.

It's not coincidental that those in our world today who are trying to push us back to a more top-down social system—who want to push us back to a time when violence kept those who were on the bottom in their place—that for these people a top priority is to get women back into their "traditional" place. This is of course a code for subservience, just as the "traditional family" they keep talking about is code for a "male-dominated," top-down family where children learn that it is very dangerous and very painful to question orders, no matter how brutal and unjust they are or how much pain they cause.

It is not coincidental that those who are trying to push society backward have made "women's traditional roles" a central issue. But unfortunately, very often if you talk to progressive peace activists or progressive economic activists today, the vast majority still think of women's roles as "women's issues," without looking at the much deeper social, political, and economic connections.

It is our job to make these connections visible; to show that the way a society structures the roles and relations of the two halves of humanity—women and men—is foundational to what kind of society is built. In order to build cultures of peace, we need foundations that support partnership rather than domination.

Women's rights are human rights. We need an integrated theory of human rights that begins with the majority, which includes women and children. We need to look at the human rights violations in intimate relations and change traditions of violence and abuse against women and children. We cannot build cultures of peace otherwise.

> *I know that*
> *every one of*
> *us can make*
> *a difference.*
>
> *—Riane*

If you take nothing else away from this talk, please take this: every one of us can raise consciousness to this very simple fact. It's really just common sense, isn't it, except that we're not used to thinking about it this way.

Progressive social movements have focused primarily on trying to dismantle political and economic systems, which I call the top of the domination pyramid. But they have not addressed the foundations on which that pyramid rests, and on which it continually rebuilds itself.

It is not coincidental, for example, that the 9/11 terrorists came out of a culture where women and children are literally terrorized into submission. Such relations are training for the use of violence to impose one's will on others.

Similarly, the Nazis said the emancipation of women was a Jewish idea and that they were bent on getting women back into their "traditional place." They passed laws that forbade women from being judges; they passed laws that imposed a dual pay scale. I bet you didn't know that Hitler said to his troops that, just like some Muslim men have more than one wife, as a reward for their heroism Nazi war heroes would legally get more than one wife. You should know this not only because it's fascinating but because it shows you a configuration—a configuration in which authoritarian rule, brutal violence, and rigid male dominance are key.

In the Soviet Union we see that although with Lenin it wasn't exactly a partnership regime, there were some efforts to equalize the status of women and men. But with the rise of Stalin to power, with the shift to a brutal authoritarianism and the killing of millions of Russians, these efforts were reversed. Children again became illegitimate. How can a child be illegitimate? A child is a child. But children who were born out of wedlock became illegitimate again, abortion again became a crime, and Stalin was so brutal to his own wife that she committed suicide. So our job is to build a better culture from the ground up. We have to build foundations for cultures of peace. You're going to say to me: "That's huge!" and "How can I do anything?" I used to think that way myself. It's from my own life experiences that I know that every one of us can make a difference. Because it was only because women fought against discrimination that we have some of the rights that young women today are just taking for granted. They are not taught the history of the struggle for women's rights—a struggle in which I was able to play a part starting in the 1960's.

Reexamining Our History and Cocreating Our Future

Indeed, it's only because women and men like you and I envisioned a better world that we moved from the European Middle Ages to the more democratic society we live in today. If you look back in Western culture about five hundred years ago, which is really not a long time in terms of human evolution, you see something very interesting. You see that the European Middle Ages looked a lot like the Taliban. You see the Inquisition, the Crusades, the witch burnings. And of course whether a woman is slowly stoned to death or burned to death, it's exemplary public violence to keep women terrorized. In the Middle Ages, men were legally entitled to chastise their wives, which means to beat them if they didn't do what they wanted. And of course, "spare the rod and spoil the child" was a motto that came out of a time when children were viewed as evil little creatures who have to be tamed.

Remember that metamythology of "we are evil, we have to be controlled"? And those at the top of the dominator pyramid, whether it's in the household or the state, were entitled to punish, to inflict pain. That's the domination system.

Just a few hundred years ago, you couldn't have a conference like this. First of all it would be unheard of, and second, we'd all be burned at the stake. The shift toward more of a partnership orientation didn't happen by itself; it happened because of women and men just like you and me. If we are to build a better future, we need to act. So I'm going to talk to you about some basic interventions.

We have already discussed the first intervention—the need to stop intimate violence, and to make our friends in the peace movement and in the economic justice movement aware that they have to focus more on changing these primary human relations, whether it's here or in India or all over the world. Because we're in this together. We can't just change things here; we have to work with our brothers and our sisters elsewhere. There are people from all of these cultures who want to move to the partnership side of the spectrum, and we have to support them.

This is why I cofounded the Spiritual Alliance to Stop Intimate Violence. You can find out about it at www.saiv.net or on the Center for Partnership Studies website, www.partnershipway.org. You can download the statistics and analysis showing that violence against women and children in the home, and the international violence of war and terrorism, are as tightly bound together as the fingers of a clenched fist.

This Spiritual Alliance is trying to engage the world's religious leaders. Why? Because while the victims of intimate violence have started to break their silence, the leaders of all the world's major religions are still silent. They have not made stopping intimate violence a major issue. But they must. If they won't do it for the sake of the millions of women and children who are brutalized and even killed, maybe they will do it once they understand the relationship between intimate violence and international violence.

They're not going to understand this link unless you bring it to their attention. So I am asking you to work on this, because this is foundational. I know you're probably not going to try to enlist the Pope, or even the Dalai Lama, right away, but every one of you can talk to your local rabbi, to your local mullah, to your local priest.

The second intervention is to raise awareness to the fact that it is *possible* to create cultures that are more peaceful. Let's take Saudi Arabia and Norway. They're both countries with wealth, but the quality of life in those countries—and not just for women, but for everybody—is very, very different. Saudi Arabia is a nation that still orients very much towards the domination model, whether it's in the family or in the state. It's an absolute monarchy. Women can't even drive, much less vote. They can't travel without a male's permission. Saudi Arabia has a very large underclass. They import people to do the dirty work, and do not treat them well. Saudi Arabia also has *madrassas*, schools where they teach little boys hate and violence. That's very important in a country like Saudi Arabia, because how else are you going to deflect rage against those on top unless you scapegoat others, be it Jews or Americans?

Now look at Norway, which orients more towards the partnership model. Instead of this top-down authoritarian structure, there is much more political *and* economic democracy.

The status of women is much higher. And that's an understatement. In the Nordic countries, not only Norway but Sweden and Finland, women have not only been heads of state, but they make up about 35 to 45 percent of the national legislature. Just having a token woman or two on the top doesn't change much. The United States has moved a lot toward the partnership model or we wouldn't be here. But on the other hand, women are still a miniscule percentage of the national legislature. And on top of that, we're now in a period of regression, with the rise of religious fundamentalism here as well as elsewhere in the world.

But back to the Nordics. It is not coincidental that as the status of women rose, the policies of these nations shifted to give financial support to more stereotypically feminine values and activities: caregiving, nurturance, universal health care, universal child care. You get a child care allowance in the Nordic countries whether you're married, single, poor, or rich.

It's not coincidental that these countries also pioneered the first Peace Studies programs in the world. It's not coincidental that they have the first laws that prohibit physical discipline of children in families. And it is not coincidental that they have a strong men's movement focused on disentangling "masculinity" from its stereotypical association with domination, control and violence.

So it is possible to move to a more equitable and less violent way of life!

A Fresh Look at Our Prehistory

There are other partnership oriented societies. There's a book by anthropologist Peggy Reeves Sanday called *Woman at the Center*, about four million people living in Sumatra called the Minangkabau, whose culture has more of a partnership configuration. In the Minangkabau communities, women have high status, and nurturance is valued in men, not just women. They have good conflict resolution systems as well.

As those of you familiar with *The Chalice and The Blade*, *Sacred Pleasure*, and other works I have written know, in our prehistory there were cultures worldwide that oriented more towards the partnership model. These were not ideal societies, but power was conceptualized not so much as the power of the blade—the power to dominate, destroy, and control—but as the power of the chalice. The chalice is a stereotypical female symbol, but not exclusive to women. It is the vessel of life, representing a life-giving, life-nurturing, and life-illuminating power.

Every world tradition has legends of these earlier societies. The Chinese *Tao Te Ching* tells us that there was a time before the yin, the feminine principle, was considered subservient to the yang, the male principle. And it's very specific. It tells us that it was a more peaceful time when the wisdom of the mother was still honored. I should add that after *The Chalice and The Blade* was published in Chinese, a group of scholars at the Chinese Academy of Social Sciences in Beijing tested my cultural transformation theory in Asian prehistory, and found that there were earlier societies orienting more to the partnership model in Asia as well.

It was a more peaceful time when the wisdom of the Mother was still honored.

—Riane

If you look at the most well-known story in Western civilization, the story of Adam and Eve in the Garden of Eden, what does it really tell us? It tells us that there was a time that woman and man lived in harmony with one another and with nature, before a male God supposedly decreed that henceforth woman would be subservient to man. When I was little, I always wanted to know what it was like before the "henceforth"—but nobody wanted to talk about that.

The emergence of the domination model literally stood the earlier myths and realities on their heads. It also led to a split between sexuality and spirituality that is very important to recognize. As men came to dominate women and as the "masculine" came to dominate the "feminine," so too did men and the masculine begin to dominate nature, and deny the divine qualities of the Earth, of our own bodies, and of our sexuality— aspects associated with women and with the Goddess.

When we look at the story of Adam and Eve, we see a sudden shift from a time of harmony between the sexes and between humans and nature to a time of shame and conflict. Suddenly Adam and Eve are ashamed of their bodies. We all have a body, don't we? So why should anyone be ashamed of the body? Does it make sense? None of these stories make sense, but they're very political; it's the politics of dominator mythology.

The garden in the Adam and Eve story is very interesting, because it could be a reference to the Neolithic period. Neolithic peoples planted the first gardens. From the first agrarian societies of the Neolithic period, we find images such as the Gulmenita lovers. In this image the vulva is very clear and the phallus is erect. It is the sacred union of the Goddess and the God. There is no shame of sexuality, the body. There is harmony between man and woman, between the sacred masculine and the sacred feminine.

We see a very similar depiction in a frieze in Chatal Huyuk, which is one of the biggest Neolithic sites ever found. It's actually like a sexual lesson. It's about eight thousand years old, and it shows a woman and man embracing, and then right next to them is the woman holding a baby. It tells a story about the sacred family.

This is very different from the sacred family story that we hear

artwork

Women of Wisdom Art Series

Deborah Koff-Chapin ©1995

in our contemporary religious traditions, which is such an extraordinary story, if you think about it. Only the males are divine. There is the Father and the Son. Where is the Mother? Where is the Goddess? The woman, the mother of God, she's the only mortal in this picture. Of course it's the Goddess, only she got demoted.

Reclaiming the Divine Feminine

There is another story—an ancient story, one that we have been taught to forget. It is the story of sacred sexuality and divinity that includes women and the Goddess. We've had clues to this even in the Judeo-Christian Bible, in Genesis. Of course we also have this in some of the Hindu iconography, the pre-Aryan society. Before the Indo-Europeans came in there were Goddess worshipping societies, as you know. In these societies, they must have noticed that life emerges from the body of woman, and preceding that is sex.

In these early societies, sex was a central religious mystery in the belief system of the cycles of sex, birth, and death. We know that some of the funerary rites included sexual elements about rebirth. Symbolically then, death was a return to the Great Mother's womb, to once again be reborn.

There was a time of sacred sexuality, and at a certain point in history many societies shifted from this model to a domination model. We see this shift in the story of Genesis, from a time of harmony to a model of separation and domination.

These early societies were not ideal; they were not violence free. But they were structured differently, beginning with an equal partnership rather than a ranking of one half of humanity over the other. Violence wasn't institutionalized or idealized. What we are trying to leave behind are *traditions* of domination and violence in intimate relations. Consider the saying "spare the rod and spoil the child." The practice of beating children has been part of a tradition of violence and domination built *into* the system.

And violence against women—we used to joke, "If rape is inevitable, relax and enjoy it, ha, ha." And do you remember the cartoon of the caveman with a club in one hand dragging a woman by the hair with the other? This was a joke, a cartoon. But we don't joke anymore, do we? We have discovered that

CD: *Gaia Rocks*, Shawna Carol
©2005 Pagan People's Music

Every Woman

*Every woman is a flower
And she offers the sweetest nectar
Every woman is a river
And her sweet love ends all thirst.*

*Every woman is a mountain
Lay your head down
And seek your rest.
Every woman is a fire
She will answer all your desires*

*You don't have to steal it
You don't have to own it
You don't have to take it
You don't have to buy it.*

*It's a gift freely given,
All you gotta do is honor it.
Just honor her.*

*Every woman is the Goddess embodied
A sacred vessel of divine love.*

*Every woman is a flower
And she offers the sweetest nectar.
Every woman is a river
And her sweet love ends all thirst.*

*It's a gift freely given,
All you gotta do is honor it.
Just honor her.
Sweeter than honey
When you honor her.
Flows so free.
All you gotta do is honor her.
Honor her,
Honor her.*

> This ancient
sexuality was
passionate,
but at the
same time,
it included
honor and
respect
for the
human body.
>
> —Riane

this is a tradition. A tradition with a beginning and an end, a tradition that can change, that *must* change.

And the evidence suggests it can change, for it was not always this way. Cave men did not drag women around by the hair. In fact, early cave drawings paint a much different picture.

The rise of the domination model includes a spiritual model of men as divine and women as merely carnal. If we have the divine Father and Son, but no Goddess to worship, then it follows that men are above women and therefore have a right to dominate us. If the divine is male, then all that is female is not divine. What is lost then? The female, the Earth, the sensuality and sexuality of the body are all left behind to be denigrated and dominated.

But we can reclaim the sacred feminine. In fact, we even have clues to this earlier time in the Bible. Take the Song of Solomon. Now why it's called the Song of Solomon is another part of dominator politics, because Solomon is never mentioned. Neither is God, Jehovah, Yahweh—nothing. So let's call it as some people do, The Song of Songs.

The primary figure that is named in the Song of Songs is the beautiful Shulamite, the Rose of Sharon. And she sings an erotic song to her lover about how his kisses are sweeter than wine, and how he shall sleep all night betwixt her breasts.

Now that erotic sacred union, as we saw, has very ancient roots. And we even find empirical evidence of this tradition in the first written records of western civilization, the cuneiform tablets of Sumer. There we find the hymns of the Goddess Inanna, the Sumerian Queen of Heaven and Earth—the same Queen of Heaven that Jeremiah rails against in the Bible, although in the Bible we're told that there never was anything except a male God.

In the hymns of Inanna, the Sumerian Goddess of love and procreation, we read of her sacred union with her divine lover Damuzi. The passages are explicitly sexual—some people today would call them pornography. She says, "Who will plow my vulva?" Not only that, but today many would find it very unseemly to speak like this, because women are not supposed to have desires. It's silly, but it's not silly because it has caused so much pain and so much grief to us and continues to cause it.

The Inanna Hymns are also tender because they came from a time before sexuality had been severed from intimacy. There is a passage that says, "Sweet is the sleep of hand to heart. Sweeter still is the sleep of heart to heart."

These hymns do not depict a mild, bland sexuality. This ancient sexuality was passionate, but at the same time, it included honor and respect for the human body—the kind of sexuality that we are trying to reclaim for ourselves, for our children, for our daughters, for our sons. The kind of sexuality that we *can* reclaim, but only if we are very vocal, very active, and very political in the real sense of the word, where we educate people.

artwork

Sacred Marriage Series

Meinrad Craighead
©1997

The Movement Toward Partnership

Then came the shift to the domination model in our prehistory. And that model informed religion. By the time we get to the Christian Middle ages, we find that the medieval church never condemned sexual violence, but instead condemned sexual pleasure!

They emphasized the idea of original sin. St. Augustine was canonized for developing the concepts of original sin and justifiable war. It is not coincidental that these two concepts go together. One only needs to look to the Bible to see that after original sin comes war, because the next story after Adam and Eve is the story of Cain and Abel, the warring brothers.

The idea of original sin—the connection between sin and sexual pleasure—is key to the dominator model. Because if you've got the idea of original sin you can control people's sexuality. And if you control people's sexuality, you can control everything. And if you can convince people that women are evil and dangerous, and sexuality is sinful, you've got a cornerstone of a domination system, don't you?

But from studying archeology and ancient myths, we discover a time before the domination model. This reminds us that something else is possible. Just by looking at the contemporary movement toward partnership, we know that sacred sexuality is possible; we know that harmony between the sexes is possible. We know a partnership model is possible.

Every single social movement over the last three hundred years has been one challenge after another to traditions of domination. These include the Rights of Man movement, challenging the divinely ordained rights of kings; the women's movement, challenging the supposedly divinely ordained right of men to rule over women and children; the environmental movement, challenging man's once hallowed "conquest of Nature"; and the Civil Rights movement, challenging the right of one race to rule over another.

The struggle for our future is not between religious and secular, right and left, capitalism and socialism, East and West. It's the struggle between the partnership and domination models as two basic human possibilities. And our job today is to build the

Patty Zeitlin ©1990 Bullfrog Ballades
Art: *Dreaming*, Kris Steinnes ©1998

Long Ago, Right Here

Sometimes in my dreams I seem to go
Back to woods and streams of long ago.
When there was no anger, there was no fear.
Long ago, right here.

There were lots of friends I used to know
With lots of time to spend, in that long ago.
We talked to the animals, there was no fear.
Long ago, right here.

But here's me and you, here and now.
What are we to do, tell me how,
When there's just a memory
Echo and a tear from long ago, right here?

Dreams, dreams, dreams, dreams
Waterfalls and streams of dreams.

Life is full of change and long ago
Seems beautiful but let it go.
And bring all the love that you can carry
Year after year from long ago, right here.
And bring all the love that you can carry,
Year after year from long ago, right here.

foundation for cultures of partnership and peace.

As I said, there are some key interventions. The first intervention pertains to stopping intimate violence. The second has to do with knowing that partnership models are truly possible. A third is education, including materials on partnership parenting and partnership education. Because we can't just tell people that what they're doing is bad! We have to show them a better alternative.

> Stopping violence against women and children is a core foundation for a peaceful and sustainable society.
>
> —Riane

A key intervention has to do with changing the status of women worldwide. At the Center for Partnership Studies, the nonprofit organization I direct, we did a study called *Women, Men and the Global Quality of Life*. It is a statistical survey of eighty-nine nations, looking at whether there is a correlation between the status of women and the general quality of life. What we found in many cases is that the status of women is a better predictor of general quality of life than Gross Domestic Product or GDP, the conventional measure of a nation's economic health. At the time of our study, Kuwait and France had the same GDP, but the infant mortality rate was twice as high in Kuwait than in France, where the status of women is of course much higher. So you can again see the partnership and domination patterns here.

In parts of Southeast Asia women are so malnourished compared to men and boys, that the infant mortality rate, and even the sex ratio, which usually favors women, is skewed in favor of men. But this is not only terrible for girls and women; it's terrible for the general quality of life. We know that women who are malnourished give birth to children who are robbed of their full mental and physical birthright. So this is not a "women's issue," is it? It is a basic human issue.

It is absurd to talk about caring for children when the work—the women's work of caring for children—is so devalued that it isn't even included in Gross Domestic Product, in productivity. Consider for a moment that we include making cigarettes that kill, making weapons that kill, in GDP. Yet the work of caregiving, without which we would be dead, without which there wouldn't be a workforce, is not included. Well, if it's not included, it's not visible, and policy makers will not see it, and will not support it. So we've got to change that.

These are not complicated things. They can be done once we begin to see how it all fits together. Of course we also have to change the economic system, which takes us to another intervention. Marx wrote about the alienation of labor, and I write about the alienation of caring labor. We can't eat gold, right? But we value it. Yet we don't value the work of caregiving. So in the labor market, people pay more for the care of their cars than they pay to the people to whom they entrust their children. And they don't expect the child care workers to be as well trained as the mechanics!

That is crazy, and we need new social and economic inventions. Paid parental leave is an economic invention that gives attention and value to caregiving work. If we don't give value to that work, it's not realistic to talk about a more caring economy! That's one of the central themes of my new book, *The Real Wealth of Nations: Creating a Caring Economics.*

So there you have it—we can all make a difference. Stopping violence against women and children is a core foundation for a peaceful and sustainable society. Partnership parenting and education are a core foundation. Raising the status of women is foundational. Changing the economic system is foundational.

Let's do what we hear so much about—let's think outside the box. Let's leave behind old categories like religious vs. secular, capitalist vs. socialist, East vs. West, and look at the whole system—including our primary gender and parent-child relations. Let's not just keep putting our fingers in the dike of dominator regressions—we don't have enough fingers, and the dike is breaking everywhere. Let's build the foundations for the partnership world we so want and need. Let's do it for ourselves, for our children, and for generations still to come. And let's start doing it right now!

artwork

Goddess Raising

Montserrat
©1987

Empower Your Self

explore your dreams and spirit...

1   Where in your life do you experience the
     dominator model?

2   Where do you still see the female denigrated?

3   Where are you experiencing the partnership model?

4   Where and how can you introduce a partnership model?

5   How can you reclaim the feminine and sacred sexuality?

6   What can you do to help build a peaceful culture?

_____

_____

_____

_____

_____

_____

_____

_____

_____

_____

_____

_____

_____

_____

_____

_____

_____

_____

_____

_____

_____

_____

_____

_____

_____

_____

_____

_____

_____

_____

_____

_____

_____

_____

_____

_____

_____

Feel the heartbeat of the planet,
this is the feminine.

this is the feminine
this is the feminine

this is the feminine
this is the feminine

CHAPTER 11

Marion Woodman

Biography

Marion Woodman, LLD, DHL, PhD, is a Jungian Analyst, teacher and author of *The Owl Was a Baker's Daughter; Addiction to Perfection; The Pregnant Virgin; Ravaged Bridegroom; Leaving My Father's House; Conscious Femininity; Dancing in the Flames* (with Elinor Dickson); *Coming Home to Myself* (with Jill Mellick); *The Maiden King* (with Robert Bly); and *Bone: Dying Into Life.* A visionary in her own right, Marion Woodman has worked with the analytical psychology of C.G. Jung in an original and creative way. Marion is the Chair of the Marion Woodman Foundation. Learn more at: www.mwoodman.org.

Reflections Today

Our home, Earth, is being torn to shreds by patriarchal greed, lust, and power. Both men and women are unconsciously identified with the patriarchal principle, with little or no consciousness of our feminine instincts. Patriarchy destroys masculinity as it destroys femininity. The feminine principle of relatedness is betrayed. Power rules.

Creating a safe space (*temenos*) in which both men and women can allow their true Being to emerge, we begin to relate to essence, to reality, to soul. Bodywork creates a strong container for the ego while dream work brings the metaphors that we understand and implement as our spirit guides holding body and soul together as transformers of energy. Dreams are honored as divine gifts and their metaphorical language connects us to the new fields of neurobiology, neuroscience, and quantum physics.

Surrendering to the love that opens the body to receive spirit, we invoke Sophia as the consciously embodied sacred feminine that will allow the impregnation of the divine masculine in an inner marriage as the source of individual creativity.

–Judith Harris, Jungian Analyst

artwork

Mary

Robin
Maynard-
Dobbs
©2002

Waking Up With Whom?

a talk with Marion Woodman

> *Inner marriage*
> *—the new*
> *masculine*
> *with the*
> *new feminine*
> *in divine*
> *embrace.*
>
> *—Marion*

It is such an affirming experience to feel the luminosity of the feminine spirit at a cellular level, and to see the manifestation of the feminine side of God in every possible way during this week—music, dance, cooking, relating. Yet I do feel a certain anxiety that I've been feeling around the feminine movement for some time, a feeling that we have come to a certain place, and we're not quite sure where to go or how to go, or even what questions to ask.

It will take a long time to get rid of the patriarchal structure and find out who we are, our Beingness, our ground in our body. It will not be easy to stand and say, "This is who I am. I have been through my experience, hourly, daily, and here I stand."

Through the years, some of us have worked hard incorporating this, but when it comes to putting it into life, new issues arise. There is a backlash coming from the other side: many people have found the price of living the feminine immense. Some have had to lose a marriage or a relationship; some have lost their jobs; some have had difficulties with their children. The bludgeoning comes at a personal level, at a social level, and certainly at a political level.

We are caught in these backlashes from many directions. Those of you who work in hospitals, in education, and in legal professions face a patriarchy that is so strong, that trying to break in with a feminine value is almost worth your life, certainly your job. It's extremely important that we not lose our courage.

I sense that there's a moment of creative pause going on: the feminine is on the move; the archetype is coming to more and more people in their dreams; more people are recognizing what it's about. It is important to articulate it; not only to sing, dance and paint it, but articulate, "What is it?" Now is the time when we're going to start moving fully into life, and I think this is manifesting itself in dreams of the pregnant virgin. The pause is waiting for the new masculine, and the baby is in the womb. There's danger that the baby is coming into a world of Herods who are waiting to kill it, but the child is going to be born, and with it comes a new consciousness and a new paradigm.

I believe that this new masculinity will honor the feminine, understand the values of the feminine, protect the feminine, and have the courage to confront the patriarchy. The new masculine is as vulnerable as the feminine. This new meeting is the inner marriage—the new masculine with the new feminine in divine embrace. It's an ancient, ancient image. You who are familiar with the Hindu world, you know that Shiva and Shakti are often in the divine embrace of lovemaking, and they are in bliss. And the book of Revelation in the New Testament is full of the divine marriage between the masculine and the feminine. The marriage of spirit and soul, the embodied soul, the sacred matter, conscious enough to open to spirit. This is the divine marriage. I see us working towards this marriage, but we are far away from it yet. So I have as a title for this talk, "Waking up with Whom?" You all know the story of the couple who have been to a party, and their instincts have run away with them. They have gone to someone's place, and slept with each other, and woken up with each other, and wondered who on Earth is in the bed with them. Most people "sleep" with another person. They go straight into the unconscious. Lovemaking should be a most conscious act, but most people tend to turn off the lights, get under the sheets, and go unconscious. That's all part of our culture. That becomes an addiction, because it's totally unconscious. It's time for us to wake up. But what are we waking up to?

Now you may laugh, but if you've woken up, it's no funny thing. It usually throws you into an all out depression. Something has happened that has forced you to face the reality of your life. The suffering is so immense that you cannot do it alone. That's why so many people go into analysis. The analyst works as a companion on the path, to help a person to endure reality.

You know the old, old Sumerian story of Inanna, three thousand years before Christ. Inanna wanted to go down to the underworld to visit her sister Erishkegal, because Erishkegal's husband, the sky god, was dead (notice the sky god was dead). So she wants to go to the underworld to bring her sister comfort. This is a story of initiation and sacrifice, and it is a story of waking up.

Inanna descends; she has to go through seven portals, and she has to sacrifice some part of herself—clothing, jewelry, whatever it is—at every stage. Each sacrifice symbolizes part of herself. By the time she reaches the last gate, she is naked. She has to go to her sister naked and she ends up on a meat hook, dead. Now, of course, she has to be resurrected, but her path is the sacred descent to the pit of darkness.

We wake up by making the descent, by passing through gates of awakening. Think back through your own life, and ask, "Where was my first awakening? What did I have to sacrifice at that point? Where was my second, my third? Did I ever come to the point of nakedness?" Now some of you may say, "I've only been through two or three portals." That's fine—there's no right or wrong. Some of you may find your eyes are more open than you thought. Some of you may say, "I've been down this way three time. I've been naked and hung on a meat hook three times."

You can meditate on this. Take the awakening that's most important to you; follow the path that the unconscious has taken you on. Go very quietly inside, have your feet flat on the floor, and try to visualize that still point inside, that still point that is connected to the God and Goddess, the central axis of our life. Breathe into your belly and check your shoulders and your hands. Are they relaxed? Breathe into them; let them go. Remember, the transformation is on breath; keep asking yourself, "Am I breathing into my belly? Is my belly soft?"

See yourself walking down a road, on your journey. You see a huge door. It has a lotus with many petals. As you approach the door, you are met by a beautiful creature who asks for a sacrifice. Think back in your own life—what was that sacrifice? How were your eyes opened by making that sacrifice? What are your feelings having made that sacrifice?

~Pause~

Quietly go on again. How does your body feel? As you move on, what do you see? Do you see any differently? Do you hear any differently?

> Sophia will be with us, fill our hearts with love for each other, and open our eyes wider to Her reality.

—Marion

This continues—threshold after threshold, sacrifice after sacrifice. The sacrifice might mean giving up ideals; it might mean giving up an addiction. But how do you feel having passed through that gate? Some of you may not pass through a gate. Do what is right for you. Check your body. Does it feel any different? Let the breath drop right into your belly and start on your path again.

How are you moving now? Do you smell anything? Did your sense of smell change in any way, or your sense of hearing, your sense of touch, your sense of taste? As you move, again you see a threshold coming up and a divine figure asks you for a sacrifice. Your eyes are opened wider. How do you feel this time? Go on your way through whatever kind of terrain comes to you in your imagery. Let it be your meditation.

Different lights are associated with different thresholds and different gates: you can visualize purple, blue, green, orange, yellow, red. Perhaps they change somewhat from comforting, but firm, to more and more threatening. This red threshold is the really frightening one for most of us. The Goddess in both her attributes is behind this door—positive Mother and dark Mother. The sacrifice is demanded, and given. The eyes are opened wider.

As you move through that last passage, can you distance yourself sufficiently to see the seven thresholds? Can you move through and circumambulate to create a circle of the thresholds and the way back into life? The thresholds are a descent to reconnect with your soul, and then return into life. Feel your own breath. Stay with it until you are reconnected. Feel your own breathing connected to your own still center. Sophia will be with us, fill our hearts with love for each other, and open our eyes wider to Her reality.

It is not easy passing through these thresholds. The veils fall away; we sacrifice a great deal. We go through adolescence and give up our need for direction and our neediness for approval. Symbolically, our mothers are taken away from us. The nourishment of the mother and of the breast is taken in order that we stand on our own feet. But we are not babies any longer, and God's not running a kindergarten!

We all have sacrifices to make. We might have to let go of our inner critic. Some of you, I'm sure, had to face the loss of your ideals. For example, I work with eating disorders, and I know a woman who wants to be thin. She comes from a big family, a family of Scotch farmers, and it's not in her genes to be a sylph. But she would kill herself with anorexia in order to become that. For her to give up her ideal is almost impossible. It feels like death.

Sooner or later, one has to accept one's own humanity, and some people fail to do that. They do not want to believe that they are human beings. They have such highfalutin ideas about who they are and who they are married to and who their kids are, that they project God onto their husbands, or Goddess onto their wife. Then they try to live up to these crazy God-like projections. Now if they're doing that, their shadow is black, because the more light they're living, the more black is their unconscious shadow. So for people who've got that kind of constellation, it's extremely painful when their eyes start to face the truth that they are not as intelligent as they thought they were; they are not as good as they thought. They are not God after all, and they are not married to a Goddess.

Now this may be only words to you, but how many people do you know who have a perfectionist attitude towards the person they "love"? Really, they don't love the other at all; they're simply in love with their own image of God. They're very narcissistic, but they are compulsively bound to that person. This is an addictive relationship. It's not based on reality; it's based on projections. So another part of waking up to reality is recognizing our projections. Of course some people never work it out at all; it's much easier just to keep their eyes shut and stay asleep. Like Lady Macbeth, whose "eyes are open... but their sense is shut." The hardest thing in the world is to pull that projection back, and recognize it's our own unconscious projection that is blinding us to our own inner reality—our own life.

CD: *She Carries Me*, Jennifer Berezan ©1995

She Carries Me

She is a boat she is a light
High on a hill in the dark of night
She is a wave she is the deep
She is the dark where angels sleep
When all is still and peace abides
She carries me to the other side
She carries me, she carries me
She carries me to the other side

And though I walk through valleys deep
And shadows chase me in my sleep
On rocky cliffs I stand alone
I have no name, I have no home
With broken wings I reach to fly
She carries me to the other side
She carries me, she carries me
She carries me to the other side

A thousand arms, a thousand eyes
A thousand ears to hear my cries
She is the gate, she is the door
She leads me through and back once more
When day has dawned and death is nigh
She'll carry me to the other side
She carries me, she carries me
She carries me to the other side

She is the first, she is the last
She is the future and the past
Mother of all, of Earth and sky
She carries me to the other side
She carries me, she carries me
She carries me to the other side

Trust in the transformation which takes you through the death.

—Marion

There's nothing like an addiction when you want to stay asleep. The pain for some people is too much. They can't deal with it. Every time they come up to the threshold of pain they get drunk, or get themselves into somebody else's bed, or go shopping and spend all their money, or work compulsively. So one of the sacrifices we must make may be the sacrifice of an addiction. To stop the addiction is to open our eyes and face our suffering. Those of you who have been through that know how painful it is. But you probably know that it is in that pit where you met the Higher Power.

If you are willing to face it, addiction can bring you to your knees. It can bring the death of the old way of living, and for most of us the birth of the feminine. You may not call it that; in your tradition you might call it the Higher Power. But this experience has qualities of the feminine: receptivity, presence, paradox, openness; trust in the transformation, which takes you through the death, the embracing of the dark to the new life.

I know I can say, "Thank God for my addiction," because without the addiction I would never have known Sophia. Life was going on quite pleasantly. Suddenly it wasn't going on at all. I had to change my whole relationship to life. I had to recognize the slowness of the feminine, the beat of the heart, the earthy imagery of the feminine. I had to take time to love nature, to be with my body, to honor the soul in my body, and come to love Her through suffering. The suffering broke my heart open. It put me on my knees, in front of the wall, and smashed my heart open. And that was the end of compulsive control.

It seems to me that one of the things we're really working with in our culture is the power paradigm. We're trying to build one country on this planet. We've got to. Technologically, we are one country now. But we haven't got the wildest idea how to be neighbors with each other, how to get along with each other. Most of us can't even get along with ourselves, let alone the people in Bosnia or any other place.

So you see the paradigm we are moving toward has to be one of love. We must let go of control dynamics. Again looking at addiction, look at the fierce control and discipline of an anorexic: "I will have 200 calories, I will cut my meat into sixteen pieces. I will control..." And though she is the weakest person in the house, she is controlling the house. Will she eat or will she not eat? Will she live or will she die? These are the questions.

Much of our addictive behavior in this culture is an expression of our need for the real feminine. If you are a food addict, for example, certainly you worship the Mother, but you worship her in a concrete form. As you eat and eat and eat you are trying to commune—that's where 'communion' comes from. You incorporate; take into your body, the God or Goddess in order to take the Divine in as part of yourself. Where the addict goes wrong is in the concretization of the God and Goddess. Food without love is not the Mother; nourishment is the real Mother. When we are addicts, we do not know what real nourishment is. We do not consider the reality of the soul that is starving for soul food.

Ironic as it is, our culture worships a stone Goddess. We call ourselves a patriarchy, but our patriarchy consists of little boys worshipping Mother. Mother is matter; matter is materialism. Our materialistic culture has concretized Mother. And one of the realities we have to wake up to is that we cannot go on with our greed and materialism and get away with it. We are killing ourselves. And we are turning ourselves into rigid stone that isn't free and spontaneous and able to move, cherish and create generous relationships.

What happens to the energy of life when we try to concretize it? Watching the world news, some of you must think, "What chaos are we in?" We see the floods, the Earthquakes and think, "What is She doing?" Well, what is She doing? Great energy is being expressed through these natural phenomena. And I see this in dreams all the time. For example, some people are dreaming that they have been poisoned with plutonium. Or they've got some kind of atomic energy in them that could become either positive or negative. In other words, they can be destroyed by this huge energy or learn to use it creatively.

We must learn to work with these great energies without being driven by them unconsciously, the way addicts are. Instead of going for spirit in the spiritual sense, alcoholics go for "spirit" in the bottle. Or instead of going for union in the inner marriage, sex addicts are into compulsive sexuality, and they can't stop, because they yearn for that sense of wholeness. Locked into the addictive behavior, they are driven by the archetypal image. But – and here is the tragedy of our culture. We concretize imagery.

We concretize the archetype. For example, our children are hungry, but they are dangerously fat. Yes, they are hungry – they concretize love in food. Does anyone suggest it is their soul starving for love?

Giving up archetypal identifications is another sacrifice we are asked to make. We are not asked to give up our relationships with the archetypes, because life isn't worth living without a relationship to them. When we're dancing, for example, and those marvelous rhythms come pouring through our body and we feel that we are being danced, this is the numinosity of the archetype coming through. But we have to be strong enough to know that although we might feel like Sophia for five minutes, we are not Sophia.

Some people don't know that! Many men and women think that they're the Great Mother. And they go on feeding and feeding everybody but themselves. Somehow they think that they have limitless milk. Or a mother makes herself a martyr for her family, believing she has limitless milk for her husband and children. The archetype has to be recognized as archetype so that we relate to it, but don't identify with it. In this way, we release ourselves and our partners from the perfection of the God and Goddess. None of us has to be God or Goddess. Isn't that a relief?

How many of you know that moment when you say, "He's only a human being—what was I doing?" Or "She's only a human being, magnificent as she is." Really, she is far more interesting as a human being than as a Goddess. Far more interesting. It's alarming at first, but then you realize how magnificent it is to love a human being.

If we can acknowledge our own humanness, we can enter into the appropriate relationships with the archetypes. I see the paradigm of the feminine coming through in this reality. I know many people who are dreaming of a woman, sometimes ten feet tall, certainly bigger than life, with immense energy, and often chocolate colored skin, or some color of chocolate. She is very sexual, luscious, firm, feisty, with a wonderful sense of humor, and we have the opportunity to meet her, learn from her, and serve her.

CD: *Feet On the Ground,* ©2009
Music & lyrics Drai Bearwomyn McKi ©2003
Art: *The Awakening,* Nancy Bright ©1993

The Song of Being

Place your feet on the ground and know the Mother.
Spread your arms to the winds and know your past.
Cast your eyes unto the skies and know your future.
Know at last. Know at last. Know at last.

Place your feet on the ground and plant your roots here.
Spread your arms to the winds and cleanse your soul.
Cast your eyes unto the skies and gather wisdom.
You are whole. You are whole. You are whole.

Place your feet on the ground and claim your space here.
Spread your arms to the winds and speak your name.
Cast your eyes unto the skies and thank Great Spirit.
No more shame. No more shame. No more shame.

Place your feet on the ground, begin your work now.
Spread your arms to the world, dare to be seen.
Cast your eyes unto the skies, sing declaration...
I've come to being. I've come to being. I've come to being.

"When Sophia holds the still point the dance of life can go on.

—Marion

I can always remember when she came to me and said, "Okay, Marion, that's the end of the lecture notes." I told her I couldn't let the notes go. "Well," she said, "You can, and you will." I was afraid I would stand in front of people, open my mouth, and nothing would come through. "No," she said, "Let me speak."

I wasn't sure that she would speak, and I actually have stood in front of an audience with my mouth open, and couldn't think of a thing to say. I have to trust that the audience thinks I'm having a mystical experience. Eventually She comes through. You see, that way something new is happening all the time. When I use lecture notes it's the same every time—nothing new happens. Whereas if I'm just standing up here, I pick up your intuition, and I move with that intuition; I look into your eyes, and I see what you're sending to me—sometimes it's good, sometimes it's not so good—and I take it in, and respond in a new way, and you in turn respond to a new atmosphere in the room.

When the feminine is present, something new is happening in every moment. She is very kind, very firm. I remember once she came in a dream, and she said, "Okay Marion, where are your pearls?" (Pearls being an essence of the feminine.) I said, "Upstairs, upstairs in the drawer." I was in the kitchen at the time, and she walked back and forth sampling things as she went, eating them. She said, "They're not in your drawer upstairs." I said, "Yes they are." She said, "Go and get them."

So I went, and sure enough they were not in the drawer upstairs. She said, "I found them in the ditch. I brought them. Here they are." And I was very ashamed. I said I would not lose them again, but of course I have lost them, many times since. I don't mean to; my intention is good. But I felt that I had been thoroughly swatted. As she was going out the door she turned around, smiled, and said, "Keep flossing!" That's exactly her quality—stern and funny. She is so human on one side, and so divine on the other. She puts you in that still place—and the more you work with her, the firmer that place becomes. When Sophia holds the still point the dance of life can go on.

Now, her other qualities? In a dream a woman went home and found a big party in process on her front lawn. She hated this great party, so she went to the back garden. There was a ten-foot high cage, and a chocolate colored woman was huddled in the cage looking out. In the dream she said, "What are you doing in this cage? Who are you?" And the dark woman replied, "Who do you think is giving the party?"

When spring comes, and you see the daffodils, and the blossoms and sunshine, say to yourself, "Who do you think is giving the party?" You will feel the energy of Sophia move right through your body, which is the numinosity of the feminine made manifest in matter.

It is important to have a relationship with the archetypes. Jung said the healing is in the archetype. If you cannot get to the archetypal level, any

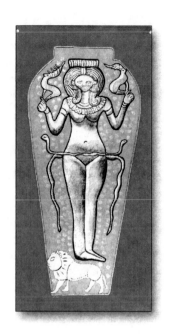

other healing is simply a band-aid. It isn't strong enough to transform the infected energy. I learned this through my experience with cancer. I had a dream that made it perfectly clear that if I could visualize strongly enough the power and love of the Goddess in the bones in my back, and allow that love to fill my sacrum, then I could heal.

All my life I've been trying to bring matter and spirit together, but I could never get into the depth of my body. The sacrum is the holy bone that connects us to the ground and is the container that holds the light. That is the amazing energy that I am working with: the numinosity of the archetype of the feminine as the healing power.

You must realize that by healing, I don't mean, "getting better." There's a huge difference between curing and healing. One could be cured and not be healed. From the medical point of view, I could be cured of the cancer and be dead from the radiation. And that is no exaggeration. That was one of my big fights—having to get my masculine together to defend the feminine. There were times when my body would go to the doctor and say, "I don't like this. I'm not staying here, Marion. I'm just not staying. I'm not." And my feminine voice was like a kid about five years old. I'd step up to the desk to sign in, and

artwork
Ashtoreth
Lydia
Ruyle
©2005

my child would say, "You can sign all you like, but I'm not going in there." And she wouldn't; I would leave. I learned to listen to the symptoms, to the little shrieks and screams and giggles that came out of her, and followed the voice of the feminine. And she would be right; the doctor would later tell me I'd had too much radiation right then.

Of course my life was turned inside out as a result. I had cut my job back to practically nothing, given up my practice. Many sacrifices were made. But I know there's a new direction ahead. And again, I don't know exactly what it is. But there the feminine steps in and says, "It's okay. Wait. You don't know what you're doing. Just wait." And that's hard for me. I like to be on the button and on the go. So the illness has forced me into a feminine pattern of being which is magnificent. It gives me time to relate to nature in a way I never did before. I always related to nature, but now I relate at a cellular level, hear at a different level, see, taste, think, and feel at a totally different level and everything is one.

The awareness that we are all one—we, the animals, each other—and that we are en-souled in one loving energy, is the Goddess. The Goddess is a manifestation of God. The two go together. To feel this in your body, and to feel the heartbeat of the planet, this is the feminine. From my point of view, the creative imagination is the healer—it's healing the Soul, so that even if I die, the healing is taking place.

Our task now is to allow the sacred to pour through matter and illuminate it. I don't think we have any idea what the body is capable of.

If you have read any of the subatomic physicists, they know that psychology and science are talking about the same thing—the consciousness of matter. The physicists are bringing consciousness to matter and the people who are doing bodywork consciously are bringing consciousness to the cells. In illness, the cells literally have to change their metabolism to move from disease into health. So through prayer, through active imagining, through opening totally to that love that pours in, the healing takes place.

I have learned so much about prayer and the sacredness of matter through having cancer. There were times at home in my living room, or late at night lying in bed, when I did not know what I was facing. Yet I would feel myself upheld. I imagined a net, and the net had little lights glowing—prayer groups here, there, from east to west coast, literally. When I couldn't go on my own strength anymore, I could feel this immense energy holding me. One day while we were sitting in the living room, my husband, who's a very sensitive man, said, "What is going on in this room?" I said, "It's got to be a prayer group." It was as if the molecules in the room were going around, and the room was golden in color, as if there was a Christmas tree with golden lights. And you know the wonderful feeling you have on Christmas Eve? That was the feeling that was in our home during those days. That is the numinosity of the feminine made manifest in matter. What I think we're working on, and what we have to work on consciously, is the sacredness of matter.

I remember one last dream of a tidal wave coming in. I am a droplet in the tidal wave. It's moving very fast toward the land. Morning is coming. On the top of the wave is a huge chocolate colored woman. She has her hand uplifted, and she is moving magnificently and triumphantly on the top of the wave, and the wave is thousands of droplets of people who are carrying her into shore. Dear Friends, let us wake up. Let us wake up to our own personhood, our own life to be lived on our magnificent Earth. Let us go with Her into the Dawn.

artwork

Women of Wisdom Art Series

Deborah Koff-Chapin ©2003

Empower Your Self

explore your dreams and spirit...

1   Has there been a price of living the feminine for you?

2   What does it mean for you to be feminine?

3   Where was your first awakening and what did you have to sacrifice?

4   Describe your experience with the meditation and connecting to Sophia.

5   What unconscious projections blind you to your inner reality?

6   What things do you turn to for nourishment and what are you really looking for?

7   Do you ever misplace your pearls (the feminine) and how will you recover them?

_____

_____

_____

_____

_____

_____

One woman, one circle at a time...
the world can change.

the world can change
the world can change
the world can change
the world can change

the world can change
the world can change

Photo, Valeria Andrews

CHAPTER 12

Jean Shinoda Bolen

Biography

Jean Shinoda Bolen, MD, is a Jungian analyst, psychiatrist, and internationally known lecturer and workshop leader. She is also a clinical professor of psychiatry at the University of California Medical Center in San Francisco, and author of the best-selling books *The Millionth Circle, Goddesses in Everywoman, The Tao of Psychology, Gods in Everyman, Crossing to Avalon, Ring of Power, Close to the Bone, Goddesses in Older Women, Crones Don't Whine and Urgent Message From Mother*, as well as *Gather the Women, Save the World*. She has been an advocate for women, women's issues, and ethics in psychiatry. Jean is a former board member of the Ms. Foundation for Women, and a Distinguished Life Fellow of the American Psychiatric Association.

Reflections Today

This article was transcribed from the talk that introduced the idea and book of *The Millionth Circle* to Women of Wisdom. Since then, I have come to think of it as a seed packet in the guise of a thin book. The seed ideas are the visionary premise of how circles with a sacred center can save the world, and instructions about how to start and maintain these circles. It seeded many new circles and inspired many already formed groups to morph into circles with a spiritual center. Like seeds carried by the wind, the ideas were carried and spread. One place it took hold was in the imagination of several visionary women who had the idea for an organization, The Millionth Circle Initiative. When I was asked if the name could be used and if I would come to the first organizing circle, I said yes. The result is an organization—www.millionthcircle.org.

In the intervening years since I gave this talk, the author aspect
of my life has been productive. I published four new books and
saw three of my books printed as anniversary editions. Besides
writing, I travel frequently, usually for short trips to give talks
and workshops, and I continue to maintain a limited private
practice in Mill Valley, California. Insights flow from one into
another. In each there are challenges, but characteristically, there
is a kairos quality of time in the doing.

–Jean Shinoda Bolen, M.D.

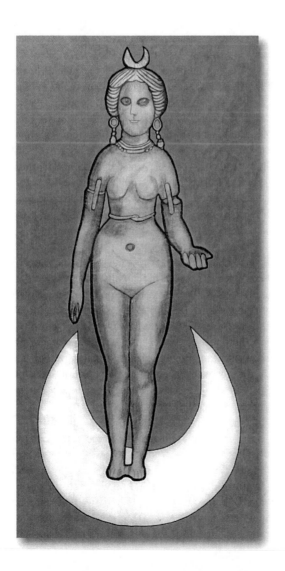

artwork
Astarte
Lydia
Ruyle
©2005

The Millionth Circle: Transforming Ourselves and the World

a talk with Jean Shinoda Bolen

> "The resultant circle with a sacred center becomes the vessel of transformation for individuals and culture.
>
> —Jean

If we are ever to have a post patriarchal world, it will begin in the United States, and it will begin with the generation of women over fifty. There has never, in the history of the world, been such a generation of women in numbers or potential. There are over thirty million of us, who, thanks to the women's movement, medical advances, and reproductive choice, have had opportunities, access to resources, education, travel, a range of know-how, and connections with each other and to others in the world. Each of us may have two or three active decades in which to make a difference. The fate of our planet also hinges on what humanity does—or what women individually and collectively can and will do, in this same short span of time.

It's our turn. If we do not make it into a post-patriarchal world, then we will have failed. That's really the message that I have felt in my bones. We have been under patriarchy for four thousand years—from the time history has been written—and it is time for the circle. Patriarchy is about hierarchy. It is a structure that enforces and expresses authority and power. In contrast, the circle is egalitarian and collaborative. To have a place in the hierarchy is about persona, often about posturing and the need to be aggressive. To seek power over others doesn't nourish the soul.

Male leadership cannot change the fundamentals of masculine hierarchy. For there to be a balanced world where those without power matter, empowered women, such as we can be, need to speak for the children, women, animals, and for our beautiful planet itself. Women's wisdom, experience and compassion are missing when decisions that affect us all are made.

In the time that I've been a woman in the world as an adult, I've been influenced by two different streams: the women's movement, in its primarily political, activist, feminist form, and the women's spirituality movement. I have been involved in both, but they have seemed separate. Now, brought together through the circle, they can become a grassroots movement that can change the world. The resultant circle with a sacred center becomes the vessel of transformation for individuals and culture.

I think back to 1980 to a pivotal day in my life. I was in Washington, D.C. for a meeting of the Board of Trustees of the American Psychiatric Association. On the agenda was a motion to rescind the Board of Trustees decision, made just six weeks before in San Francisco, to support the Equal Rights Amendment by refusing to hold the annual national meeting in an ERA-unratified state. With Gloria Steinem's help, Psychiatrists for ERA, the organization I had led, had brought this about. I had become an activist because the APA was not supporting equal rights for women, and the annual meeting was to be held in my hometown. If something were to be done, I felt it was up to me, and I could not disregard an inner voice that said, "Silence is consent."

We had been successful, but the issue had not been settled. There had been a backlash from male psychiatrists who accused board members of having come under some kind of feminist spell in San Francisco. I was there to witness what would now happen, and perhaps to speak as I had in San Francisco. They were back on home turf in Washington, D.C., and the question was: would the APA rescind their support of the ERA? With very little debate, the vote was rescinded. This meant that the next annual meeting would be in New Orleans, in a non-ERA ratified state. My stint as an activist was not over. This time, I would need to lead a boycott of my own professional organization.

That same day, outside of the room where the Board of Trustees was meeting, I received a call from my agent in New York, who said that the publisher Harper and Row had accepted the book proposal for *Goddesses in Everywoman*. On this particular day, the disappointed and angry feminist activist which I was, took on the role of a reluctant warrior to lead a boycott of my own professional organization; while the Jungian analyst author, which I also was, took on a commitment to write a book about Goddess archetypes. Though unintended and unexpected,

Goddesses in Everywoman would become a major influence in the women's spirituality movement.

I was one of five women in my professional organization aware of the situation with the ERA, one of five women who were part of an ad-hoc organization called Psychiatrists for the Equal Rights Amendment. The other four were all based on the East Coast. We were often on the phone in the early morning hours, and as I look back on what we were doing on the phone, I can say that we circled—we met as if we were in a circle. We talked about what was happening and how we felt, and what each of us would do. I led in San Francisco because I was there; we really had operated non-hierarchically with shared leadership, which made it a circle. I look back now and realize in retrospect that when the five of us met, which was mostly on the phone, my political inclinations joined with my spiritual inclinations. The two streams came together. They came together in a circle.

What happens in a circle? In this particular case, we were creative, we laughed, and we enjoyed the struggle we were in because it was meaningful and because we were doing it together. It was an experience in how the circle can empower, be effective and be fun.

I have a daughter, who is twenty-nine now, and when I look back to when she was very much younger, I realize how the circle model worked for her and her friends. They didn't call it a circle, but in many ways it had circle qualities. They spent time together and talked, which girls do, but when one of them was being a problem or creating problems for herself, I was impressed that they took on the responsibility of talking directly to her and didn't exclude her. In a circle, your women friends or girl friends are friends, and not rivals or backbiters. You can trust them and learn from them. In a circle, we are each mirrors in which we can see ourselves more clearly and role model in some aspect for each other.

The consciousness raising groups of the sixties and early seventies did not consider themselves circles with a spiritual center. Sometimes, without defining themselves as such, they were. In consciousness raising groups, women told the truth of their own lives, often for the first time ever. They spoke about what really happened to them and how they really felt. They were real. Compassion is generated and soul connections are made when such is so, and it could be said that they were meeting in sacred space. On the other hand, women also were "trashed" in some consciousness raising groups when they were judged and attacked verbally for not being feminist enough, or accused of elitism. In most, information and readings were shared and discussed. Many others were organized for a specific purpose or cause, such as a march, a conference or a confrontation. "Sacred" or "spiritual" were never-heard words in this era of activism.

Activism and circles with a spiritual center now can and do come together. They can tap into invisible support generated in silence, meditation, prayer, or ritual—all of which is centering. Talk may occupy most of the time together, as in any meeting, and yet when it is a circle with a sacred center, the energy feels different. Energy is generated and women are nourished and feel better for having attended. I have seen how well organization business can be conducted when the underlying structure is this kind of circle. The Women's Sanctuary Forest women modeled this for me. They decided that they would save old growth redwood trees by purchasing several acres of northern California forest, with the intention of keeping the trees safe in perpetuity; and committed themselves to raise the money that came due on their purchase twice a year.

artwork

Inside this Shell of Mine

Nancy Bright
©1990

> *Each person has an equal responsibility to be present and to be true to herself.*
>
> —Jean

They met one day a month. First they met in a sacred circle. I think they had their own usual ritual beginning, after which they checked in with each other. Check-in is taking the time to share the journey we are each on. If we don't know what really matters to the people in our particular circle, it's really not a circle as a growth medium. Because trust, and vulnerability, and knowing what the journey truly *is*, is the essence of how we grow in a circle. The personal circle was the foundation of their activist tasks, which they then tackled in the business part of their day. Raising funds, holding events, having retreats in the forest, sending the request out to cover the next payment; who would do what was never a problem. I've observed in circles such as this, where the cause is motivated by love and the women are competent and committed, that additional help seems to come from synchronicity.

The women's spirituality movement as I experienced its beginnings in the San Francisco Bay Area emphasized beauty, music, and ritual. Meetings were held in a circle with a definite sacred center. There was an altar cloth with a candle at the center. Usually, symbolic objects were placed on the altar cloth, often flowers. The lit candle in the center was instinctively chosen. It is the symbolic representation of Hestia, the ancient Greek Goddess of the Hearth and Temple. Hestia was one of the twelve original Olympians who we usually do not recognize, because she doesn't have a persona, and she never took part in the romances, intrigues, or wars that abound in patriarchal mythology. She was considered present in the fire itself, at the center of the round hearth. It was her fire that made a home and a temple sacred.

In Jungian terms the circle with a center is a symbol of the Self, the source of meaning, the center of the psyche. For the Tibetans, the spiritual realm is painted in the shape of a mandala, a circle in the center of a square. Jung described the mandala as a geometric symbol of the Self. Hestia's fire in the center of a round hearth provided warmth and illumination, and since cooking was also done here, nourishment as well. The candle in the center of a circle touches on these archetypal meanings in us. Also, when we are in a circle, it's like each of us is on the rim of an invisible wheel, each connected like a spoke to the center, in touch through our hearts both to the center and to each other. Each person has an equal responsibility to be present and to be true to herself. In a circle, there is a level in which symbol and

Coleen Renee with Pamela Gerke ©2004

Take It Out to the World

In sacred circle we heal
In sacred circle we grow
In circle we can become all we know
And take it out to the World.

Earth dances with Air,
My body and breath sublime
Renewed and inspired
I claim my journey divine

In sacred circle we heal
In sacred circle we grow
In circle we can become all we know
And take it out to the World.

Fire dances Water
My passion, rebirth align
Dreaming and creating
A world of orgasmic design

In sacred circle we heal
In sacred circle we grow
In circle we can become all we know
And take it out to the World.

We center in Spirit
We're weaving the web so fine
Loving and supporting
Across all space and all time

In sacred circle we heal
In sacred circle we grow
In circle we can become all we know
And take it out to the World.

> She learns to speak up, to speak out—not with anger, but with clarity and with her real voice.

— Jean

feeling come together. We can journey to a collective place of soul where we can meet other people in depth.

I realize that there are many men who are in circles, and yet I really think that it is the proliferation of women's circle that is going to change our world. From the women's circle, each woman learns and practices what it's like to be in an egalitarian society. And she learns to speak up, to speak out—not with anger, but with clarity, and with her real voice. She learns how to be both truthful and direct, and to be concerned and compassionate at the same time. This is not all that easy when you're worked up about something. But there are other women in the circle who can help hold it, mediate, model and do the kinds of things that help a circle work. In a circle, you have the experience of practicing what it's like to be present in an egalitarian way, and then you can take that out into the world. You can bring circle to your family. You can start another circle. You can use a circle model at work. When I think about how this experience can change things, I get an image of strawberry fields and strawberry runners. You know how strawberry plants grow? Strawberry plants send out runners, and where they touch down in fertile soil, another plant begins to grow that in turn will send out runners, and so on until there is a whole field of strawberry plants. This is how geometric progression works. This is how consciousness raising groups led to the decade of the women's movement.

Women's experiences and qualities make circles a natural form for us. It's not a natural form for most men. But most women are used to talking about themselves and their vulnerabilities and sharing their stories with each other. It's what we do from the time we're very little. This is how we form friendships—by speaking about what really matters to us. We learn about holding confidences; we feel betrayed when our friend doesn't. Many things having to do with making friendships work are what make circles work. That kind of ability to be in circle is much more natural for women. Of course, our empathic talent also makes us susceptible to becoming codependent as well.

A lot is happening in the world that we care about, that men as a gender have not cared very much about. And these things have to do with the ways women and children are treated. We're able to have compassion, because we can so easily imagine ourselves being in the position of a poor woman with children. There is something about our common experience, which I think has to do with the vulnerability to pregnancy and menstruating, that opens us to others. I think our vulnerability to being raped, and the fact that we are physically not as strong as men, give us considerable compassion for vulnerable people.

When I see, politically speaking, the kinds of issues raised in a presidential election, I wonder, "Where are the women and the women's concerns?" Emily's List might be the beginning. Did you know Emily's List is the most powerful, political action organization in the U.S.—more important than the American Medical Association? Through Emily's List women have raised more money than the AMA to support Democratic women in office. And that was because it wasn't enough to support Democratic men—they just did not have the same agenda as women do.

When Gloria Steinem responded to my invitation to support Psychiatrists for the Equal Rights Amendment by speaking at the American Psychiatric Association meeting, I was very surprised at how nice she is. I found her to be a generous, solid good person who is outraged at things and sees the evils of patriarchy, but hasn't been poisoned by it. Coming from the West Coast with its focus on women's spirituality, I had assumed that this attitude must have been the result of some kind of spiritual practice.

At that point, in the 1980's, "*spiritual*" was not a word that was used in the New York feminist circles much. It is now. It's changed. Some time later, I said to her that I would like to interview her about her spiritual life for a magazine I wrote for occasionally. She looked at me rather puzzled, so I thought maybe I had better ask the question from another angle. "Well, you know, most of the feminists I've read about, and some I've seen close up, get burned out. They're angry. They don't seem to last on the barricades. And here you are able to keep going on, and you're not angry. What is the secret, if it's not spiritual?"

She said that it had to do with the women at *Ms. Magazine*. She explained that they shared a common vision. They put the magazine together and together worked to change women's lives. She was the one who went out into the world, and she might run into difficulties, or she might not, but she was carrying a message shared by the home base at *Ms. Magazine*.

It's important
to have faith
in our
contributions.

—Jean

Home base knew that it wasn't always easy for her; that speaking was something that she learned how to do over time; that her feelings *could* get hurt, and she *could* feel betrayed and let down. Home base knew that. She went out into the world, and she came back. And her home base, whether she called it a circle or not, had the essentials of a circle: an egalitarian model sharing vision, taking care of each other, and loving each other. I think that the secret of activist circles that really work is that there is truly both vision and love, and a capacity to model for each other what is possible.

If you think about the circles you have been in over the years, most likely there have been some that hurt you, and became too tension ridden, and didn't work. And there were some that were wonderful. Maybe you are still continuing in one. I think of the one that I am still in, and I hope that it will last the rest of my life. I can also think of some that came, that had a significant life for a time, and then it was time to dissolve. And I think about the dysfunctional ones that I learned from. I learned as much from the dysfunctional ones as I have from the one that has continued. Circles are like that. They're just like relationships. You know, if your first relationship did you wrong, did you give up on relationships forever? There is something about the circle that is very much like that. They differ, and yet they offer each of us support and empower us to be who we truly are—a circle with a center.

It's important to have faith in our contributions, even though the results are not always visible. Sometimes a shift in consciousness is not immediately evident. Remember the story of the hundredth monkey? It's an allegory that helped activists intent on stopping the nuclear arms race to keep on keeping on, when they had nothing to show for it in the outer world.

The story describes monkey colonies on islands off the coast of Japan. In order to study them, scientists dropped sweet potatoes on the beach for the monkeys to eat. One day, an 18 month-old female monkey they named Imo started to wash her sweet potato before she ate it. Then she taught her friends, and they taught their mothers, and more monkeys began to change their behavior by washing their sweet potatoes, until it was the habit of all the monkeys on the island.

Then the scientists saw that the monkeys on the other islands were also washing their sweet potatoes, even though there was no direct contact with Imo's island. It was a story that supported the intuitively grasped idea, that when a critical number of any species changes a habit, a way of thinking, a way of acting, the habit of the entire species changes too. The tipping point for change is the critical mass, when one more is added and tips the scales. This was the metaphoric "hundredth monkey," that monkey who learned the new thing, after which all monkeys might do it.

Rupert Sheldrake, a British biologist, put forth the theory on which the story of the hundredth monkey is based. Members of a species pick up on patterns of behavior among others within that particular species through their shared morphic field. This is a collective field of unconscious patterns or instincts. The human morphic field would be Jung's collective unconscious and archetypes. Sheldrake added an emphasis on morphogenesis, or how new behaviors come about when a critical mass or number of a species change. In his books, he provides many examples in biology to support this.

"The Millionth Circle" as a title and premise was inspired by the story of the hundredth monkey, which made ordinary people think that they could bring about an end to the nuclear arms race. They persisted, and what we know is that the United States and Russia did sign a non-nuclear proliferation treaty, followed by the collapse of the Berlin wall and the end of the cold war.

We have been in a patriarchal era for about four thousand years. At times I find myself outraged when my consciousness is raised about the state of things under patriarchy; how I was misled when I was taught history and religion to cheer for the wrong team, or think that advances in civilization applied to me as a woman. In college, for example, do you remember the freshman course History of Western Civilization, in which we were taught about those wonderful Greeks bringing democracy to us all?

Well, they brought democracy to men. It had nothing to do with women. In classical Greek times, a woman could manage property equivalent to only one bushel of wheat. She could never testify in court. She had the status of property. A daughter could be sold by her father into slavery, provided that she was not a virgin. The status of women in this "cradle of democracy" was appalling.

We now know that there was once a goddess culture that was peace loving, created art, didn't war on each other, and lived where there were rivers and fertile land. They did not live on fortified mountaintops. When somebody important died, they did not put all the stuff that that person had acquired into his grave, often with his wife and servants. Warrior peoples with sky gods destroyed this culture and absorbed goddesses into the mythology of ancient Greece, subjugating women and establishing patriarchy.

Something very similar happened to goddesses and women when the Israelites went into the land of Canaan, the land of milk and honey, and did battle with false gods and triumphed. I was led to believe that this was a good thing, only to find that it was another capitulation similar to what had happened in Old Europe. The land of Canaan was a Goddess land of milk and honey—a place of abundance. There was no word for Goddess in Hebrew, so of course the divinity there was described as a false god. If there isn't even a word for feminine divinity, it's no wonder She disappeared.

Then there was Asthoreth, another "false god." Asthoreth was associated with the Syrian fertility Mother Goddess Astarté. All the Mother Goddesses were named differently depending on where you were. Just as we have our own personal mother, wherever you worshipped there was a particular name for the Mother Goddess. Asthoreth was also the name applied to sacred groves that the Israelites cut down because people worshipped the Goddess in those sacred groves. And here we are again with Julia Butterfly Hill, sitting in Luna for two years among the old growth redwoods, carrying a cause that goes back as far as Canaan and probably before.

artwork
*Great
Mother*

Lydia
Ruyle
©1995

Back to morphic fields and the millionth circle. Every species has its own morphic field. Ours is the collective unconscious, within which exist archetypes that have nothing to do with space

CD: *I Walk with the Goddess*, Kellianna ©2007

Art: *Snake Goddess*, Lydia Ruyle ©1996

Ancestor's Song

Honoring the ones who came before us
Honor them with song

To women back 1,000 generations
Grandmothers, daughters, mothers, aunts and sisters
Who worked towards securing our survival
I want to thank you for every sacrifice

You chose to live together not in war but peace
By observing Mother Earth you learned to plant the seeds
And cultivated food to meet the family's needs
I want to thank you for your courageous hearts

You passed along the skills to heal with plants and seeds
Of birthing and of death and women's mysteries
By teaching what you'd learned you helped us to succeed
I want to thank you for your legacy

> **We might also be tapping into every circle that ever was.**
>
> —Jean

and time. When we activate an archetypal pattern, we align ourselves through emotions and images. It is possible that we can align ourselves with an awareness and a sacred energy that existed over four thousand years ago.

Might it be true that when we form a sacred circle, we are not only forming a model to change patriarchy in the here and now, but that we might also be tapping into every circle that ever was, including circles prior to patriarchy? That would be the thesis of the morphic fields theory. It fits right in with the idea of the collective unconscious. But the morphic fields theory also says that when we align ourselves with a new habit, we are influenced by what has gone on before, and we in turn contribute to that morphic field.

So every time you form a new circle, you draw from the circles that have existed before, and you add to that morphic field so that it becomes easier for the next circle to form, and the next circle to form, and the next circle to form.

I remember when I was an activist that it used to seem perfectly obvious to me that I might choose "feminism" as my ground. But the people who were doing anti-nuclear stuff, and the people who were doing ecological stuff, and the people who were cleaning up the Bay—we were really all doing the same thing. Each of us chose a particular concern, where our heart was, where our spirit was, to make a difference. And as we looked over at the others who were doing what they were doing, they were contributing to the same shift in culture.

When there is a critical mass shift in the morphic field, something that was ridiculed, opposed, considered impossible or unnatural becomes a new norm. Five women friends in Seneca Falls began the first conference for women's equality in 1848. That circle led to the movement that became the women's suffragette movement, which at last achieved the vote for women in America when the 19th Amendment passed in 1920.

Eleanor Roosevelt was thirty-five years old, when she was allowed to vote for the first time. This was not very long ago. Now we take it for granted: haven't women always voted?

I recently read an article in the paper about a twenty-nation survey that found that one in three women are seriously abused.

What happens when women are abused? What do their children see? It just goes on and on and on. But if you stop abuse in one generation, the reverberations improve the generations to come. So, if you remember that silence is consent, and you decide not to be silent, you will need a circle to help support you. If you join in a circle with other women who are not only witnesses, but tell their own stories of how it is for them—if we do this, one woman, one circle at a time, and then take that influence to the men in our lives, and into the institutions in our world, the world can change.

The Grail legend tells us of the wounded Fisher King whose kingdom was a wasteland. Only the Grail could heal his wound, and only if his wound healed would his kingdom become green again. The wound was in his genitals. The wounded king could not stand or be sexual; symbolically, he could not be creative or generative. He is a symbol of a wounded patriarchy that has brought our planet close to becoming an actual wasteland.

artwork

*Women of
Wisdom
Art Series*

Deborah
Koff-Chapin
©2001

If patriarchy is to be healed and the planet restored, might women's wisdom be needed? Just as the Grail Maiden holds the grail, women are the carriers of feminine wisdom and the sacred feminine that has healing power. This healing can start with women's circles. Each one is like a pebble thrown in a pond. The effect on women in the circles themselves, and the concentric rings of influence sent out into the world and into our collective unconscious, is vast and innumerable. See one. Do one. Teach one. Be an influence where you are.

Remember history? Remember how one age ends and another begins? The Age of Faith, the Age of Reason, the Reformation, the Renaissance. Historians break time into ages and epochs, acknowledging that major shifts take place. What "was and always will be" in one age is outmoded, superceded, and revised in the next.

A peaceful revolution is going on—a women's spirituality movement hidden in plain sight. Through circles of women healing women, might the culture come around? There is no "always was, always will be" in human affairs. Something like a teeter-totter effect happens at certain points in time. Rupert Sheldrake's morphic fields theory is enacted, and history changes. When a critical mass—the hundredth monkey, or the millionth circle—tips the scales, a new era will be ushered in and patriarchy will be over.

artwork

Sophie
Wisdom
Mother
Church

Lydia Ruyle
©1998

Empower Your Self

explore your dreams and spirit...

1   When did you first experience being a circle in your life and what did you gain from it?

2   When are you most comfortable expressing your voice?

3   What holds you back from speaking what you feel?

4   Have you been hurt in women's circles?

5   How can you stop abuse from past generations and break the silence?

6   Is there a circle calling you? What would be the focus and who would you call to invite to join you?

_____

_____

_____

_____

_____

_____

_____

_____

_____

_____

_____

"your sacred circle partners will
encourage you to blossom.

encourage you to blossom
encourage you to blossom
encourage you to blossom
encourage you to blossom
you to blossom

Six of Water, Joanna Powell Colbert ©2007

encourage you to blossom
you to blossom

CHAPTER 13

Women of
Wisdom Circles

Circles

a sharing by Kris Steinnes

> We honor each other in the circle.
>
> —Kris

Circles are a universal symbol of connection. There are several important elements associated with a circle: the rim, which creates a container holding the energy inside; the center, which creates a focus point; and all the space in between for infinite possibilities. At WOW's circle, our vision is at the center of the circle. This vision is our purpose, and as we focus on the center we remain connected to that vision. This allows for us, as we sit in the outer rim, to explore all the limitless possibilities, and for creativity to occur.

Women are familiar with the structure of a circle. We will instinctively sit in this format when we gather, formally and informally; it allows everyone to see each other as equals and encourages everyone to participate.

Women of Wisdom is planned and organized in this circle format. Through the years we've developed connections with each other and there's a flow of people, new and seasoned, who join the committee. People come and people leave as life moves them on to other things. We each take on different roles, and we each vote for our choice of events to include every year.

As we begin our circles, we welcome and honor each other, usually with us standing joined by hands, led by whoever feels called to do so that day. She might read a poem, teach a song, and lead us around the circle so we each can voice our intention for our gathering. We share what's happening in our life–how we are that day, that week, that month. Even if we're just having a meeting, we will do this ritual to draw us together. It allows us to shrug off the day, be present to what is happening in this circle of friends, and strengthens our bonds with each other.

Even at our events we will set up the workshop room in a circle of chairs, to create these same elements in a learning, experiential environment. This allows for a sense of equal participation by everyone, including the presenter, acknowledging we all learn from each other.

Women of Wisdom uses Christina Baldwin's *Calling the Circle, The First and Future Culture* as our guide to operate our Council meetings that direct the organization. Christina has been a presenter at Women of Wisdom and has many years of experience in directing and training people in this operating system for a wide range of purposes, including support groups, committees, seminars and businesses. She has defined three main principles of circles: rotating leadership, shared responsibilities, and relying on spirit, which are Women of Wisdom's guiding principles.

Working in a circle encourages us to listen with heart, honor everyone's voice, and speak with respect. When we run into difficulties, we revisit the ground rules and remind ourselves of our purpose, returning our focus to the center.

Women of Wisdom's logo also is a circle. Within this circle are seven arches that form the symbol of Sophia. In the center is another circle with a triangle and three swirls, all representing the feminine archetypes of Mother, Maiden, and Crone.

Jean Shinoda Bolen has a lovely little book, *The Millionth Circle,* which encourages all of us to create circles to change the world. From her book, friends created The Millionth Circle Initiative. At the end of this book is information on how to start a Women of Wisdom Circle. We want to encourage you to start a circle; whether it be a Women of Wisdom Circle, or your own circle with a theme you choose.

Life long friendships can form from these circles; they will support you and be your anchors as you support them in return. They will witness and validate your journey. They will acknowledge the legacy you are leaving for the world. Stepping into a circle itself is a sacred act, and as we sit in a circle of friends we bring divinity down to Earth to nourish life with our presence. Everyone has a gift, and your sacred circle partners will encourage you to blossom.

Connecting with others is a human need, and that need for community is even stronger now in our disenfranchised world, where many of us feel separated and isolated. It seems there's less of a sense of community now more than ever, and yet there's more opportunity for community with our 21st century communication. When we sit in circle we have a sense of connection with others. It validates our lives, and we can find meaning in our dreams when we find people of like minds. It can empower us to do the things we feel called to do.

More and more exciting things are happening in the world, and yet at the same time it seems people are staying at home, cocooning, trying to stay protected from a world that seems spinning out of control. It's a paradoxical situation, and a dangerous one, for if we are to truly change the course of our world and stop destroying the Earth, we have to bring ourselves together in community.

Together we can create strategies for new ways of living that save the environment, end war, and bring peace and coexistence in an exciting new way. There is an urgent need for connectivity with others now. I think people feel it, and there is an excitement in the air if we can connect to hope for our Earth and not to despair. But we must be willing to step forward, to speak, to take action, to listen, to be with others, and to bring spirit and meaning back into our lives. The circle helps us to do this; it creates a vehicle for our voices; a vessel for creating new possibilities, and empowers each of us to do our work.

> *Together we can cocreate strategies for new ways of living...*
>
> —Kris

In a circle, leadership is developed in a supportive community, as it allows you to practice leadership, make your mistakes, feel supported, and also provides mentors. As you develop your leadership skills, you will gradually bring them to other places in your life: at work, with your family, and in organizations, and ultimately benefiting society. Many leaders have been birthed out of Women of Wisdom.

A Model for Circle Leadership

I have been the founder and leader of Women of Wisdom for 16 years, and yet for a long time I wanted to create a different kind of leadership. I had a desire for what I call "triad leadership," where three of us would work equally together to run the organization. I wanted this so I wasn't the only person shouldering the responsibilities of running an organization, and I enjoy working with a team of people.

One day, while I was on a personal retreat at Whistler in British Columbia, I was meditating by a river. I looked down at our Women of Wisdom medallion that I wore as a pendant. And then I had the big "Aha!" moment. I saw the structure there in the logo. There was a triangle and three swirls contained in that circle. What I was looking for had been in front of me for years, right there in our logo.

I wanted to create this system at WOW. The center circle would be the board; the triangle in the center would be the new triad leadership; the swirls were staff, and the arches surrounding this center became interlocking circles, which were our committees. However, it was not possible to make it work right away. We were short staffed, had a small board, and I still wasn't able to create a triad leadership. I held onto this dream believing that someday I would find a way.

A couple of years later, during an intense emotional time, I had another "Aha!" experience.

Retiring one evening after a stressful day managing the WOW conference, I picked up a book to read. On the page I opened to, there was a paragraph describing the movie *Groundhog Day*. Something in that rang a chord in me. I picked up another book,

artwork

Women of Wisdom Art Series

Deborah Koff-Chapin ©2000

and opened to a page that also described the movie *Groundhog Day*! I felt like I had been hit on the head with a two by four! This was not a coincidence.

I said to myself, "I'm in this movie and I want to get out!" I felt like I had been repeating a cycle over and over again and it wasn't going anywhere. Then the true vision of the logo spoke to me—I was reading the logo backwards. The circle leadership had to evolve from the outside circles, the community, the teams, and the membership. They create the core of the organization, the leadership. I picked up my paper and pen and went to work immediately, drawing this Circle Leadership Model starting with the design I had created from our logo.

At that moment I decided it was time to resign as Executive Director. The membership would elect our board members, who were previously chosen by the board. The board would become a Council, and would replace the Executive Director position. The Council would also consist of a representative from each team who acted as a liaison between the team and Council. Finally I was able to see how I could develop the idea of shared leadership in the organization. I was excited!

It's been four years since that "Aha!" moment, and it is still a work in progress. There are many issues that arise as we learn a new way of being. Changing a system can't happen overnight.

It took time to develop the Council and the teams, and decide how the teams would communicate with each other and the Council. Now the Council is operating in this circle leadership model, sharing the leadership, sharing responsibilities, and rotating the various roles, so we all can become adept at them. We're closer as a group, work more on purpose and even though it may not seem like it at times, we are moving forward. We leave meetings excited and hopeful for the future.

I have included the diagram of the circle leadership model that I created, and I invite you to play with it. My goal is that people will start to look at leadership and organizations in a new way, to see how there can be more participation in decision making with everyone's voice honored.

This system still allows leaders within the group, but it allows leadership to rotate according to the need of the moment. If the

Women of Wisdom
Organization Model

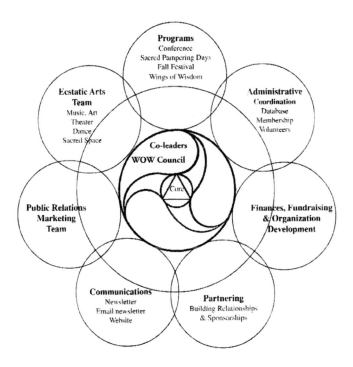

WOW Council =
1 rep from each team
& 3 elected by members
2 alternates elected

CORE=
3-4 people sharing a
leader/President's role

7 Outside Circles
represents each team. The large
outside circle connects the teams.

Middle circle connects
representatives from each team to
form the full council.

The three swirls between the middle
circle and inside circle represent the
membership–mother maiden crone.

Inside circle is the elected
members of the council from
the membership.

Triangle in the center is the
CORE leadership position of
co-presidency.

All members of the Council
have equal power.

The CORE is there to hold a
leadership position when needed
and they create the agendas for the
council meetings one week
before the Council meetings.
They don't hold any more
power at the Council meetings than
anyone else.

–Kris Steinnes ©2004

topic of discussion is marketing, the person who has that expertise will step forward; if it's about programs, program leaders will step forward. Letting go of hierarchy doesn't mean you don't have leaders anymore. The circle model simply allows leadership to be flexible.

Many of us have voiced our interest in moving out of a patriarchal era, and adopting a circle system of management is one way to do so.

Change will not be handed to us on a silver platter. I encourage you to make the changes where you have influence in your life.

When you see patriarchy and hierarchal thinking—speak up, change it, and offer new solutions and new possibilities for how to do things. Start now!

I hope that you will explore how you might be able to make use of the circle leadership model in your life. I invite you to dialogue with Women of Wisdom about your thoughts and explorations in circles and leadership. You can contact us at Women of Wisdom if you would like to start a circle, or a Women of Wisdom Chapter in your city. www.womenofwisdom.org

> " *Letting go of hierarchy doesn't mean you don't have leaders anymore.*
>
> —Kris

There is no time but now,

There is no place but here.

In the sacred we do stand,

In a circle hand in hand.

–There is No Time But Now–
Veronica Appolonia ©2003

Gather the Women

Gather the women
Gather the women
Gather the women
Let the circle begin
Gather the mothers
Sisters and daughters
Come to the waters
Where the circle never ends

Women of vision, women of wisdom
Gather the women, let the circle begin
Women of sorrow, women of longing
Come to the water where the circle never ends

Women of birthing, women of dying
Gather the women, let the circle begin
Women who falter, women who weary
Come to the water where the circle never ends

Gather the women...

Women of colors, women of courage
Gather the women, let the circle begin
Women of chaos, women of change
Come to the water where the circle never ends

Women of anger, and of compassion
Gather the women, let the circle begin
Women of fear and doubt, women of action
Come to the water where the circle never ends

Gather the women...

She is experiencing her own
creativity as a life force.

creativity as a life force
creativity as a life force
creativity as a life force
creativity as a life force

creativity as a life force
creativity as a life force

CHAPTER 14

Barbara Marx Hubbard

Biography

Barbara Marx Hubbard is a noted futurist, author and public speaker. She is founder of the Foundation for Conscious Evolution and a founding board member of the World Future Society and the Association for Global New Thought. Her books include: *The Hunger of Eve, The Evolutionary Journey, The Revelation*, and *Conscious Evolution and Emergence*. In the 1970's she cofounded the Committee for the Future, codesigning twenty-five SYNCON (Synergistic Convergence). In the 1980's she presented a fourteen-part television series, *Potentials*. In 1984 her name was placed in nomination for the Vice Presidency on the Democratic ticket, proposing a Peace Room. She is now producing a DVD series called *Humanity Ascending: A New Way Through Together* (www.humanityascending.com). She has created an educational program, *Gateway to Conscious Evolution*, (www.evolve.org). She is developing The Barbara Marx Hubbard Library for Conscious Evolution and The Center for a Positive Future. Out of this work she is inaugurating the first Chair in Conscious Evolution for Wisdom University.

Reflections Today

Feminine consciousness has transformed my life. It has unlocked the creative impulse within me and given me the awareness to become an "evolutionary woman." This means that at seventy-seven I sense within myself an evolving life force that continues to be ever more creative. I am no longer chronologically specific! I recently returned from a large family reunion, with my five children and eight grandchildren, and my sister's five children and her many grandchildren. I realized that I had done something "right" in a deep way. I had found my vocation, and gotten a divorce when I was forty, breaking up my home and taking my children with me to Washington D.C. Painful though it was for all of us, the result is that five out of five children have passionate vocations. They are all dedicated to their life purpose. And all support one another completely. I credit some of this to good luck, but also I believe that when a woman gains her feminine consciousness and gives birth to her authentic feminine self, she enters a second phase of motherhood, both giving birth to her self, as well as offering to her children (and many others) a model of her own life of meaning and passion.

–Barbara Marx Hubbard

artwork

Summer

Meinrad
Craighead
©1985

The Feminine Cocreator: Women's New Role in the Transformation of the World

a talk with Barbara Marx Hubbard

The very first time I experienced the power of feminine energy was in 1972, when I spent a day with Jean Houston and Hazel Henderson. Hazel is a global economist with a PBS television series called Ethical Market Place, where she interviews socially responsible investors who consciously work with a triple bottom line—the person, the profit and the planet. At that time I was still "under the thumb of a man." I will never forget the scene—we sat on the floor of Hazel's living room in Princeton, New Jersey, and we began to talk.

I had never actually met any two women like Jean and Hazel, and this was the first time I had fully heard the authentic feminine Self. It was a revelation to me, because even though I was a liberated woman, a Bryn Mawr graduate, married with five children, there was something in me I wanted to express but that hadn't come out yet. I realized when I met these women that part of the problem was that I hadn't had any role models— I had never met a woman who was able to fully express her Self.

As we sat there talking, Hazel's husband was quite distressed, as it was obvious he was not the center of attention. He had gallantly said that he would be very happy to help us, and as he served us coffee, made us breakfast, lunch and dinner, we began to see this reversal of gender roles, and I don't think he ever recovered from the event. He was not the same again, and in fact neither was I, because after the influence of these two very powerful cosmic women, when I went back to my relationship I realized the degree to which I assumed, even though I was leading and supporting everything, that the man knew better. That was a deep imprint in our generation.

Barbara McAfee ©2006
Art: *Sun*, Joanna Powell Colbert ©2001

When Women Awake

When women wake, mountains move.
When women wake, mountains move.

When women rise, the world rises with us.

So women wake, women wake
Women rise, women rise, women rise . . .

Now, a generation later at the dawn of the third millennium, what was so revelatory to me in the early seventies is now the birthright of your generation. There has been an amazing shift in understanding feminine identity over the last thirty years. Many things have regressed in this world; many things are breaking down; but if I had to identify perhaps the greatest thing that is breaking through, it's the evolutionary woman, what I call the feminine cocreator. I would like to spend some time telling the story of this emerging woman and how extraordinarily vital this feminine energy is for the regeneration of planet Earth.

I believe we have not seen the fully expressed, authentic feminine Self for thousands of years. Perhaps never fully, because the cultures of the past did not support our emergence as individual cocreators. That's quite a bold statement, but in just about every culture, once the patriarchal structure was established it was impossible for this feminine to fully express itself. When it did come out, it had to be behind the scenes. Women had to be aggressive; we had to be subterranean; and finally in the last one hundred years the women's movement has come forth in the most astonishing way. I think we're in the third phase now.

The first phase was the suffragette movement. It's remarkably hard to imagine that barely a hundred years ago we had no vote, and no opportunity to speak out in public, and that women were almost killed to get this precious right. Then in the sixties, an amazing decade, there was a phenomenal birthing period that brought the emergence of the second phase of the feminine movement, the feminine cocreator. She is experiencing her own creativity as a life force.

In the sixties one major event really helped wake me up, and this was the space program. Now this seems an odd thing to be talking about in the context of the Goddess and feminine cocreator. I remember when I was having my fourth or fifth child; I was vacuuming when I saw John Glenn go up into outer space on the television. I had a most amazing experience. I was catching my breath and tears were coming down my face as I heard these words on the inner plane: "We're being born; we're penetrating the blue cocoon of Earth; we're becoming universal. We're like tiny amphibians when they came out of the early seas on to the dry land; there was no biosphere. We're penetrating out there; we're being born."

If you remember when the Apollo rockets went off and we landed on the new world in 1969, we looked back at Earth and we saw ourselves as one living body. That picture from outer space of our Earth as one whole living body awoke a mystical experience for myself and so many others. We saw that we are all connected, we are all part of one, and there are no boundaries. It awoke as a physical, tangible fact. In 1969 we had the lunar landing and in 1970 we had the first Earth Day. The entire environmental movement woke up right there in the late sixties.

artwork

Gaia

Montserrat
©2000

> Women...
> woke up to
> the fact of
> their own
> identity.
>
> —Barbara

What also happened was that the women in the consciousness raising movement woke up to the fact of their own identity. This was a major step, although it seems so obvious now. In 1963 Betty Freidan wrote her book *The Feminine Mystique*, for which she interviewed hundreds of Smith graduates and others from the more or less educated part of the feminine gender. She discovered that these women had no self-image after the age of twenty-one. No matter what our education was, what our aspirations were, there was no self-image other than the identity as wife and mother—not that there was anything wrong with being a mother and wife—but she discovered that people were depressed. There was this kind of malaise, and she called it the disease without any name: the feminine mystique.

I will never forget when I was in my early thirties and I had my fifth child; I had a deep sense of depression, a sense that something was missing in my life. I went to my local psychologist, a Freudian analyst, but he had no idea what was wrong with me. He thought it was my sex life and it definitely was not that. When I read Betty Freidan, I realized that after I graduated from Bryn Mawr in political science, I immediately got married, and got pregnant. When I became pregnant that desire for self-development, that desire to go to Washington to get a job, was actually transformed into the longing for a child.

I yearned for the unborn, unknown child more than I yearned for the development of my self. I was giving birth, which was the most dramatic and exciting experience, and then nursing, and during this period I was freed from my drive for self-expression. But when the baby was weaned, the drive to find out why I was here on this Earth came back and it made me miserable. I had nothing to go on as to what that was about, and I got pregnant again. Margaret Mead called this "mindless fecundity."

Not that it wasn't good to have the children, but when you become pregnant the hormones that go into self-development, self-evolution, and self-expression are absorbed into self-reproduction and the nurturing and caring for the child. So when I was pregnant and nursing, I would be freed up from that unknown malaise, but when the baby was weaned it would come back. In that whole decade of the 1950's in Lakeville, Connecticut, I did not have a clue that there was something more for me to do. So the depression that sunk in was a deep depression.

I've learned from experiences in many others and in myself that when depression comes, it means there's something more to be expressed; there's something being suppressed. I didn't know what it was. But when I read Betty Freidan, I could see I had not found the identity that was unique to me. In my culture in that time, that seemed like a neurosis. So this is the history of how we started to evolve.

Abraham Maslow was the next author I read who helped lay the foundation for the emergence of the feminine cocreator. That was also in the sixties, when the entire human potential movement came to birth. It wasn't there in the fifties; we didn't know about it.

In his famous book *Toward a Psychology of Being*, Maslow writes that every well, joyful, productive human being has one thing in common: chosen work that they find intrinsically self-rewarding. Beyond the human needs for security, shelter, and self-esteem, we have a need to find our deeper life purpose—our calling or vocation—and give expression to it. If we don't do so, we become depressed, alienated, ill, violent, or we go into many forms of addiction.

I realized that the feminine evolutionary woman that I was, but didn't know I was, did not have an identity or vocation. And I realized that I wasn't neurotic; I was under-developed. That put a different signature on my depression and on my feeling that there was something more, and I was able to say, "All right. I need to find this vocation. It isn't something that is wrong with me; it might be something good."

The next person to help lay the foundation for the evolutionary woman, the evolutionary man, the evolutionary possibility, was Pierre Teilhard de Chardin. He wrote a book called *The Phenomenon of Man*. He saw God in evolution leading to ever higher consciousness and ever greater freedom through ever more complex order—from molecule to cell, to animal to human. And he saw the complexity of planet Earth as a living organism.

It's been over fifty years since he recognized that a new "superorganism" is being born out of Earth. First there was the geosphere, then the hydrosphere, then the biosphere, and now the noosphere—the "thinking layer of Earth." It is composed of the collective consciousness of humanity, combined with our systems, languages, and technologies all woven together into a new whole that is giving us collective power that we used to attribute to our gods. We can create little new worlds; we can blow up our world. This is precisely the time in human history when the rise of the feminine cocreator is essential to the survival and thrival of humanity. The dominator structures of the current world cannot handle this degree of power. This is the time of the "second coming of Eve." This is the time when the whole woman is emerging. She holds the code of our evolution as a species. She can give birth to babies. So too, she can give birth to herself as a new archetype, a whole woman, a feminine cocreator.

Teilhard de Chardin said that when this conscious, thinking layer evolved to a certain point, there would be a time of massive connection of heart to heart. It would be a quantum transformation, which he called the Christification of the Earth. He foresaw that there would be an awakening in the hearts and in the minds of all humans culminating in the maximum level of consciousness, which he called the Omega Point. And this higher consciousness would reflect the divine nature of all things and the great union and connection between them.

It may well be that the rise of feminine consciousness is a vital, organic factor in the awakening of the noosphere.

This immediately felt right for me, as I felt this urge within me to connect, to reach out, and to participate. Far from being a neurosis, it was actually the universe within me expressing itself towards higher consciousness and greater freedom.

In other words, the evolutionary woman in me shifted from a neurotic housewife to an expression of the universe evolving. And I began to see that I had some vital and natural role to play in this creative process. This was a huge shift, because every single one of us is actually an expression of the process of creation. The deepest aspect of our identity is the divine Self that holds within it our unique frequency. We are an expression of divine potential. So I realized in the sixties that this yearning for more life, for more connectivity, was actually part of the natural process of evolution and that it was moving towards something great.

CD: *Heart of the Child*, © Betsy Rose

Coming Into My Years

I'm a grey haired woman and I'm comin' into my years
I'm a weathered woman and I'm comin' into my years
No more holding back, no more tryin' to please
Got the will and the power to get off my knees
I'm an aging woman and I'm comin' into my years

I'm a street wise woman and I'm coming into my pride
I'm a fight back woman and I'm coming into my pride
No more shrinking with fear when they whistle and jeer
I got a fist that's hard, a mind that's clear
I'm a night walking woman and I'm coming into my pride

I'm a loud mouth woman and I'm coming into my voice
I'm a talk back woman and I'm coming into my voice
There's an ocean of words that got caught in my throat
Gonna let loose the waters, gonna learn how to float
I'm a sing out woman and I'm coming into my voice

I'm a big boned woman and I'm coming into my size
I'm a take space woman and I'm coming into my size
Now some of it's muscle, some of it's not
But all of it's me and it's the best I got
I'm a boundless woman and I'm coming into my size

I'm a light hearted woman and I'm coming into my Joy
I'm a fun loving woman and I'm coming into my Joy
The weight of the world is off my shoulders
I'm getting lighter as I'm getting older
I'm a laugh aloud woman and I'm coming into my Joy

I'm a loving woman and I'm coming into my own
I'm a heartbeat woman and I'm coming into my own
I'm gonna go for passion, go for strength
Go for the moment gonna go for the length
I'm a hot blooded woman and I'm coming into my own

> We're going to see that the crises on this Earth are actually evolutionary drivers.
>
> —Barbara

Like so many others, I intuitively understood that out of crisis something great was coming. Does anyone feel that there's something new coming, that something has been revealed in mystical insights of oneness, of wholeness, of transformation, of immortality, of a universe filled with life? I've come to understand that those mystical intuitions are actually revelations, not necessarily of life after death, but of life after this phase of evolution, of life after this phase of life.

Teilhard describes the unfolding of the cosmos through jumps in consciousness and freedom—from molecule to cell, to animal, to human, to Buddha, to Christ. So the drive in you and me for greater consciousness, greater freedom, more complex order, more harmonious connectivity, is not idealism, is not neurosis; it is the universe in you showing up. And when the universe in you shows up like that, there is nothing that can stop you if you say yes to it.

I began to feel empowered through this understanding that my own personal yearning to express and expand was completely natural, and that it was connected to everybody else's yearning to express and expand. It was going to lead to a transformation on this planet that would collectively empower us way beyond where we are now. I got imbued with the evolutionary potential movement.

So I'm laying the groundwork for what I mean by an evolutionary woman, a feminine cocreator. Not only is she awakening to her equality, but she doesn't want to be equal to men in a dysfunctional world. We do not want front seats on the Titanic. So we have a role to play in creating this new world.

I actually think that this quantum transformation—what Teilhard de Chardin describes as the Omega Point, and what Jean Houston calls Jump Time—this radical, non-linear exponential connectivity of what's emerging, will happen in our lifetime. I think we're going to see it, we're going to feel it, and we're going to be it. We're going to help cocreate it.

We're going to see that the crises on this Earth are actually evolutionary drivers pressing us to give birth to what's emergent in every one of us. Let's think for a moment of the significance of women en masse not having the maximum number of babies they could have, and living longer because of it. I work with women in their thirties and forties who have chosen not to have any children; and they are passionate women. Where will their energy go? This is what I call the shift of the feminine from maximum procreation to cocreation; from self-reproduction to self-evolution. This shift happens through choosing a vocation with life purpose and through expressing the authentic feminine self.

Teilhard de Chardin described a new type of person on Earth called *homo progressivus*. He said that when the idea of evolution came to human attention, it gave rise to a flame of expectation carried within certain people. These people feel there is a future emerging towards the unknown, and they are attracted to it. He contrasted this type of individual to the bourgeoisie who want to keep everything under control. Does that sound familiar?

He said the people who try to keep everything under control would become more and more agitated, more and more distressed, because you can't keep everything under control. People who were attracted to what's emergent, and within whom the flame of expectation burns, would become ever more vital in the process itself, until they become the emergent species of humanity. I liked that a lot, and the problem was I never met anyone like that.

When I used to go to cocktail parties in Connecticut, people would say to me, "You know Barbara, we really don't want to hear how you are." I was this questing evolutionary spirit. I started to reach out in many ways, and I called or wrote letters to people I liked. I wrote a letter to Dr. Jonas Salk about the meaning of what he was doing. Then one day I got a telephone call and the man on the phone said, "Mrs. Hubbard, this is Dr. Salk. We are two peas in the same genetic pod. May I take you to lunch?"

I will always remember the day he came to pick me up. I had just had my fifth child, and I was sitting outside on a beautiful fall day. He looked me in the eyes and said, "This is like the Garden of Eden." I said, "Yes, I'm Eve and I'm leaving!"

Dr. Salk was the first evolutionary man I met. I started to feel the tears coming and I pretended to have hay fever; and then I proceeded to describe all these things that were wrong with me—this attraction to the future, this desire to participate.

One's place in life is not just a profession or a job; it's part of a universal process of creation.

—Barbara

He said, "Barbara, that's not what's wrong about you, that's what's right about you. You combine the characteristics needed by evolution now. You are a psychological mutant. I spent twenty-five years trying to find people like you and I will introduce you to them." At that time there was no hint or sign of this culturally.

It was hard to believe, and I was completely ecstatic. Because what I've learned about the evolutionary emergent human is that we need to be seen, we need to be recognized; we need to be recognized for that in us which is emerging, is growing, is delicate, and hasn't fully manifested yet.

So when he introduced me to these four or five men, we all fell in love with each other simultaneously. I was this married housewife in Connecticut with five children, totally in love with at least four or five other men. I coined this word—one of the better-known words in my evolutionary glossary—called suprasex; and suprasex comes along with vocational arousal. In puberty you have sexual arousal and nature is getting you excited to join your genes to have a baby. That's a great thing nature's doing, whatever the lovers think they're doing. Nature is joining sperm and egg to get a baby. When I met Jonas and these few others he introduced me to, I discovered that the vocational arousal was the awakening of the genius code.

Everyone has genius code; it is the set of creative qualities unique to you. When you meet others who have the same frequency of this emergent exciting potential, your genius code starts to get turned on and you want to join—not your genes to have a baby—but your genius to give birth to something else. When a genius joins with two or more other geniuses, each person's genius expands. Have you had that experience? The awakening of your unique creativity and the joining of that with others is a natural impulse as great as the impulse for self-reproduction and procreation. It's my intuition that the world is going to evolve by suprasexual cocreation.

Suprasex is the rising up and the extension of the sexual drive into the creative drive. That creative drive is unique for every single human being, and it is held within the essence of the person as a code relating to his or her unique way of participating in the world. If you're really attuned, you will discover that code of unique vocation.

The evolutionary woman is evolving now into the cocreator, and her genius code, her unique creativity, is being aroused, just as her procreative capacity to reproduce the species was aroused in pregnancy and birth. It's now aroused to give authenticity to the feminine self and allow its expression to join in the world. That feminine cocreator is the third phase of the women's movement.

First we had to get just the basic rights; then we had to get the sense of equal rights; our identity and the freedom of our own bodies; the choice of reproducing ourselves or not; or evolving ourselves, or both. And now, we have a certain work and purpose that is larger, having to do with all humanity and with the evolution of the Earth. Because may I ask you, who else is going to lead this world? Who? It cannot be those trapped in the existing dominating structures, whether they're men or women. It's not even about men—it's about the structures, wherein you have to dominate and control in order to lead.

I believe the feminine cocreator is the evolutionary type that Teilhard mentioned so long ago, before he probably even had a clue that this was going to happen. The feminine cocreator is awakened from within, through the heart, by a passionate desire to express her gift, her vocation, and her purpose for the evolution of self and humanity. It is done out of love. It's loving; it's passionate.

Yes, yes! The feminine cocreator is loving, and she's awakened from within by a suprasexual drive to express her unique creativity for the good of the self and for the whole.

In my own mapping, I always draw the evolutionary spiral as the universe, Earth, life, animal life, and human life. Now we are going around this turn in the spiral, and right at the core of the spiral I think we find God manifested as the creative process within that evolution. God—that implicate order, that divine intelligence, is now breaking through into the consciousness of millions of people, not as a new religion, not as a new ideology, but as a new person.

This is a person awakened from within by the desire to express their creativity, and that creative desire contains within it the frequencies of one's place in the universe. In other words, one's place in life is not just a profession or a job; it's part of a

> We are
> liberated to
> reinvent
> ourselves in a
> new image of
> our full
> potential
> selves.
>
> —Barbara

universal process of creation. The greatest gift that I was ever given in my life was my calling. The greatest blessing that happened to me is my sense of vocation.

I realized that as I discovered my own vocation I began to access the vast untapped regions of my own potential. I met people, starting with Jean Houston and Hazel, who like myself have been turned on to a passionate vocation. Two or three years ago I noticed in myself an amazing thing happening. While it was true my body was aging and my body was programmed to degenerate and die, I was going the other way. I could feel symptoms of it—the spirit, the vitality, the vocation—the sense of emergence seemed to be accelerating. I said there has to be a word for what I was going through. I asked for the word and here it is: regenopause. Regenopause is the shift in a woman's life cycle as her body declines; she enters menopause, and she is no longer producing eggs.

The body that could transform itself to give birth to the child has untapped potential. When a woman is no longer producing eggs and has fallen in love with a life purpose, a vocation, a calling, it activates her at the cellular level. The deeper you go into life purpose, the more the juices are turned on at the cellular as well as the psychic and spiritual level.

Nobody expects anything from women over fifty. This is good. We are free from current social expectations, liberated to reinvent ourselves in a new image of our full potential selves. A friend and I invited women to "regenopause dialogues" to share their experience of the energy, the higher quality of being, and the intimate sense of identity they felt happening in them. Almost without exception, the women expressed that an energy they had never felt before was rising up in them, and it was more dynamic. As you reach menopause, if you recognize that your purpose is now to have the freedom to give birth to your self and its expression, you begin to activate almost a cellular memory of the emergent potential of the feminine, to tap into a universal force that will actually not simply regenerate women, but regenerate the planet: the feminine cocreator.

The regenopausal woman can be a wonderful mentor to younger women. They are facing a new world. They may or may not have children. They may live to one hundred and beyond. They are growing up in a world in crisis that has to be

The Change

Discarding her past
In the inbetween time
Where it is murky and grey
though golden hues hint
of the magic she has acquired.

She recreates herself
From once a beautiful butterfly
Comes a soul deepening
Growing a new kind of wings
Wings with wisdom and vision

repatterned. The old systems are breaking down. The new systems are being born. We are at the beginning of the first Age of Conscious Evolution. This means the evolution of evolution from unconscious to conscious choice.

Women are at the threshold of conscious evolution, both self and social. As older women in regenopause, we want to be mentors and guides to the younger women, take their hand and let them lead us too. We're all one great generation at a threshold that has never existed before on planet Earth. A new species is emerging—a species of universal human beings connected through the heart to the whole of life. And the feminine cocreator is a pioneer in the emergence of this universal humanity.

Empower Your Self

explore your dreams and spirit...

1 What influenced you to awake to your own identity?

2 What are your passionate about?

3 What is your calling; your vocation for your life purpose?

4 What is your genius code and how can you express it?

5 What is your picture of the new species that is emerging?

6 How can you help cocreate this conscious evolution?

" Tell the women the world over that
they must embrace their power.

must embrace their power
must embrace their power
must embrace their power
_____ their power

Women of Wisdom Art Series, Deborah Koff-Chapin ©2001

must embrace their p___
_t embrace their power

Photo, Christopher Briscoe

CHAPTER 15

Jean Houston

Biography

Dr. Houston is the best-selling author of many books, including *The Possible Human, The Search for the Beloved, A Mythic Life, A Passion for the Possible, Jump Time: Shaping Your Future in a World of Radical Change* and her newest book, *Mystical Dogs: Animals as Guides to an Inner Life*. An internationally renowned scholar, philosopher and teacher, Dr. Houston is the codirector of the Foundation for Mind Research in Ashland, Oregon, and the International Institute for Social Artistry; as well as a consultant in human development to the United Nations and other international agencies. She has also founded the Mystery School, a program of cross-cultural mythic and spiritual studies now in its twenty-fifth year. She is the founder and principal teacher of the programs in social artistry, which explores human development in the light of social complexity.

Reflections Today

In our time we have come to the stage where the real work
of humanity begins. It is the time where we partner with
Creation in the creation of ourselves, in the restoration of the
biosphere, the regenesis of society and in assuming a new type
of culture: the culture of kindness. Herein, we live daily life
reconnected and recharged by the Source, so as to become
liberated in our inventiveness and engaged in the world and in
our tasks. In my international work, training leaders in many
countries to develop their human capacities in the light of social
change, I find that women are generally the ones doing the work
of consciousness, social healing and innovation. In ways both
large and small they work as teams: training themselves to make
a difference, overcoming the shadows of millennia, behaving as
artists of the possible and midwives of social transformation. In
this most critical time in human history, women have taken the
lead both locally and now globally, as the world faces the great
Either/Or of history. In the broad and deep meetings of the
WOW conferences we experience the physical, mental, and
emotional symbolic as well as spiritual dimensions of ourselves
as we prepare to take on new ways of doing, being and sharing
in the world.

–Jean Houston Ph.D.

artwork

*Our Owl
Wisdom*

Meinrad
Craighead
©1983

Wise, Wise Women
in a Wild, Wild, World

a talk with Jean Houston

The Millennium brings many of us to the table. Some of you are radical visionaries, proposing utopian global housecleanings; others are reformers devoted to addressing old wrongs; but each of us is attempting to push through the membrane that wraps us in the cloud of unknowing. And with all our various practical skills and accomplishments, we are humble before the mystery of a world in transition. What a grand place to be and what a grand time to be: just to be. The most interesting time in human history, wouldn't you agree?

At the State of the World Forum, a United Nations official from Italy said to me, "It's as if we're all in a giant womb, you know? And we're all trying to figure out what happens next." Now I was very startled by her remark, because that morning I had been driving around San Francisco at six in the morning with a Bulgarian cab driver, and we'd been talking about politics. He said to me, "I have just been present at the birth of my daughter. I was very afraid because I have never seen such a thing. It was very, very messy, and very, very beautiful, you know? After all the hours of my wife's contractions: a new life. Maybe that's what is trying to happen in our world. A new life. A new life."

I think he is right. It truly is a time of new life. The old maps no longer fit the territory. The only thing to be expected is the unexpected. Everything that was, isn't anymore. Everything that isn't is coming to be. We are experiencing the most radical deconstruction and reconstruction that the world has ever seen. More and more history is happening faster and faster. It's extraordinary, isn't it? You don't know what is going to happen.

It's as though we are guests at a wake for a way of being that has been ours for hundreds, if not thousands, of years. Most of you probably live anywhere from five to ten to a hundred times the amount of sheer experience that your ancestors lived. And there are challenges that come with this speeding up of experience. How do we educate ourselves to be stewards of this extraordinary time? How do we nurture ourselves, our clients, our professional friends, our deep friends, our various cultures? How do we midwife the birth of this new life?

One thing we can do is to recognize that we are in a unique system of change, what I call "Jump Time." Jump Time is related to what evolutionary biologists call "punctuated equilibrium." Evolutionary theorists tell us change doesn't happen gradually. Things go along hundreds, thousands, even millions of years in the fossil record looking much the same— and suddenly *whoop*! In a few generations a species has jumped to a new state that includes significant changes in its structure and even its function. Why do we evolve this way? Is it because the species is living at the edge of its tolerance? Is it bored with itself? Has it experienced enough ferment and stress to punctuate the equilibrium with a sudden jump to a whole new order?

We can see evolution as jumps from the Big Bang, to supernovas, to the forming of our planet, to protein and cells forming, to organisms, to communication, to where we are today with jet propulsion, electricity, telephone, radio, television, power, laser power, solar power, computers, vaccination, sanitation, medication, refrigeration, anesthesia, air-conditioning, weather forecasting, air travel, space travel, satellite news, cloning, life extensions, world links, world banks, world culture, global village—and now here we are, at the conference of the wise women, because we are in Jump Time.

The jumps continue coming faster than ever. It is the changing of the guard on every level, and every tradition is up for grabs. The momentum behind the drama of the world—the breakdown of every way of being, knowing, relating, and governing—is shaking the foundations of all and everything. And it is allowing, literally, for another order of reality to come into time. What is looming before us is a collective jump, vaster and more complex than any the world has ever known. We find ourselves in the midst of the most massive shift of perspective humankind has ever known.

And while the old forces, traditions and fears seek to restrain us,

> The most
> significant
> change is
> women rising
> to full
> partnership
> with men.
>
> —Jean

we know there is no going back. Our complex time requires a very, very wise use of our capacities; a richer music from the instruments we have been given. The world will thrive only if we grow. The possible society will become a reality only if we learn to be the humans we are capable of being. We can no longer afford to live as remedial members of the human race. New values: holistic, syncretic, relationship and process oriented, organic, and spiritual, are rising within us and around us.

And these are what? They are *women's* values. They are women's genius, and they are women's gifts. As women—and as some very nice men, too—we are the pilgrims and the parents of this new emerging world. And no old formulas or stopgap solutions will do.

In the past, men in government and private sectors have been the authorities in determining how the world works. Women, who are the majority of people on this Earth, have been largely excluded. It is now time to focus on the roles that women should play in the developmental process. The biggest change in human history is upon us, and the most significant change is women rising to full partnership with men in the whole domain of human affairs. And this is absolutely indispensable if we seek a future that is different from the past.

You and I know that if ninety percent of what you think today is exactly like ninety percent of what you thought yesterday, and ninety percent of what you think tomorrow, we're in big trouble. And it's not just about *what* we think. I've been hearing from certain conversations among you that the thought process *itself* is being dramatically shifted. So you are not the same as you were yesterday, or the day before. And you need occasions like this to provide stimulus, passion, verve, greening, and fecundity, to switch those little mind receptors so they can take in the depths of what is trying to happen.

Women are an absolutely critical force within the changes taking place: the repatterning of human nature, the regenesis of human society, the breakdown of the membrane between peoples, the breakthrough of the depths. This is why the rise of women in our time, and in this new century before us, is the most important happening in human history.

CD: *Edge*, Holly Near ©2000 Hereford Music

Planet Called Home

Can you call on your imagination
As if telling a myth to a child
Put in the fantastical,
wonderful, magical
Add the romantic, the brave and the wild

Once upon a time there was a power
So great that no one could
know its name
People tried to claim it and rule with it
Always such arrogance ended in shame.

Thousands of years would pass
in a moment
Hundreds of cultures would
come and go
Each generation with a glorious calling
Even when they were too busy to know

Then one day after two millennia
Which after all was a small part of time
Hundreds of souls found their
way out of nowhere
To be on Earth at the threat of decline

Let's all go, they moved as one being
Even though each would
arrive here alone
They promised to work
in grace with each other

to brave the beautiful planet
called home

There was no promise that
they could save it
But how exciting to give it a try
If they each did one or
two actions beautifully
Complex life forms on Earth
might not die

And so they arrived in a
spectrum of colors
The population on Earth did explode

Some threw themselves in
front of disaster
Others slowly carried their load

Some adopted small girls from China
Some lived high in the branches of trees
Some died as martyrs,
some lived as healers
Some bravely walked with
a dreadful disease

They mingled among each
class and each culture
Not one of them could be identified
But together they altered
just enough moments
To help the lost and the terrified

To step outside our egos and bodies
To know for once that we truly are one
Then quickly we would
forget to remember
But that's OK, their job was well done

And Earth went on for another
millennium
And now it's time for my song to end
This magical story of hope and wonder
Invites you all to wake up
and pretend to be

Fabulous creatures sent from the power
Souls that have come with
one purpose in mind
To do one thing that
will alter the outcome
And maybe together we can do it in time

Can you call on your imagination
As if telling a myth to a child
Put in the fantastical,
wonderful, magical
Add the romantic, the brave and the wild

The Souls are coming back!

Let's take a look at the repatterning of human nature. For a new world to be born, we have to bring a new mind to bear. But where does this new mind come from? Well, a rich mind-style of women has been gestating in the womb of preparatory time this many millennia, and is rising; and with it rises a tremendous change in how we do things.

The emphasis here, friends, is on *process* rather than on product. On making things cohere, relate, and grow. The relationship *between* people and things becomes much more important than the final outcome. There is no final outcome! Things are always ongoing. So, the world within—the subjective world—becomes as important as the world without.

Clearly, we are living in a time in which our very nature is in transition. The scope of change is calling forth patterns and potentials in the brain-mind-psyche system, which, as far as we know, were never needed before. Knowings that were related to the unconscious have become conscious. How many of you are aware that your unconscious has just risen and flooded the gates of consciousness? Experiences that belong to the extraordinary have become ordinary. I mean, thirty years ago you rarely spoke in public about certain experiences—parapsychological experiences or experiences of radical intuition. Now we just talk about them over lunch. With the intersection of so many ways of being, from all over the planet, the maps of the psyche and of human possibilities are undergoing awesome change.

Years ago Margaret Mead sent me out all over the world with letters of introduction to the women and men elders of various tribes. She said, "Go out! And gather in the human potential." So she sent me to a tribe in West Africa. She said, "Go look at these people. They don't have any of our kinds of neurosis and little or no warfare as far as we know. Find out what's going on."

So I took myself to West Africa, and I sat there for day after day, and I watched them solve problems. Their problem solving was nothing like problem solving in the West, where we say, "Yes, A, yes, subsection 123, yes, addendum B, item 3, yes."

No! Not at all. They faced a problem about sanitation—they *sang* it back and forth: "Hey, yah yah yah"—"Hey, yah yah yah"; "Hey, *yah* yah"—"Hey, *yah* yah." They *drummed* the problem. They got up! And they danced the problem with their great chicken dance, which opens up the thoracic cavity. "Hey, yah yah yah"—"Hey, yah yah yah." And then they closed their eyes and they dreamt it and they danced it and then they talked about it a little bit and they danced it some more and then they all had the solution.

Now, what were they doing? They were cooking on more burners. They were using kinesthetic thought, they were using visual thought, rhythmic thought, auditory thought, and of *course* they all came up with a solution. Instead of "A, subsection 1, paragraph..."

artwork

We Never Left Eden

Montserrat

©2006

Margaret sent me to other cultures, where the inner life was

> Every one of us is a roiling cauldron of creative process.
>
> —Jean

equal to the outer life. She sent me to cultures where people would pray down the rain, and pray up the crops and it would happen in remarkable ways. Then I saw her do it. I myself gave her Rorschach tests, and she was right down the middle, fifty percent, between what we would call fantasy and action. She taught me a lot about what you would call luck—what I would call radical synchronicity. I never saw anybody so lucky in my life. I mean I never saw *anybody* like that.

One day we were walking along, arm and arm in Central Park, and she says "Arrgh. I need to know about this particular taboo with regard to the Arapesh; I can't find any papers relevant to my inquiry. Arrgh." Well, along comes a lady and says to Margaret: "Dr. Mead, I'm sure you don't remember me." And Margaret says, "Certainly I do, you're Linda; you were in my class in 1947 and you never finished your paper." The woman replied, "But, Dr. Mead, actually I pursued it in different ways, and I went on to graduate school and now I'm closely studying Arapesh customs." "Huh!" Margaret said to this woman, "Come home with me!"

I said to her, "I've never seen anybody so lucky in my life." She said, "Yes, I am blessed." "Why are you so blessed?" I asked. And she replied, "Because I *expect* to be!"

I studied Margaret along with other research subjects of mine such as Joseph Campbell, Buckminster Fuller, and Jonas Salk. I asked, "Why do they have this sustained creativity?" And I understood that they were all archaeologists in their own mind. They were spelunkers in the caves of their creativity. Their inward life was equal to their outward life. They had developed internal imageries to such an extent that they were like holograms in their mind. They could drop in ideas—whoom!— and then the inner life would take them and bring in more associations from memory and even from beyond their own memory, from the collective unconscious.

These people could literally enter into a realm beneath the surface crust of consciousness, which is called the Realm of the Automatisms of the Creative Process, the self-creating works of art, which are there *all the time*. These people were pioneers in unique modalities of the creative process, but this creativity is an aspect of what is emerging now, and in the future, in all of us.

Every one of us is a roiling cauldron of creative process. It's just that we haven't developed the hooks and eyes to catch the creative idea as it emerges. But that doesn't mean it can't happen. Do you hear what I'm saying? Wherever there is the impetus, the passion, the *yearning* that reaches a certain point of passionate possibility, you will tend to do it. It can work in the opposite emotional form as well. Take the level of disgust or nausea before the stuckness of things. One of the advantages of being a woman in our time is that the disgust level has gotten so high, that we are willing to take up housekeeping in the depths of ourselves, where the new orders of creation can break through. There we've got all this God stuff yearning at the threshold of space and time to enter through our lives. But you have to get to either a level of exultation or disgust; radical nausea or radical delight, whichever is your preference. Then you are open to something new.

As we develop our sensory systems, external and internal, to help the depths break through, there still is that whole issue about what to do with personality. Well, personality is flexible too! It does not have to be static and stuck; it does not have to hold us back.

How many of you have changed your names, radically? You know, I would much rather be Alessandra than Jean Houston. The thing that I'm trying to say is that we are in a state of changing where and who we are. I mean, we certainly change our bodies, we change our minds, but we are also in the process in Jump Time of developing alternative personae. If schizophrenia, the disease of split personality, is the disease of human condition, then polyphrenia, the orchestration of our many, many selves, is our expanded health.

The frail craft of ego is too brittle to sustain the complexity of our time. For example, I *hate* to write. I am phobic, big time, as I cannot write worth a darn. My New Age friends say, "Do you channel your work?" I respond with some heat, "No, I fight for every damn word." Jean cannot write. But Jean can cook! So, Jean the cook can write. I literally have to think totally in cooking images of stirring up the mélange of the stew of ideas, adding the spice of associations and all kinds of things to do with cooking, otherwise I can't do it.

I'm suggesting that as you begin to develop different personae, you also give them biographies. I've given myself as a cook a huge biography, where I did not go off and do the things I did—I went off and became a chef. And I have about six or seven lives going simultaneously!

We all have these different personae, and they have different skills—different skills gestating just beneath the surface crust of consciousness. If you give them some attention they will come forward to do the kind of work that your local, habituated, existentially trashed self can't do. And it works. It truly works.

And when you shift personae, you have not only different skills, but in some ways you have a different body, because your local self activates a lot of your adrenal activity. For example, certain experiments have shown that when a person terribly allergic to poison ivy moves into a new personae that isn't allergic, you can in some cases put them into a deep trance where they identify with the other persona, touch their bodies with poison ivy and nothing happens. The same thing is true about different skills, and different energetic systems.

I witnessed this with someone who had a very bad case of Epstein Barr. I said to her, let's live for a week as a persona that doesn't have Epstein Barr. And she had plenty of energy! She was stunned! But then she wanted her Epstein Bar back—it was her dear friend, so there was nothing I could do.

What we do know is all of these personae need a guide. And the guide is not the ego. The guide should be what I call entelechy—that great Greek word which means the dynamic purpose of self, the highest self, if you will. It is the entelechy of the acorn to be an oak tree. It is the entelechy of a baby to be a grown up human being. It is the entelechy of you and me to be God knows who or what. But when you get into the flow of that entelechy and you have that sense of great dramatic alignment and attunement, then you begin to articulate worlds you did not know existed.

Get into entelechy, its essence, and you will understand a great deal. I mean, not only do you have all systems go, but you have access to the rest of the world. You have access to the depth, to the strange mysteries of life. You have access to compassion because you feel the pain of the world more acutely.

Many years ago Margaret Mead took me into companies where

CD: *Testimony,* ©℗Ferron,
Nemesis Publishing 1980

Art: *Sleeping Lady*, Lydia Ruyle ©1997

Testimony

There's godlike
And warlike
And strong
Like only some show
And there's sad like
And madlike
And had
Like we know
But by my life be I spirit
And by my heart be I woman
And by my eyes be I open
And by my hands be I whole

They say slowly
Brings the least shock
But no matter how slow I walk
There are traces
Empty spaces
And doors and doors of locks
But by my life be I spirit
And by my heart be I woman
And by my eyes be I open
And by my hands be I whole

You young ones
You're the next ones
And I hope you choose it well
Though you try hard
You may fall prey
To the jaded jewel
But by your lives be you spirit
And by your hearts be you women
And by your eyes be you open
And by your hands be you whole

Listen, there are waters
Hidden from us
In the maze we find them still
We'll take you to them
You take your young ones
May they take their own in turn
But by your lives be you spirit
And by your hearts be you women
And by your eyes be you open
And by your hands be you whole

> "You must continue to tell stories.
>
> —Jean

women were coming into leadership positions. She said, "Let's go practice cultural anthropology in the corporation!" So we did. And often we saw women who were modeling themselves along male lines in order to get ahead. "What a stupid thing to do!" she said. "They're becoming second-rate men, and they'll stay in second-rate jobs."

Then she encountered a woman executive whose style was different. With the executive's permission we followed her around and observed her style of work. Margaret said, "Look, Jean, look how she braids her work. She's attending to how the process of things are done as well as to getting the task done." And indeed, this woman, who was overseeing the company's quarterly report, was very sensitive to the environment of feelings among her employees. She noticed who felt left out, who was not voicing an idea. She was probably being guided by her entelechy, her higher self.

Later, over lunch, the executive, Margaret and I spoke about how women all over the world were challenging the most sexist of institutions—from the medical establishment to organized religion, and replacing them with a new social order in education, career, marriage, recreation, business, inventions, investments, and government. And they were changing the results.

Margaret said, "You'll see Jean. Within the next decade women will be both priests and presidents. Why? Because women's resourcefulness and resolve increases as circumstances become more difficult." And the executive woman said, "You know, I do see this with women business owners. They're more likely to succeed, because women are more likely to admit that they need allies and partners, and they surround themselves with good people. Also, women don't want to work in pyramids of power. They want to pull people out of the pyramids and work in clusters—circular investedness. That's the way it works." And she said, "It's working."

I said, "Well, what about sexism and violence against women and backlashes—they're bound to increase as women become more powerful." "Well of course they'll increase!" Margaret said grimly. "You can't turn around the social order of thousands of years in a few decades without expecting a backlash." She said, "Oh, I wish I could live to see it! I'd know how to fight the backlash. It's a matter of transforming our values and priorities.

It's a matter of midwifery."

With that magic statement she went to go to a doctor's appointment, and she died some ten months later. But even on her deathbed she said, "Jean! When the time is right, you go out and you tell the women the world over that they must embrace their power! They must challenge the way things are done. They must build a new social order! And because of their emphasis on process, coherence, and growing things, women are more geared toward team building and leading enterprises through natural growth stages."

She said to me, "Governance, games, education, work, health, and society itself can be held to a new standard. One that promotes and honors the fullness of who and what we can be, rather than just collective rights and liberties."

And so, my friends, I would have to say that you are part of that, you are critical to that. And I am moved to celebration and gratitude for what you have done here, for what you have shown me, and how you have served.

You are telling your stories, and you must continue to tell stories, because solutions to the problems facing the future will arise from the subjective world, from the unfolding of levels of understanding, from the implicate order that is held in the metaphysical womb that you all contain, which is gestating a world to come. This nonlinear mind we hold is the Mother mind. It is not analytical or sequential, but is by and large circular, empathic, and narrative.

Our feminine mind view is supremely concerned with the networking of the individual with the larger social organism and with the blessed planet herself. So our approach will be systemic rather than systematic; we will see things in constellations rather than as discrete and disconnected facts.

The shift that I am describing, the jump if you will, is toward a different mind. Call it feminine, call it the Mother mind, it does not matter. It is emerging from within us. It is the joining together of the geographies of the mind and the body that have never touched before. It is weaving this new cultural fusion; it is weaving together synapses and sensibilities to create people who are fused into a world mind, with its unlimited treasures, its empowering capacities.

" Become
what you are
meant to be—
Cocreators.

—Jean

The Internet is the objective form of what is happening internally in the intranet, calling up new functions, new personalities; it is the world mind. It is changing the way we think, but it is high tech, high touch. It is activating a spiritual level that is so powerful.

This new mind is even changing the nature of myth. I was in India when they put on the Ramayana. Every village had one television set and I was sitting there next to the old Brahmin lady who had the TV. People tied up their water buffalo and came in to watch the Ramayana, this gorgeous story of Rama and Sita, and how they're betrayed so that they cannot take on the rulership of their land. They live in exile in the forest, and Sita is abducted to Sri Lanka by the demon Ravanna, and Rama has to rescue her. Everybody's watching this glorious presentation of the principal mythic legend of India, and I'm thinking, "What a gorgeous, marvelous, beautiful thing this is. I wish we had something like it in the United States."

And then the old Brahmin lady turns to me and she says, "Oh, I don't like Princess Sita; she is too passive. We women in India we're much stronger than that. My husband's name is Rama, my name is Sita—very common in India. He is a lazy bum. Anything happened to me, I would have to rescue *him*. We have to change the story!"

I said to her, "But madam, the story's at least three thousand years old!" And she said, "All the more reason why we have to change it! It is a very terrible thing for women to see. You know we really have to change it."

Guess what followed the Ramayana, downloaded from the satellite? What were three hundred million Indian people watching? Dynasty! I was so embarrassed, but the old Brahmin lady said to me, "Sister, don't be so embarrassed. Can't you see it's the same story? You've got the good lady, you've got the bad lady; you've got the good man, you've got the bad man. Good versus evil—oh yes indeed it is the same story."

The myths are changing. Change the myth, and you change the matter. The old myth used to be about the lonely hero. But now the women's movement is bringing us back to the basic quantum principle of the universe where everything is dynamically related to everything else. The lone mythic hero is leaving us. The myth of interconnection is coming into consciousness. Our stories are coming together.

I think of this group of New Yorkers following a shaman up the mountain in Peru, dressed in Abercrombie and Fitch, to be drummed into trances, to eat visionary vegetables, and be brought to another state of consciousness. I think of some of my Jewish friends, who are mostly Tibetan Buddhists or Sufis now. I think of a wonderful Catholic retreat center in Montana run by aged nuns, who say: "Oh, do come in, come in to St. Mary's, yes! Yes, before you go to mass would you like to go to the sweat lodge? And we will have the powwow later on."

The only way I can put it is—zeit is getting geisty!

Someone should do a brilliant paper about women's religion and the new quantum physics, and you would really see something fascinating. You would see that a whole new natural theology and philosophy is emerging. We are becoming mystics.

Mysticism is the art of union with reality. The mystic knows that life is about leaving lackluster passivity and going into creative exuberance, where you stop boring God or the Goddess and you stop living a life of serial monotony. You enter into the energetic continuum and you become what you are meant to be— cocreators in this incredible divine process.

artwork

Great Goddess

Lydia Ruyle
©1995

Where will it go, how will it end? Perhaps a clue is given in the marvelous words of Edna St. Vincent Millay*, from "Huntsmen, What Quarry?" when she said:

Upon This Age, That Never Speaks Its Mind

Upon this age, that never speaks its mind,
This furtive age, this age endowed with power
To wake the moon with footsteps, fit an oar
Into the rowlocks of the wind, and find
What swims before his prow, what swirls behind—
Upon this gifted age, in its dark hour,
Rains from the sky a meteoric shower
Of facts…they lie unquestioned, uncombined.
Wisdom enough to leech us of our ill
Is daily spun; but there exists no loom
To weave it into fabric; undefiled
Proceeds pure Science, and has her say; but still
Upon this world from the collective womb
Is spewed all day the red triumphant child.

Those words were written decades ago. But now, in a new millennium, we have the weavers. They are women in business, women in arts, women in sciences, women in religion—the artisans of many cultures who together with men are rebuilding that loom. The threads you bring, the songs you sing, the tastes you savor, are the strands of the potent moment when the fabric of Jump Time begins to take form.

Oh, thank God/Goddess that our time is now, when wrong comes up to meet us everywhere, never to leave us till we take the longest stride of soul that folk ever took. Affairs are now soul-sized. They are the exploration into God/Goddess. What are you making for her? It takes so many thousands of years to wake. But will you wake, for pity's sake?

Of course you will! You are Women of Wisdom!

Stretching Time

We are racing with time
Stretching it and folding it
Traveling within and without
Retrieving the essence
That is vital to the survival
And wellness of all beings

Empower Your Self

explore your dreams and spirit...

1   What is your role in the developmental process
       of the Earth?

2   Who can you ask to be your mentor?

3   What do you yearn for in your cauldron of
       creative process?

4   What different personae would you like to develop?

5   Write a biography for these personae.

6   Who surrounds you that you can partner with?

We now need to focus on embodiment—fully supporting women to be powerful women and leaders.

powerful women and leaders
powerful women and leaders
powerful women and leaders

Where the Rainbows are Born, Montserrat ©2003

powerful women and leaders
powerful women and leaders

EPILOGUE

Connection With Women of Wisdom

Epilogue

connecting with Women of Wisdom

> "You are a Woman of Wisdom! We honor you and welcome you to our circle.
>
> —Kris Steinnes

Women of Wisdom Foundation's mission statement:

Women of Wisdom is a non-profit organization for the empowerment of women through programs that offer healing, spiritual awareness, personal development and community. WOW celebrates the sacred feminine and is creating a new paradigm through a circle structure of shared leadership.

Our vision is beginning to shift from empowering the dreams and spirit of women to helping women embody their dreams and spirit. We realize that we now need to focus on embodiment—fully supporting women to be powerful women and leaders.

WOW invites you to join our community and become a member of Women of Wisdom! Please go to our website to find out how you can join and to learn about what we offer. Basic membership begins at $35 a year. You can sign up to receive our monthly enewsletter on our website, www.womenofwisdom.org.

If you are visiting Seattle, we invite you to connect with us; perhaps you can attend one of our monthly events or join us for our annual Women of Wisdom Conference, held each February.

Women of Wisdom Foundation has created bi-monthly events to bring WOW to the community throughout the year. We call these events Community Connections with three presenters offering workshops around a theme. This has been a great way for women to connect with each other during the year. We've also begun sponsoring quarterly dances for women.

WOW also created Wings of Wisdom, our community service program where we take our presenters to transitional shelters, such as Ratcliff House, which is a work release shelter in Seattle. This work has been very satisfying and meaningful for recipients and presenters. We're committed to the development of this program.

WOW donates 10% of our profits to two microlending organizations, Global Partnership, focused on helping women in Central America, and Washington Cash, working locally to support women in business through training and financial support.

Women of Wisdom's Council desires to make connections with other women's organizations. We believe collaboration is important as we move into the next generation of women's spirituality. Please contact us if you'd like to connect us with other women's organizations with similar interests and mission.

If you have an organization or service related to women you can send us your link to be on our website and offer WOW a reciprocal link on your website.

Are you interested in a Women of Wisdom chapter in your city? Are you interested in creating a Women of Wisdom Circle? Please contact the WOW Council of your interest.

Perhaps you'd like to license the name and have a Women of Wisdom Conference or a Retreat such as the one at Big Bear Lake, California? Founder, Kris Steinnes, is interested in talking to you and can work as a consultant to make that happen.

artwork

In the Beginning

Montserrat
©2000

Invite Kris to come to your city for a book signing and workshop, especially to a women's center or organization. She can provide workshops on: Empowering Your Dreams, Manifesting your Purpose, Circle Leadership and Leader of Your Own Life in addition to consulting on organizing women's events.

Kris Steinnes hopes to write a second Women of Wisdom book – there are more presenter talks to share with you, and if you're interested, please send her your art, poetry and empowering stories!

However you would like to participate with Women of Wisdom, we would love to hear from you. Please contact us at:

wow@womenofwisdom.org
www.womenofwisdom.org
Women of Wisdom
PO Box 30043
Seattle WA 98113
206-782-3363

WOMEN OF WISDOM CD
Commemorating Ten Years of Inspirational Music!

Don't miss this outstanding collection of well loved songs performed by women artists who have shared their music at Seattle's renowned Women of Wisdom Conference in Women's Spirituality over the first ten years.

National and regional artists are supporting WOW Foundation's work with women and community through this recording. Featured artists are Holly Near, Ferron, Libby Roderick, Rhiannon, Cris Williamson, Lisa Thiel, Susan Osborn, Jami Sieber and Shawna Carol. Our regional artists are Lorraine Bayes, Marybeth Saunders, Marita Berg, and Pamela Gerke leading the Women of Wisdom Sacred Fire Choir.

artwork

Spirit of Singing Hill–WOW CD Cover Art

Deborah Koff-Chapin ©2000

You can order a CD from the WOW website:

womenofwisdom.org

Paula Walowitz ©1979
Art: *She Calls to the Soul,* © Denise Kester

She's Been Waiting

She's been waiting, waiting
She' been waiting so long
She's been waiting for her children to remember, to return

Blessed be and blessed are the lovers of the Lady
Blessed be and blessed are the Mother, Maiden, Crone
Blessed be and blessed are the ones who dance together
Blessed be and blessed are the ones who dance alone

She's been waiting, waiting
She's been waiting so long
She's been waiting for her children to remember, to return

Blessed be and blessed are the ones who work in silence
Blessed be and blessed are the ones who shout and scream
Blessed be and blessed are the movers and the changers
Blessed be and blessed are the dreamers and the Dream

CD: *Rising of the Phoenix*. Lisa Thiel ©1990
Art: *WOW Ecstatic Arts Team Mural* ©2005

Star Maiden

As I look into the great night sky
I see the Star Maiden waiting
Among the many worlds she stands
And she always gently beckons
For me to look among the heavens
And remember my beginning there
She calls me to return in dreams
And to follow the path of the Bear

For the sky is like a lover
To whom you've always belonged
Whose eyes hold all the secrets
For which you've always longed

So I take the Star Maiden's hand
And fly among the stars
And meet my ancient relations there
In the Dreamtime where they all are
Eternally keeping the Light
And the wisdom of all time
My soul drinks from their shining waters
That heal my heart and mind

For the spirit is a lover
To whom you've always belonged
Who holds all the secrets
For which you've always longed

Contributor's Resource Guide

With gratitutde…I honor and support these amazing women who have contributed their gifts to this book. Please visit their websites, discover more about them, and support their livelihood through purchasing their art, music and books.

Photo, Self Portrait ©2006

Ashley Adams
Denver, CO. Multimedia "life" artisan, musician, and writer.
ashadenver@yahoo.com

Photo, James A. Nelson ©2007

Lorraine Bayes
Whidbey Island, WA. Award winning singer, songwriter, ceremonial leader and rainbow medicine woman. Founding Director of Tickle Tune Typhoon.
passageway@whidbey.net
tickletunetyphoon.com

Photo, Lori Barra ©2007

Isabel Allende
Author, *isabelallende.com.* The Isabel Allende Foundation supports organizations that help women and children in need, by providing education, healthcare, protection and the means to empowerment.

Photo, Self Portrait ©2007

Drai Bearwomyn McKi
Denver, CO. Founder, Wild Redhead Design. Mother. A Celtic, Earth-spirited ceremonialist, drummer and Keeper of the Song. *blog.myspace. com/wildredheaddesign*

Photo, Linda Steen

Veronica Appolonia
Seattle, WA. Singer-songwriter, artist and manager of BodySong Healing and Arts Center.
bodysongcommunity.com

Jennifer Berezan
San Francisco, CA. Singer-songwriter, activist and teacher whose innovative blend of folk, rock and country tackles contemporary issues with insight and striking melodies.
edgeofwonder.com

Photo, Marianne Gontarz York

Angeles Arrien
Cultural anthropologist, author, educator, President of the Foundation for Cross-Cultural Education and Research.
angelesarrien.com

Photo, ©1999

Marita Berg
Wenatchee, WA. Singer-songwriter, music educator, nursing student.

Christina Baldwin
Whidbey Island, WA. Author of *Storycatcher* and *Calling the Circle*, and cofounder of PeerSpirit Inc., specializing in facilitation and community building.
peerspirit.com

Photo, Valeria Andrews

Jean Shinoda Bolen
Jungian analyst, psychiatrist, and internationally known lecturer and workshop leader.
jeanshinodabolen.com, millionthcircle.org

Nancy Bright
Eugene, OR. Watercolor artist widely recognized for her deeply moving spiritual imagery, inspired by personal life experiences, dreams, and visions.
brightcreationsart.com

Photo, Frank Coccia ©2006

Sue Coccia
Edmunds, WA. Animal lover and artist whose intricate and colorful drawings depict animal images, or totems, from around the world.
earthartinternational.com

JoAutumn Brock
Oregon City, OR. A visionary artist and writer who works in various mediums. She specializes in nature and spirit centered art.
rising-earth-images.com

photo unavailable

April Cody
Seattle WA, chalk artist, created chalk drawing of WOW logo.

Shawna Carol
Kauai, HI. Internationally recognized composer, recording artist, sound healer, author and creator of the ritual theater piece "Goddess Chant".
goddesschant.com

Joanna Powell Colbert
Bellingham, WA. Artist and writer known internationally for her Goddess portraits and mythic art.
jpc-artworks.com,
gaiantarot.com

Photo, ClaireKriofske ©2007

Linda Castine
Seattle, WA. WOW member, Poems with a Purpose.
linda_castine@yahoo.com

Photo, John Holzwart ©2007

Linda Conroy
Sheboygan, WI. Founder and Proprietress of Moonwise herbs, Earth wisdom programs.
moonwiseherbs.com

Susan Chiat, MA
Seattle, WA. Writer, holistic counselor, neurofeedback practitioner,
seattlehealingarts.com

Photo, Valeria Andrews

Meinrad Craighead
Albuquerque, NM. Visionary artist who sees with the "All Seeing Eye of the Mother" and knows that all she sees is sacred...connecting the visible and the invisible in the soul of nature.
meinradcraighead.com

Diana Denslow
Poulsbo, WA. Artist with over 40 years experience in a wide variety of subjects. In recent years the children have transformed into fairies and the women into goddesses—as it should be.
ddenslow@embarqmail.com

Photo, Jadina Lilien

Hilary Hart
Whidbey Is. WA, author of *The Unknown She* and *Pearlie of Great Price*. She owns a small retreat house and leads meditation retreats for women. hh@hilaryhart.org
hilaryhart.org

Photo, Michael Collopy

Riane Eisler
Cultural historian and evolutionary theorist, President of the Center for Partnership Studies, cofounder of the Spiritual Alliance to Stop Intimate Violence.
rianeeisler.com, partnershipway.org

Photo, Christopher Briscoe

Jean Houston
Author, scholar, philosopher and teacher, codirector of the Foundation for Mind Research and International Institute for Social Artistry. Founder of Mystery School,
jeanhouston.org

Ferron
Kalamazoo, MI. Singer-songwriter, poet, influential writer and performer of women's music. Cocreator The Fen Sanctuary in Three Rivers, MI.
ferrononline.com

Barbara Marx Hubbard
Futurist, author and public speaker, founder of the Foundation for Conscious Evolution,
barbaramarxhubbard.co evolve.org

Suzanne Cheryl Gardner
Poulsbo, WA. An internationally known artist who paints the Sacred Divine Feminine and metaphysical principles.
suzannesart.com

Kellianna
Montague, MA. Accomplished singer-songwriter performing powerful Goddess and mythology inspired folk music and chant, and a certified teacher of SpiritSong.
kellianna.com

Photo, Holly Warren ©2005

Pamela Gerke
Everett, WA. Composer, arranger, playwright, choral conductor (Sacred Fire Choir and Seattle Women's Ensemble), author of books on children's drama, music and arts educator.

Denise Kester
Ashland, OR. Artist, writer, master printmaker of viscosity mono-printing, and teacher. Owner of "Drawing on the Dream" art line distributed world wide and Kester Studio.
drawingonthedream.com

Photo, Ross Chapin ©2005

Deborah Koff-Chapin
Whidbey Is. WA. Artist, originator of Touch Drawing process, vocalist, author, teacher, independent publisher, creator of Soul Card decks. Conference interpretive artist.
touchdrawing.com

Robin Maynard-Dobbs
Seattle, WA. An Aware Eating ™ personal coach and artist, whose paintings on silk express her personal journey and the Sacred Feminine.
awareeating.com

Photo, Grace Seidel ©2007

Simone LaDrumma
Seattle, WA. Professional drummer, teacher, and founder of Ladies Don't Drum world beat percussion ensemble.
LaDrumma.com

Barbara McAfee
Twin Cities, MN. Singer-songwriter, speaker and coach, Barbara's music and presentations inspire audiences to create fulfilling lives and meaningful work.
barbaramcafee.com

Photo, Richard Rowe

Frances Moore Lappé
Author, activist, cofounder Food First and Center for Living Democracy, coleader Small Planet Institute,
smallplanet.org

Brooke Medicine-Eagle
Author, healer, visionary, sacred ecologist, Earth heart Sanctuary Montana,
medicine-eagle.com

Photo, Colette Hinkle ©2007

Rev. Judith Laxer
Seattle WA. Spiritual counselor, Priestess of the Goddess, ceremonialist, psychic, hypnotherapist and founding minister of Gaia's Temple,
gaiastemple.org.

Montserrat
Bellevue WA. Artist from Barcelona who paints images of the Goddess and Faeries and creates one-of-a-kind meditation and ritual candles.
thesacredfeminine.com

Photo, Kathy Admire ©2007

Melissa Layer
Port Townsend, WA. Writer, studying for an MA in Counseling Psychology at the Institute for Transpersonal Psychology.

Photo, Susan Keeler

Marcia Moonstar
Seattle, WA. Poet, performer of unique style of poetry, astrologer and artist, publisher of three poetry books, CD and greeting cards.
marcymoonstar.com

Holly Near
Ukiah, CA. Singer, composer, teacher and social activist who brings to the stage an integration of world consciousness and spiritual discovery.
hollynear.com

Photo, Susan Wilson

Coleen Renee
Ellensberg, WA. Works as a healer, teacher and dreamer.
coleenrenee.com

Julie Charette Nunn, Crow's Daughter, wise woman teacher, shamanic herbal apprenticeships/classes for women, mentorships for girls, gardener and crafter of nourishing herbal creations.
crowsdaughter.com

Photo, Taddeusz Charette Nunn ©2007

Rhiannon
Point Reyes, CA. Vocalist, performance artist, composer and master teacher whose musical vision embraces jazz, a cappella, improv, world music and storytelling.
rhiannonmusic.com

Judith Orloff
Psychiatrist, intuitive, and author, assistant professor of psychiatry at UCLA, *drjudithorloff.com*, free mini video classes at *youtube.com/judithorloffmd*

Photo, Kathy Kenney

Jenn Richards
Big Bear Lake, CA. Artist and workshop leader. She concentrates on the inner and outer female form usually including a poem with her work to help viewers to "see" her focus.

Photo, Kris Steinnes

Susan Osborn
Orcas Island, WA. Internationally recognized singer whose styles range from classical to jazz, pop, and folk melodies. Teacher of Silence and Song seminars around the world.
susanosborn.com

Libby Roderick
Anchorage, AK. An internationally acclaimed singer-songwriter, poet, activist, teacher. Turtle Island Records. libbyroderick@gmail.com 907-278-6817.
libbyroderick.com

Photo, Irene Young

Rev. Rosa Redtail
Pistol River, OR. Ordained Minister, Spiritual teacher, Original Hippy and self proclaimed "Spiritual Junky." revrosaredtail@gmail.com

Betsy Rose
Singer, composer, and leader of women's song circles around the Bay area and the Northwest. Her recent CD includes both original and collected songs sung for and by women.
betsyrosemusic.org

Lydia Ruyle
Greeley, CO. Artist and art history instructor at the University of Northern Colorado. Her sacred Goddess icons and spirit banners celebrate the Divine Feminine in all cultures.
lydiaruyle.com

Lisa Thiel
Monrovia, CA. Visionary artist and ceremonial singer whose healing song prayers and chants emphasize the Sacred Feminine.
www.*sacreddream.com*

Nicki Scully
Author, metaphysics teacher, Alchemical Healing, and the Egyptian Mysteries. guide to an extra-ordinary world of mystical tours to sacred power sites and within the inner planes.
shamanicjourneys.com

Paula Walowitz
Chicago, IL. A freelance writer, songwriter and professional counselor with a focus on GLBT issues.

Chandra Smith
Big Bear Lake, CA. Psychotherapist, ceremonialist. Founder of Women of Wisdom, CA Women's Wellness Retreat. Teacher, writer, sailor and skier.

Cris Williamson
Seattle, WA. Singer, composer and activist who helped pioneer the genre of "women's music", and founder of Wolf Moon Records.
criswilliamson.com

Annalisa Steinnes
Seattle WA. Creative writer, music teacher, reading and language arts tutor, political activist. Enjoys mentoring young women.

Marion Woodman
Jungian Analyst, teacher and author. Chair of the Marion Woodman Foundation supporting BodySoul Rhythms Intensives.
mwoodman.org, mwoodmanfoundation.org

Kris Steinnes
Seattle, WA. Founder of Women of Wisdom Foundation. Minister, teacher, author, artist.
womenofwisdom.org wisewomanpublishing.com

Patty Zeitlin
Seattle, WA. Author, songwriter, playwright, teacher of Nonviolent Communication, MA in Human Development.
pattipaz@juno.com

Women of Wisdom Presenters

through the years, 1993–2008

in memoriam to Janine Ellison and Elaine Childs Gowell

1993 Vicki Noble, Jennifer Berezan, Luisah Teish, Meinrad Craighhead, Choquosh Ah– Oh-ho, Vivienne Hull, Marilyn Strong, Renie Hope, Diane Zimberoff, Joanne Harmon, Victoria Castle, Rev. Karen Lindbig, Sharyn Rose White, Peggy Nomura, Alexandra Kovats, Flor Fernandez, Ann Thomas, Rita Bresnahan, Terri Gaffney, Jeanne Eldere, Marita Berg, Anila Prineveau, Melodie Blair, Sheila Belanger, Chandra Smith, Lucinda Herring and Laura Cameron Fraser.

1994 Marlo Morgan, Demetra George, Libby Roderick, China Galland, Evelyn White, Nikki Louis, Karen Lindvig, Nancy Kahn, Generessa Arielle, Alexandra Kovats, Joan Staples-Baum, Ester "Little Dove" John, Charmell McLoughlin, Kimberly White, Judith Kahn, Deborah Koff-Chapin, Lillian Susumi, Dudley Evenson, Linda Grieschel, Renie Hope, Marilyn Strong, Ratna Roy, EagleSong, Waverly Fitzgerald, Lucinda Herring, Mary O'Malley Chandra Smith, Terri Gaffney, Jane Comerford, Susan Little, Chrystos, Lani Wynne-Hampton, Dr. Geri Marr Burdman, Linda Sewright, Flor Fernandez, Charlotte Sherman Watson, Sheila Belanger, Rev. Karen Lindvig, Elaine Childs Gowell, Chris Stafford Sabbatina, Laura Cameron Fraser, Thora Hess, Rita Bresnahan, Marita Berg and Emily Day.

1995 Jean Shinoda Bolen, Marion Woodman, Susun Weed, Betsy Rose, Nikki Louis, Toni Douglass, Marita Berg, Kelly Kerr, Patt Lind-Kyle, Generessa Arielle, Melodie Silverwolf, Ani Haines,

Gwendolyn Endicott, Fern Feldman, Adefua, Michelle Levey, Molly Gordon, Linda Herring, Ratna Roy, Waverly Fitzgerald, EagleSong, Deborah Koff-Chapin, Karen Hughes, Linda Wolf, Simone LaDrumma, Esther "Little Dove" John, Linda Grieschel, Laura Cameron Fraser, Rev. Barbara Fox, Flor Fernandez, Frances Wood, Rev. Cindy Stutting, Rev. Karen Lindvig, Debrena Jackson-Gandy, Jan Maher, Christie Denhart, Victoria Castle, Renie Hope, Marilyn Strong, Harriett Walden, Emily Day, Adrienne Whitman, Rita Bresnahan, Dr. Geri Marr Burdman, Therese Stallings, Christina Baldwin, Ann Linnea and Sabriah Rahiman.

1996 Iyanla Vanzant, Riane Eisler, Linda Leonard, Maureen Murdock, Charlotte Davis Kasl, Cris Williamson, Tret Fure, Tickle Tune Typoon, Sacred Earth Singers, Ladies Don't Drum, Marita Berg, Renie Hope, Marilyn Strong, Lynn Dakini Marlow, Ratna Roy, EagleSong, Melodie Silverwolf, Ani Haines, Jacqueline Davis, Gwendolyn Endicott, Dr. Maxine Mimms, Donna Linn, Venita Ramirez, Sheila Belanger, Debrena Jackson Gandy, Rev. Judith Laxer, Rev. Susan Sanford, Vicky Edmonds, Karen Hughes, Linda Wolf, Simone LaDrumma, Linda Sewright, Rev. Karen Lindvig, Anita Blume, Isadora Wong, Elaine Childs, Rev. Deb Olive, Rabbi Beth Singer, Meghan Smith, Therese Stallings, Deborah Koff-Chapin, Delayna Elliott, Frances Wood, Tina Lear, Maria Glanz, Lynn Fuller, Lee Fuller, Mary Jane Koerper, Carolyn Hartness, Rita Brenahan, Adefua, Jane Lister Reis, Adrienne Whitman, Marion Moss, Barbara Koch, Madi Nolan, Ilona Selke, Krista Gemmel Harris, Ingrid Hurlen, Molly Gordon, Lucinda Herring, Ester "Little Dove" John and Michelle Levey.

1997 Angela Davis, Joan Borysenko, Judiith Cornell, Jamie Sams, Marita Berg, Lorraine Bayes, EagleSong, Starfeather, Margaret Starbird, Barbara Koch, Donna Linn, Vicky Edmonds, Lillie Terry, Sulfiati Magnuson, Shelley Mitchell, Afua Harris, Peggy Nomura, Rita Bresnahan, Rev. Karen Lindvig, Melissa West, Shanyn Emerson, Brenda River Wind Poitra, Peg Firm, Roxanne Hamilton, Alexandra Hepburn, Janelle Keane, Rev. Linda Spencer, Edre Allen-Agbro, Emily Day, Linda Greiscehl, Meghan Smith, Carolyn Hartness, Deborah Koff-Chapin, Flor Fernandez, Renie Hope, Marilyn Strong, Jennifer Haywood, Sibel A. Golden, Isadora Arevalo Wong, Daystar Jephi Sioux, Linda Wolf, Wind Hughes, Ana Kinkaid, Waverly Fitzgerald, Joanna Powell Colbert, Ani Williams, Rev. Judith Laxer, Rev. Susan Sanford, Fatimah Gordon, Kelly Kerr, Simone LaDrumma, Viso Amoo, Rossie Norris, Melodie Silverwolf, Ani Haines, Joyce Greenwell,

Sibel A. Golden, Ratna Roy, Peggy Nomura, Judith Kaftan, Beth Cachet, Dr. Debra Brammer, Leslie Menke, Diane Givens, DanaMichele, Anita Fahnlander, Stacia Valley, Mayet Dalila, Kathleen Yow and Louise Salisbury.

1998 Isabel Allende, Judith Orloff, Gabrielle Roth, Angeles Arrien, Charlotte Sophia Kasl, Rhiannon, Sobonfu Somé, Ladies Don't Drum, Joules Graves, Marita Berg, Lorraine Bayes, Anzanga Marimba Ensemble, Manueal Mischke Reeds, Cecile Andrews, Vicky Edmonds, Linda Wolf, Heather Wolf-Smeeth, Margaret Starbird, Simone LaDrumma, Michelle Levey, Therese Charvet, Waverly Fitzgerald, Joanna Powell Colbert, Annie Thoe, Mary Lynn Pulley, Rossie Norris, Karen Gorrin, Ani Williams, Renie Hope, Marilyn Strong, Rev. Judith Laxer, Rev. Susan Sanford, Linda Sewright, Fatimah Gordon, Leah Mann, EagleSong, Carol Kaye, Meghan Smith-Webster, Deborah Koff-Chapin, Sheila Belanger, Rev. Karen Lindvig, Starfeather, Katherine Hambrecht, Lynn Fuller, Lee Fuller, Willow Scheel-Kushler, Ana Kinkaid, Jan Maher, Flor Fernandez, Marlene Lesh, Rev. Linda Spencer, Jo Dunning, Melissa West, Christina Salter, Donna Linn, Julene Tripp Weaver, Carolyn Hartness, Helen Vandeman, M. Cathy Angell, Rita Bresnahan, Ratna Roy, Molly Goron, Jennifer Haywood, Sibel A. Golden, Dr. Debra Brammer, Louise Salisbury, Tracey Stover, Peggy Gilbert, Cynthia Orr, Kris Steinnes, Marita Berg, Lorraine Bayes, Christine Cave, Luna, Rev. Rosa Redtail, Janelle Keane, Anita Fahnlander and Stacia Valley.

1999 Starhawk, Luisah Teish, Jeanne Achterberg, Ferron, Elena Avila, Sandra Ingerman, Lorraine Bayes, Les Femmes d'Enfer, Helen Vandeman, Cathy Angell, Christina Salter, Annie Thoe, Sheree Seratse, Sibel A. Golden, Carolyn Hartness, Rev. Rosa Redtail, Margaret Starbird, Ratna Roy, Shanyn Emerson, Melodie Silverwolf, Rashani, Mary-Lynn Monroe, Janine Ellison, Dee Poth, Vicky Edmonds, Jennifer Haywood, Lorraine Bayes, Katherine Nelson, Starfeather, Sheila Belanger, Marline Lesh, Fatimah Gordon, Marilyn Strong, Renie Hope, Donna Linn, Carol Kaye, Deborah Koff-Chapin, Lynn Fuller, Lee Fuller, EagleSong, Teri Dianne Ciacchi, Nora Cedarwind, Peggy Gilbert, Marge Hampton, Esther "Little Dove" John, Harriett Walden, Simone LaDrumma, Gloria Burgess, Luna Crow, Maxine Norton, Leah Mann, Rev. Karen Lindvig, Rev. Susan Sanford, Christina Baldwin, Ann Linnea, Rita Bresnahan, G-Marie Miyata, Colleen Foye Bollen, Ingrid Berkhout, Delilah, Waverly Fitzgerald, Joanna Powell Colbet, Michelle Levey, Sophia, Willow Teegarden-Davis, Glynnis Osher, Wahaba Karuna Heartsun, Lynn Morrison, Carol Ladas-Gaskin,

Louise Salisbry, Therese Charvet, Corn Milk Mother, Norma Jean Young, Marybeth Mayo Olsen, Amy Van Skaik, Anaiis Salles, Kris Steinnes, Dr. Debra Brammer, Cheryl Conklin, Suzanne Soloman, Amma Anang, Cherel Harrison, Anita Fahnlander and Stacia Valley.

2000 Jean Shinoda Bolen, Brooke Medicine-Eagle, Laura Love, Mary Manin Morrissey, Susan Powter, Shawna Carol, Nadyeshda Duvan, Flor Fernandez, Patricia Lynn Reilly, Nicki Scully, Lorraine Bayes, Kate Thompson, Peggy Taylor, Michelle Levey, Patricia Perrine Virly, Marilyn Strong, Renie Hope, Rev. Susan Sanford, Marline Lesh, Christie Denhart, Christina Baldwin, Ann Linnea, Margaret Starbrid, Mary O'Malley, Waverly Fitzgerald, Rev. Rosa Redtail, Pamela Gerke, Susan Chiat, Pomegranate Doyle, Krysteen Lomonaco, Fatimah Gordon, Rev. Judith Laxer, M. Cathy Angell, Willow LaMonte, Brenda Sol, Renee Welfeld , April Reiss, Simone LaDrumma, Esther "Little Dove" John, Sally King, EagleSong, Therese Charvet, Arlene Arnold, Starfeather, Marge Hampton, Peggy Gilbert, Dawn Dickson, Mimi Weiss, Maxine Norton, Sheila Belanger, Dee Poth, Paula Houston, Kris Steinnes, G-Marie Miyata, Loretta Kemsley, Paula Pugh, Christie Denhart, Colette Gardiner, Chiyomi Yoshida, Lori DeMarre, Donna Linn, Melodie Silverwolf, Ani Haines, Peggy Nomura, Alison Slow Loris, Sally Rockwell, Lidona Wagner, Marybeth Saunders, Jo Chavez, Amy Moondragon, Rita Bresnahan, Gloria Burgess, Ratna Roy, Mary-Lynn Monroe, Keri Shaw, Stacia Valley, Amma Anang, Kristin Berg, Aemmer, Kath Raymond, Patrice Ann Hawkwood Schanck, Paulette Rees-Denis, Sibel Golden, Jean Gilbert Phelan, Leslie Adkins, Pamela Rapinan, Georgette S. Donatello-Star, Rachel Gaunt, Kim Weers and Pamela Osborn.

2001 Margot Anand, Jean Houston, Phyllis Curott, Deena Metzger, Holly Near, Debrena Jackson Gandy, Jane Bell, Normandi Ellis, Jane Goldberg, Linda Leonard, Nicki Scully, RhythMix, Lorraine Bayes, Pam Gerke, Therese Charvet, Janine Ellison, Helen Vandeman, Patricia Perrine-Virly, Sandra Sitzmann, Ceci Co'rdova, Colleen Haggerty, Melodie Silverwolf, Ani Haines, Michelle Levey, Simone LaDrumma, Jane Latimer, Elizabeth Gray, Waverly Fitzgerald, Melissa Gaye West, Lotus Linton Howard, Rev. Bev Anderson, Starfeather, Fatimah Gordon, Colleen Foye Bollen, Amy Moondragon, Marilyn Strong, Renie Hope, Amma Anang, Mary Imani, Sonya Lea Ralph, Rev Susan Sanford, Sally King, Sophia Roberts, EagleSong, Maxine Norton, Rev. Crystol Bujol, Rev. Judith Laxer, Nadyezhda Duvan, M. Cathy Angell, MargeHampton, Peggy Gilbert, Aleili, Mary O'Malley, Rev. Rosa Redtail, Janice Van Cleve, Christie Denhart, SeaHart, Leah Mann, Shawna Carol,

Lori DeMarre, Esther "Little Dove" John, Robin Maynard-Dobbs, Dawn Star Dickson, Donna Linn, Renee Welfeld, Maxinne Smith, Pamela Grace, Deborah Koff-Chapin, Sheila Belanger, Rev. Peggy Nomura, Alison Slow Loris, Peggy Taylor, Kate Thompson, Susan Chiat, Elaine Childs Gowell, Marybeth Saunders, Lilith Meurer, Ingrid Berkhout, Patrice Ann Hawkwood Schank, Paulette Rees-Denis, Margaret Starbird, Brenda Sol, Cheryl Kanner, Karen Brighton, Harriett Walden, Maria Cook, Carol Wallace, Waverly Fitzgerald, Mary Lynn Monroe, Katherine Sterling, Jan Santora, Rita Bresnahan, Paula Houston, Kris Steinnes, Sally Rockwell, Kathy McKeever, Stacia Valley and Kendra Thornbury.

2002 Margot Adler, Shakti Gawain, Patricia Monaghan, Sherry Anderson, Paul Ray, Libby Roderick, Susan Osborn, Sacred Fire Choir, Pamela Gerke, Marybeth Saunders, Ladies Don't Drum, Shawna Carol, Marita Berg, Lorraine Bayes, Normandi Ellis, Anodea Judith, Flor Fernandez, Jane Goldberg, Sobonfu Somé, Anne Waldman, Rev. Judith Laxer, Jill Schumacher, Meredith McCord, Polly Sames, Ceci Co'rdova, Coleen Haggerty, Sallie Smith, Rev. Rosa Redtail, Rev. Susan Sanford, Erica Helm Meade, Mary O'Malley, Sonya Ralph, Mikelann Valterra, Helen Vandeman, Paula Homes Eber, Ifrah Hyder, Ann El-Moslimany, Susan Tate, Rev. Crystal Bujol, Patricia Stimac, Miriam Dyak, Nefertiti, Gretchen Lawlor, Gloria Taylor Brown, Lisa Summerlot, Kaylin Keith, Marilyn Strong, Renie Hope, Kendra Thornbury, Waverly Fitzgerald, Jennifer Evans, EagleSong, Rosetta Sanz, Linda Conroy, Aleili, Pomegranate Doyle, Starfeather, Neesah Heart, Robin Maynard-Dobbs, Deborah Koff-Chapin, Dawn Star Dickson, Siobhan Riordan, Barbara Spargo, Amy MoonDragon, Janine Ellison, Patricia Perrine, Leah Mann, Marybeth Saunders, Fatimah Gordon, Joelle Lyons Everett, Sally King, Danielle Hoffman, Kathryn Ravenwood, Kathleen McKern Verigin, Coleen Rhalena Renee, Kay Lagerquist, Ingrid Berkhout, Kumudini Shoba, Donna Linn, Gloria DeGaetano, Gina Salá, Laura Green, Glynnis Osher, Simone LaDrumma, Linda Allen, Ratna Roy, Zoe Ryan, Gordy Ryan, Buttrfly, Mary Lynn Monroe, Katherine Sterling, Suzanna McCarthy, Terra Page Paddock, Diane Patton, Kris Steinnes, Christine Hopkins, Bev Anderson, Sallie Smith and Kathleen McKeever.

2003 Riane Eisler, Frances Moore Lappé, Cheryl Richardson, Cherié Carter-Scott, Sacred Fire Choir, Candye Kane, Peggy Platt, Ilana Rubenfeld, Sobonfu Somé, Jalaya Bonheim, Kris Waldherr, Jane Bell, Robin Maynard-Dobbs, Carolyn Hartness, Suzan Hilton, Gail Hudson, Ratna Roy, Monza Naff, Rev. Kathryn Ravenwood,

Gina Salá, Sheilagh Roe, Gretchen Lawlor, Danna Beal, Maria Lujan de Peralta, Carol Jeanne White Tietjen, Leah Mann, Heidi Starbird, Allison Weeks, Zoe Ryan, Gordy Ryan, Jane Smallman, Mariah Mannia, Jackie Branagan, Shiela Baker, Gila Cadry, Julie Dittmar, Mary Kay Bailey, Stacy Rice, Allison M. Cox, Maxine Manning Norton, Gloria Taylor Brown, Teresa Dietze, Deborah Koff-Chapin, Sharlyn Hidalgo, Asar Tsehai, Rev. Rosa Redtail, Bergith Kayyali, Ingrid Berkhout, Joanna Powell Colbert, Danielle Hoffman, Coleen Renee, Neesah Heart, Betty Jean Williamson, Sandy D'Entremont, Barb Putnam, Rev. Judith Laxer, Dr. Claudia Rose, D. Fatimah Gordon, Noelle Remington, Sophia Roberts, Jody Stevenson, Isa "Kitty" Mady, Tamie Kellogg, Mary Newbill, Donna Linn, Simone LaDrumma, Dr. Tanmeet Sethi, Renee Welfeld, Donna Henes, Jessie Chiyomi Yoshida, Brenda Miller, Cynthia Gayle, Helen Vandeman, Janine Ellison, Madeline Gerwick-Brodeur, Leslie Fleming, Lori Boess, Michelle Levey, Deborah Shields, Joanie Vogel, Bev Anderson, Sallie Smith, Justine Gordon, Mary-Lynne Monroe, Waverly Fitzgerald, Susan Valentine, Susan Tate, Katherine Wismer, Christine Hopkins, Pauline Le Bel and Dawn Star Dickson.

2004 Brooke Medicine-Eagle, Nicki Scully, Brigitte Secard, Rhiannon, Lorraine Bayes, Jennifer Berezan, Shawna Carol, Ann Medlock, Ubaka Hill, Jan Phillips, Sobonfu Somé, Justine Willis Toms, Maria Lujan de Peralta, Saraina Hancock, Helen Vandeman, Ratna Roy, Maria Marsala, Margaret Starbird, Elaine Childs Gowell, Soleil, Shiela Baker, Rev. Kathryn Ravenwood, Lennie Martin, Shawna Carol, Rita Bresnahan, Melissa West, Marilyn Strong, Renie Hope, Leslie Fleming, Brenda Sol, Shirley Blasé, Mary Beth Moser, Gina Salá, Miriam Dyak, Laurie Finkelstein, Danielle Hoffman, Ingrid Berkhout, Janine Ellison, Susan Partnow, Gloria Taylor Brown, Shiela Baker, Rev. Rosa Retail, Richard Little, Madeline Gerwick-Brodeur, John Tokarchuk, Fatimah D. Gordon, Carold Nelson, Selah Martha, Danna Beal, Sondra Kornblatt, Joanie Vogel, Deborah Koff-Chapin, Rev. Judith Laxer, Noelle Remington, Jane Latimer, Mary O'Malley, Kris Steinnes, Starfeather, Deborah Shiels, Linda Conroy, Aleili, Joanna Powell Colbert, Lynn Garrett, Elaine Smitha, Linda Baker, Susan Valentine, Maria Marsala, Susan Tate, Sally King, Allison Moore, Buffalo Mazzetti, Rev. Kathryn Ravenwood, Christine Hopkins, Katherine Wismer and Sheilagh Roe.

2005 Vicki Noble, Mary Manin Morrissey, Ubaka Hill, Gina Salá, Pamela Gerke, Sacred Fire Choir, Carolyn Brandy, Simone LaDrumma, Soleil, Shiela Baker, Ambika Wauters, Aum-Rak

Sapper, Terah Kathryn Collins, Sharron Rose, Tama Kieves, Leah Kliger, Deborah Nedelman, Janine Ellison, Marisah Auerbach, Carla Woody, Aleeta Van Petten, Joanne Factor, Joanna Powell Colbert, Halimah Bellows, Pamela Hastings, Miriam Reiss, Danielle Hoffman, Rev. Pamela Douglas-Smith, Alysia Trombla, Desiree Wells, Selah Martha, Betty Martin, Kris Steinnes, Colleen Foye Bollen, Elaine Childs Gowell, Norma Joyce, Lynn Garrett, Coleen Renee, Jane Comerford, Amara Pagano, Sara Pagano, Dorothy Mclean, Rev. Rosa Redtail, Richard Little, Deborah Koff-Chapin, Shanti Hartstein, Subhan Schenker, Rev. Joanie Vogel, Robin Mastro, Lydia Ruyle, Suzanna McCarthy, Maureen J. St. Germain, Janice Eng, Rev. Judith Laxer, Mary Beth Moser, Waverly Fitzerald, Colette Hoff, Rev. D. Saraina Hancock, Joanne Lee, Linda Strever, Jean Haner-Dowsett, Julie Charette Nunn, Joanne Halverson, Margaret Riordan, Renie Hope, N'Shama Sterling, Alia Calendar, Jessica Powers, Ann Christa McCormick, Susan Tate, Starfeather and Linda Khandro.

2006 Barbara Marx Hubbard, Peggy Rubin, Christina Baldwin, Connie Grauds, Gloria Burgess, Tama Kieves, Soleil, Shawna Carol, Lisa Thiel, Lorraine Bayes, Sacred Fire Choir, An-Ra-Nae Meders, Christine Hopkins, Robin Maynard-Dobbs, Sabine Grandke-Taft, Christina Eisenberg, Elaine Childs Gowell, Susan Tate, Deborah Koff-Chapin, Rev. Judith Laxer, Linda Neale, Babs Smith, Patrice D. Edwards, Maria Teresa Valenzuela, Selah Martha, Trebbe Johson, Rev. Jane Smallman, Rev. Karen Brighton, Suzanna McCarthy, Julie Charette Nunn and Travey P. Stover.

2007 Gina Salá, Fatimah Gordon, Soleil, Rev. Judith Laxer, Rev. Rosa Redtail and Cynthia Lyons.

2008 Sobonfu Somé, Ferron, Jean Shinoda Bolen, Susan Armstrong, Kellianna, Nicki Scully, Sacred Fire Choir, Zaphara, Carolyn Brandy, Claire Johnson, Karen Fletcher, Victoria Fann, Maria Teresa Valenzuela, Melisa Wadsworth, Sabine Grandke-Taft, Suzanna McCarthy, Marianne Streich, Georgia Faye, Vanessa Timmons, Jennifer Posada, Deborah Koff-Chapin, Maria Lujan de Peralta, Samantha Russell Raven, Rev. Judith Laxer, Joanna Powell, Colbert, Julie Charette Nunn, Sheresse Braun, Kathy Kali, Lauren Archer, Susan Tate, Bjah Townsend and Brigitte Sztab.

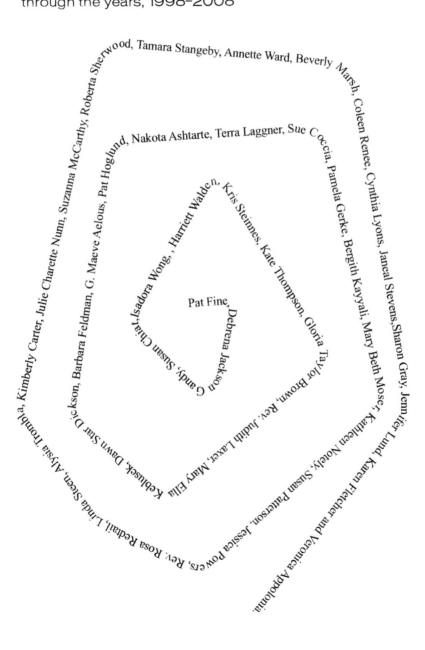

Women of Wisdom Board Members/Council Members

through the years, 1998–2008

...Sherwood, Tamara Stangeby, Annette Ward, Beverly Marsh, Coleen Renee, Cynthia Lyons, Janeal Stevens, Sharon Gray, Jennifer Lund, Karen Fletcher and Veronica Appolonia, Kathleen Notely, Susan Patterson, Jessica Powers, Rev. Rosa Redtail, Linda Steen, Alysia Trombly, Kimberly Carter, Julie Charette Nunn, Suzanna McCarthy, Roberta ...und, Nakota Ashtarte, Terra Laggner, Sue Coccia, Pamela Gerke, Bergith Kayyali, Mary Beth Moser, ...Dickson, Barbara Feldman, G. Maeve Aelous, Pat Hoglund, ...Isadora Wong, , Harriett Walden, Kris Steinnes, Kate Thompson, Gloria Taylor Brown, Rev. Judith Laxer, Mary Ella Keblusek, Dawn Star ... Gandy, Susan Chiat, Pat Fine, Debrena Jackson

Women of Wisdom Conference Comittee Members

through the years, 1993-2008

Kris Steinnes, Marianne Lewis, Charlotte Oakes, Sadie Rosholt, Faith, Marita Berg, Sharon Rose White, Kelli Miesse, Pat Fine, Chandra Smith, Barbara Thorp, Bergith Kayyali, Debrena Jackson Gandy, EagleSong, Harriett Walden, Isadora Wong, Johnnie Woods, Karin Coart, Marsha Lash, Nikkie Michael, Phoenix, D'Arice Anderson, Sabriah, Juliette Leach, Shanyn Emerson, Darlene Flynn, Jennifer Haywood, Ana Kinkaid, Valerie Smith, Charlee Williams, Rev. Judith Laxer, Rev. Susan Sanford, Gloria Taylor Brown, Susan Chiat Joan Goodnight, Terry Morton, Colleen Rose, Travey Stover, Lorraine Bayes, Dawn Star Dickson, Becky Kemery, Kathy McKeever, Marcia Makasini, Rev. Rosa Redtail, Amy Westhoff, Ingrid Berkhout, Keven Fjellman, Krysteen Lomonaco, Brenda Sol, Terra Paddock, Chalice Bailey, Charly Barker, Karen Brighton, Maribeth Moore, Sonya Lea Ralph, Melanie Richardson, Helen Vandeman, Chiyomi Yoshida, Sandy Chism, Catherine McFarland, Suzanna McCarthy, Amy MoonDragon, Deb Kennedy, Rev. Jane Smallman, Kiya Bodding, Diane Patten, Justine Gordon, Stacy Anderson, Shiela Baker, Cynthia Lyons, Cheryl Gere, Marte McCadden, Cynthia Wheaton, Cheryl Gordon, Brenda Wheeler, Vanessa Ronsse, Karen Robinson and Noreen Wedman.

Women of Wisdom Staff, Committee Members/Supporters

through the years, 1998-2007

Robin Evans, Janice Maddox, Leslie Fleming, Michele Halfhill, Carol Sorden, Deborah Drake, Pam Gerke, Linda Steen, Jessica Powers, Mary Beth Moser, Tamara Stangeby, Veronica Appolonia, Kathleen Notely, Sue Coccia, Teresa Musial, Aura Lee Honkanen, Kris Keller, Shannon Markley, Kayren Kittrick, Jan Santora, Halimah Bellows, Coral Miller, Heidi Morford, Lisa Bakke, Katherine Droden, Zoe Sturm, Eas Gooch, Pebbles Willekes, Bev Rings, Tom Flynn, Chris Prall, Meghan Smith, Peggy Jordan, Rev. Steve Towles, Rev. Karen Lindvig, Judy Jones, Joanna Powell Colbert, Susan Hoyt, Barbara Feldman, Kate Thompson, Power of Hope, Marybeth Saunders, Vulcana Wolfe, Tim Rasmussen, Luke Kehrwald, Melanie Saenz, Sharlyn Hidalgo, East West Bookshop, Susan McGinnis, Crystal Wendekier, Narayan, Jennifer Kogut, Kris Shaw, Becky Gemelli, Lois Higgins, Holly Fowers, Kim Kerrigan, Kimberly Carter, Sue Holm, Nola Nevers, Pam Foster, Allena Babosch, Crystal Carlson, Ballard Great Harvest Bread, Sandy Fox, Deverick Martin, Conscious Choice, Dr. Pat Baccili, Dr. Pat Show, New ConneXion, Cameron and Davindia Steele, Contact Talk Radio, Kathy Lowden, Voice of Choices, Krysta Gibson, New Spirit Journal.

artwork

Dragonfly
Sue Coccia
©1998

Hawk
Sue Coccia
©2007

Index Page references for artwork are called out with numbers in *italics*.

Index of Poems and Songs by Title

Biography

about the author, Kris Steinnes

Kris Steinnes is a true native of Seattle, a rarity in the city now! She loved growing up in the beautiful Pacific Northwest, having fun camping during summer vacations and taking part in Girl Scouts. Her cultural roots are Norwegian, her father having immigrated in 1929 and her mother, of Norwegian descent, having grown up in South Dakota.

Kris graduated from the University of Washington with a degree in Home Economics, studied clothing design, and was hired as a patternmaker in the clothing industry in Seattle. In the mid-1970's she designed the Seattle Sonics basketball team uniforms, a design which lasted for almost 20 years. She became part of the design team at Britannia Jeans, where she discovered her love of travel, taking several trips to Hong Kong a year. In 1983 she took off with her husband for a year long trip around the world, which stretched into three years. She fondly remembers many countries and experiences, China and Tibet being her favorite areas to explore.

Returning to Seattle in 1986, she knew she was finished with corporate life, and struck out on her own as a freelance designer and patternmaker. Having witnessed the daily spiritual life of the slower-paced countries during her travels, she yearned for something more, and finally found herself at Seattle Unity Church. After attending a couple of years, she became involved in their programs and became a board member. In 1991 she began a self exploratory journey, studying metaphysics and healing systems. After reading *The Feminine Face of God*, by Patricia Hopkins and Sherry Anderson, she had a vision of a gathering for women and in 1993 organized the first Women of Wisdom Conference in Seattle. Year after year she directed the eight-day conferences, bringing women leaders from many fields together to share their gifts with the women's community. In 1998 she founded the Women of Wisdom Foundation, a not for profit organization, and acted as executive director for six years.

Currently Kris is a minister, spiritual leader and meditation teacher, with a commitment to bringing feminine consciousness into everyday life. She continues to work with Women of Wisdom as a council member, and hopes to move into an advisory role so she can move onto her next career—as a writer, workshop leader and speaker, with a focus to promote Women of Wisdom internationally. She enjoys working with others to create new events, in addition to camping, swimming, traveling, reading, movies, and living with her husband, Chris Prall, and their two calico cats. She looks forward to what the next stage of life will bring as she approaches her sixties, and the many rich experiences that will follow in the decades to come.

artwork

Pregnant Butterfly Healing

Kris Steinnes
©1996

By your hearts be you women. —Ferron

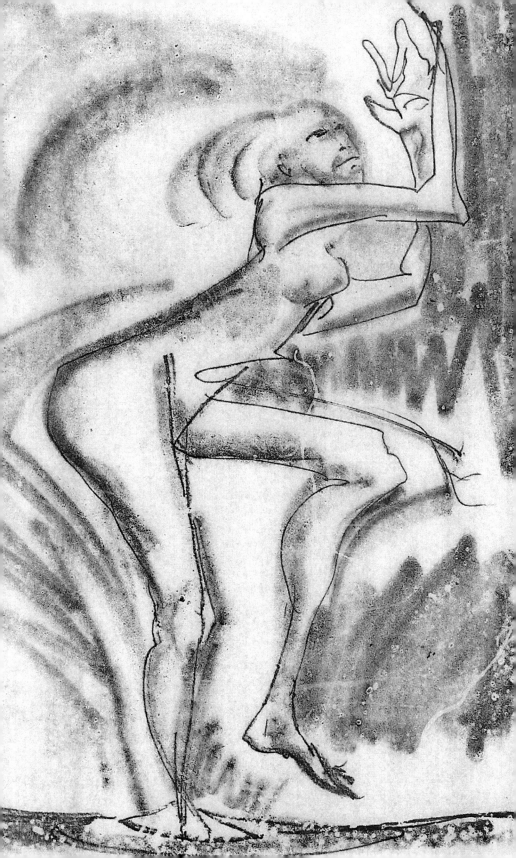

CPSIA information can be obtained at www.ICGtesting.com
Printed in the USA
LVOW121017220513

334995LV00002B/295/P